D1244161

MYTH AND POETICS

A series edited by
GREGORY NAGY

Homer and the Sacred City
by Stephen Scully

Also in the series

Poetry and Prophecy: The Beginnings of a Literary Tradition
edited by James Kugel

The Language of Heroes: Speech and Performance in the Iliad
by Richard P. Martin

Greek Mythology and Poetics
by Gregory Nagy

HOMER AND THE SACRED CITY

Stephen Scully

CORNELL UNIVERSITY PRESS

ITHACA AND LONDON

.

First published 1990 by Cornell University Press.

International Standard Book Number 0–8014–2464–X
Library of Congress Catalog Card Number 90–55130
Printed in the United States of America
Librarians: Library of Congress cataloging information
appears on the last page of the book.

⊛ The paper in this book meets the minimum requirements
of the American National Standard for Information Sciences—
Permanence of Paper for Printed Library Materials, ANSI Z39.48–1984.

To my mother and father

Contents

Foreword		ix
Acknowledgments		xi
Introduction		1
1	Toward a Definition of the Polis in Homer	6
2	The Sacred Polis	16
3	The Walled Polis	41
4	The People of the Polis	54
5	City Epithets and Homeric Poetics	69
6	History and Composition	81
7	Oikos and Polis in the Homeric Poems	100
8	Achilles, Troy, and Hektor: A Configuration	114
	Appendix 1. Nature and Technology in Place Epithets	129
	Appendix 2. Sacred Places	137
	Appendix 3. Sacred Cities of the East	141
	Abbreviations	159
	Notes	161
	Selected Bibliography	211
	General Index	215
	Index of Ancient Passages Cited	233

Foreword

GREGORY NAGY

Homer and the Sacred City, by Stephen Scully, is the fourth book in
the Myth and Poetics series. My goal, as series editor, is to encourage
work that will help integrate literary criticism with the approaches of
anthropology and that will pay special attention to problems concerning the nexus of ritual and myth.

For such an undertaking, we may look to the comparative testimony
of relatively complex societies, like the Ndembu of Zambia, and also
of the smallest-scale societies, such as the Yukuna of the Colombian
Amazon.[1] Just as important, we must pursue the varied testimonies of
the most stratified societies, including what goes under the general
heading of "Western civilization." It is precisely here that the meaning
of myth is the most misleading—and challenging. In a small-scale
society myth tends to be viewed as the encoding of that society's
concept of truth; at the same time, from the viewpoint of Western
civilization, myth has become the opposite of fact, the antithesis of
truth.[2]

Since the ancient Greek concept of *politeia* serves as the foundation
for the very word "civilization" and for our concept of Western civilization, a number of the books in the series will treat ancient Greece
and the ancient Greek city-state, or *polis.* Scully's book addresses the
polis directly, examining the Homeric concept of a "sacred city" and

---

[1]V. Turner, *The Forest of Symbols: Aspects of Ndembu Ritual* (Ithaca, N.Y., 1967), and
P.-Y. Jacopin, "La parole générative: De la mythologie des Indiens Yukuna" (diss.,
University of Neuchâtel, 1981).
[2]See especially M. Detienne, *L'invention de la mythologie* (Paris, 1981), and my review
in *Annales: Economies Sociétés Civilisations* 37 (1982) 778–80.

showing that the sacredness of the city depends on the authority of myth in the earlier stages of Greek society.

The authoritativeness of Greek *muthos* or "myth" in early Greek poetics was the central subject of Richard Martin's *Language of Heroes,* the first book in Myth and Poetics.[3] As a concept, Scully asserts, the Greek city-state is a direct reflection of this authoritativeness. And the social foundation for the validity of myth is the city-state itself—not as a concept but as a reality, the same reality that in the course of ancient Greek history will eventually undermine the very meaning of myth.

[3]R.P. Martin, *The Language of Heroes: Speech and Performance in the "Iliad"* (Ithaca, N.Y., 1989).

Acknowledgments

I am grateful to those who have supported this project during its long period of gestation. To my friend and teacher Charles P. Segal of Harvard University, I owe a special debt for his magnanimous and inspired advice. I also offer special thanks to Gregory Nagy of Harvard University for his invaluable suggestions, support, and good humor. I am no less grateful to my colleagues Rufus Fears, Donald Carne-Ross, James Wiseman, and Steven Esposito, as well as to William Sale of Washington University, Jon Rosenblatt of Providence, Rhode Island, William Scott of Dartmouth College, and Ian Morris of the University of Chicago. Without all of their nudging and nurturing this work could not have attained its present form.

I owe a different kind of debt of gratitude to the National Endowment for the Humanities for a summer stipend; to the F. Marion and Jasper Whiting Foundation; and to the Boston University Humanities Foundation, which appointed me a member of the Society of Fellows.

My final acknowledgment must belong to my wife, Rosanna Warren, whose generosity of spirit and critical intelligence have helped throughout to sustain me and support this work.

STEPHEN SCULLY

Boston, Massachusetts

HOMER AND THE SACRED CITY

Introduction

I shall assert in this book that the *polis* is the social nucleus around which life in the Homeric poems acquires meaning. Clearly the polis in Homer is not yet a state in the sense that we conventionally understand the classical polis as "city-state." As one scholar has recently shown, members of a Homeric *dēmos* are neither quite citizens in, nor subjects of, a politically organized community with a complex of institutions, laws, and customs.[1] In Homer, *politai* are not "citizens" but more simply "inhabitants of a *polis*"; that is, they are not defined "politically." They are neither conscripted nor taxed, they are not governed by a constitution (or *politeia*) and would not easily understand the concepts of specialization of governmental roles or international relations. Neither is it correct, however, to infer, as Runciman and many others have since Moses Finley's formative *The World of Odysseus* (London, 1954), that Homeric society is comprised of autonomous *oikoi* (best translated "family estates"), with no higher unifying "entity" to define the relation between self and community. Such a position minimizes the importance of urbanization, of walled cities, and of residential concentration as they are seen both at Homeric Troy or Scheria and at Old Smyrna (on the coast of Asia Minor) in the eighth century.

The prominence of the polis in the Homeric poems is most obvious in the *Iliad,* a poem haunted, if not dominated, by the fate of holy Troy. If the preeminence of the polis is less obviously true in the *Odyssey,* where themes of oikos and of reunion predominate, successful return to the oikos must still occur within the context of the larger community of Ithaca. On the evidence of the pejorative account of the Kyklopes and the uncultivated island across from their own, the polis, however it may be constituted or understood in Homer, is the implicit norm against which all societies are evaluated. In this book, I contend that the *Iliad* cannot be read in its proper amplitude without considering the way the polis "theme" magnetizes other major themes, including that of personal heroism.

For the Mycenaeans (in their prime from 1450 to 1200 B.C.), the term *polis* referred to the citadel, often walled in the last phase of the Mycenaean era, a citadel of the Mycenaean king. By the eighth century B.C., however, when the poems reached their definitive form, the same term came to refer, in a broader designation, to the entire community, or nascent city-state. There is in the word, then, a challenging paradigm shift from Mycenaean citadel to Ionian city-state. That semantic shift, or bridge, presents at once our greatest difficulty (is *polis* citadel or city-state?) and our opportunity (as the word *polis* links Mycenaean citadel and Ionian city-state). In our examination of the polis and its image in Homer, we will therefore inevitably trace both a process of transmission and an evolution.

Because a great span of time extends between the Mycenaean subject matter (ca. 1250 B.C.) and the time of poetic composition (ca. 725–700 B.C., by convention), the poems present a mosaic world picture with varying and occasionally contradictory systems of social organization. As much as the poems partake in a long epic and formulaic tradition that may reach as far back as the Mycenaean past, they also have been adapted to the period of epic performance in the 700s. In political organization, the *Iliad* and the *Odyssey* look back beyond the small tribal groupings and warrior aristocracy that characterize the Greek Dark Ages (ca. 1100–800 B.C.), to a highly centralized and bureaucratic society governed by kings, perhaps divinely ordained, of the Mycenaean era; but the poems also look forward to that form of social organization emerging in the eighth century—the polis.

The Iliadic portrait of Troy and the Odyssean descriptions of Scheria suggest at first glance that no single image of the polis may be found in Homer. Like a Mycenaean citadel, Troy is set back from the sea and rests on top of a steep hill; like the Ionian colonies being formed at the end of the eighth century and like famous Old Smyrna, Scheria is built on a low-lying peninsula. Troy has an acropolis, where royal palace and city temples are to be found; Scheria does not. Whereas Scheria is an idealized polis far from humankind and from the danger of war, Troy has been under siege for almost ten years, all its people forced to huddle behind the city wall. Yet underlying these differences is a more crucial similarity. Both for the polis at war and for the polis in a remote land of ease, the circuit wall is crucial for definition as it encloses the entire urban community. Although Homeric Troy resembles a Mycenaean citadel in other respects, in this regard it shares with Homeric Scheria a more striking kinship with Old Smyrna, whose massive walls date from the late ninth century. If the palace on the acropolis at Homeric Troy suggests Mycenaean conditions, the freestanding temples to Athena and Apollo on the city's height must be modeled on the new features of an eighth-century polis. The Homeric description of Troy therefore is not a historical portrait of a polis at any one period in Greek history but rather an amalgam, or pastiche, of old and new, its vision an essentialized, poetic creation. Integral to that vision is the sacred nature of the polis. Unlike the other major "institution" of Homeric life, the oikos, never *called* sacred in Homer or later Greek literature, the polis, or aggregate of oikoi, is sacred space and the height of human achievement.

As a poetic construct, the Homeric description of settlements is capable of reaching backward to Mycenaean times while still reflecting eighth-century realities. If, in its essential lineaments, the Homeric portrait has reshaped inherited traditions of social organization according to an urban reality developing from the eighth century onward, it is characteristic of Homeric expression to incorporate elements from other periods with a certain equilibrium and to fit them into a relatively coherent and unified image.

But this is more than a happy story of integrating old and new. It does not need to be said that the polis in Homer provides an essential context in which to read human action. Without the fate of Troy behind the foreground story of heroes at war, the *Iliad*'s depth and complexity would be greatly diminished, its epic sweep and most tragic dimensions lost. The eighth-century urban revolution in Ionia, however, adds more. These new cities not only provide a model for the Homeric vision of the polis; on a deeper level they inevitably invoke contemplation of urban definition, of urban enclosure, and of polis-oriented cult. In this new world, the inherited stories of siege warfare acquire fresh meaning. The emerging polis revitalizes old traditions, making it possible to weave, or perhaps reweave, the many episodes of the Trojan war and heroic exploit into the common story of Achilles and Hektor, Troy and its fate. We may imagine, then, the emerging Ionian city as contributing to the momentum that made the great literary quantum leap of the *Iliad* conceptually possible: monumental scale in epic composition. I anticipate here an argument developed more fully in subsequent chapters: that the city is a model for the construction of the *Iliad* as well as its essential theme.

In this book, I look primarily at the polis as the Homeric poems describe it, leaving as secondary, but not ignoring, archaeological detail of Greek settlements from the Mycenaean era down to the new polis of the Homeric period. I also consider comparative material, especially from the Near East, to show how it illuminates—often by contrast—the repeated Homeric claim that the polis is sacred; in addition I briefly juxtapose the Homeric portrait with Aristotle's definition of the polis, comparing in broad outline the Homeric city to the developed fifth- and fourth-century City-State. But my primary task is to distinguish the main features of the Homeric portrait and to argue that they are integral to, indeed, active in, the *Iliad*'s own deepest pulsations of meaning.

This is not a simple task. Just as Homeric composition tends to avoid offering detailed portraits of its major heroes, little is said about the physical background of most episodes or scenes of recurring action. As a result, we know more about a lone oak in the Trojan plain than about the plain itself, more about the walls of Troy than about the city behind them. But the task is not impossible. If the spotlight rarely falls on Troy, or other poleis, directly, these human centers are nevertheless richly and complexly described through the epithets attached to them. This book must, of necessity, proceed in part through a study of those epithets, the brushwork that meshes finally in the larger portrait of the human city.

Epithets are generally considered to be the least expressive element in Homeric poetics. I argue for a contrary view. For epithets of place, one can claim that their use in speech, and occasionally in narrative, responds to the dramatic pressure of each particular episode. In addition to their metrical utility, they can be keys to interpretation. For example, the Iliadic epithet of Troy, *euteikheos* ("well-walled"), occurs only in speech, uttered only by those eager, but thwarted, in their desire to take the city: Achilles in Book 1 is such a speaker as he describes the spoils the Achaeans might divide up "if ever Zeus permits us to destroy well-walled Troy." The line's secret power vibrates in the counterpoint of Zeus, verb, and epithet; of divine protector, destroyer, and apparently inviolable defense.

In both the *Iliad* and the *Odyssey*, epithets guide and color interpretation. Comparing these adjectival phrases, we can see a shift in focus and in theme from one poem to the other. City epithets of the *Iliad* emphasize the well-built and holy nature of the polis, while those of the *Odyssey* tend to focus both more broadly on the fatherland and more narrowly on the oikos. (See Appendix 1.) Such a shift from one poem to the other clearly befits their respective orientation, a shift that is most apparent in the epithets for Ithaca: Ithaca the polis, as opposed to Ithaca the island, is only once described by epithet in the whole of the *Odyssey*.

A shift in focus from polis to oikos, as we move from the *Iliad* to the *Odyssey*, is seen in the epithet *euktimenos*, "well-founded." In the war poem, where questions of polis supersede those of family estate, the structural strength of poleis is frequently mentioned by epithets, whereas the oikos is rarely mentioned and never in structural terms. So, in addition to being "well-built," "well-walled," "lofty," "well-inhabited," and so on, the polis, and only the polis in the *Iliad*, is also "well-founded." In the *Odyssey*, however, as the arena of action and psychological orientation shifts to the oikos, whether it be that of Odysseus, Nestor, or Menelaos, the epithet *euktimenos* modifies oikos as well as polis. *Euktimenos* is not alone in such new formulations: the epithet *eudmētos*, "well-built," in the *Iliad* describes city towers and walls (*teikhos*) but in the *Odyssey* house walls (*toikhos*). In a world of dizzying movement both toward and away from Penelope and fatherland, Odysseus' "well-founded" homestead, and his unmoving bedpost, assume primary significance. Odyssean "reworking" of Iliadic formulaic usage expresses in small brushstrokes more obvious major thematic shifts.

An examination of the epithets for Troy, in both the *Iliad* and the *Odyssey*, will direct us to consider three interlocking features of the city: its wall, its sanctity, and its people. In their sum, they compose a visual image of wall, divine presence, and human habitation, each element recorded in Nausithoos' founding of Scheria: "He drove a *wall* around the polis, built *houses*, and constructed [freestanding] *temples*" (*Od.* 6.9–10). This earthly trinity also happens to correspond with the three categories singled out by Antony Snodgrass as expressive of the emerging Greek polis: circuit wall, urbanized clusters, and, most important for him, state worship as evidenced by temple architecture.[2] This principle of classification structures Chapters 2 through 4, and provides the basis of my study in subsequent chapters. But before we turn our attention to these questions, we must consider the landscape of Troy and approach the polis itself through its various names and through generic definition.

CHAPTER I

Toward a Definition
of the Polis in Homer

Troy

Homer says as little about the city of Troy as he reveals about the physical characteristics of his major characters. Although one scholar has calculated that "as envisaged in the poems, more than 50,000 people could be accommodated"[1] at Troy, one would be hard-pressed to describe where they lived within the city. All buildings and public spaces mentioned by name are said to be on the acropolis, or "the high city" of Ilios, an area of considerable activity: houses, temples, agora. Here we find Priam's palace (both administrative center and resident hall), where the king and queen lived with sixty-two of their sons, daughters, and respective spouses, including Hektor and Andromache.[2] Within that complex, there was a barnlike building for mules, horses, wagons and chariots, and so on. In front of Priam's palace there was an agora (here referring, it would seem, to an assembly of people rather an architecturally defined space);[3] "close by" was Alexander's house "of many rooms."[4] Also in the high city were freestanding temples to Athena and Apollo ("in holy Pergamon").[5] How these buildings stood in relation to each other, we cannot say; about the rest of Troy, we know only that it was a city of wide streets. About Agenor's house, or where it stood, Homer maintains the same silence that attends descriptions of the dwellings of other families in Troy.

A principle of aesthetic economy seems to preclude enumeration of further detail in city design. When Hektor rushes back to war in Book 6, leaving his house in the acropolis, he retraces his steps "down the well-built streets, crossing through the great city [*dierkhomenos mega astu*]," until he reaches the Skaian Gate (6.390–92). Similarly, Alexander, when roused to battle, rushes "through the city" (*ana astu*) (6.505), having "come down from high Pergamon [*kata Pergamou akrēs*] . . . and then straightway encounters Hektor" (6.512–5) at the city gate. Both descriptions abbreviate detail, the first by ignoring the city height whence Alexander came, the second by juxtaposing city height with city gate. Again, a minimalist's aesthetic dominates the scene of Hekabe's attendants gathering the old women of Troy by going "through the city" (*kata astu*) (6.287).[6] Narrative description of Troy is reserved for places of critical narrative significance, namely city acropolis and defensive wall—the line of demarcation separating polis from nonpolis.

The preference for Troy and Ilios over Pergamon—the three names for Troy—sheds a little more light on the way Troy and the polis in general are perceived in the Homeric poems. Troy (Troia), referring both to "Troytown" and the country, the Troad, derives from Tros, third king of the Trojans, whereas Ilios, meaning the city of Ilos, gets its name from Ilos, Tros' son. These two names appear to be used in Homer almost without distinction. Carl Blegen comments:

> Troy was perhaps originally the more general name, applying to the countryside—the Troad—while Ilios more specifically designated the actual city. In the Homeric poems, however, this distinction is not maintained, and either name is used without prejudice to mean the city. In the *Iliad* the name Ilios appears 106 times, more than twice as often as Troy, which occurs 50 times. In the *Odyssey* Troy has an advantage of nearly four to three over Ilios, appearing 25 times, while we meet the latter in 19 instances. In the classical period and later the regular name of the city that still survived on the site had become Ilion and the inhabitants were known as Ilians.[7]

The neuter Ilion occurs only once in Homer (*Il.* 15.70–71), leading Aristarchus to consider it a later interpolation. Perhaps in support of Blegen's distinction, a Luvian text, more or less contemporary with the Mycenaean period, identifies the city as Ilium and even employs a formula popular in the *Iliad:* "steep Ilium."[8]

Unlike Ilios or Troy, Pergamon, probably derived from, or connected with, the word for tower (*purgos*), refers exclusively to Troy's acropolis and is especially associated with Apollo. His temple is "in high Pergamon"; it is from there that he watches in disgust as the Trojans give way before the Achaeans in Book 4, and he carries the wounded Aeneas there in Book 5. Pergamon is also mentioned without reference to Apollo, when, for example, Cassandra "climbs up to" (*eisanabasa*) Pergamon in order to look out onto the plain to see whether Priam is returning to Troy with Hektor's body (24.700); and, as we saw above, Alexander rushes "down from high Pergamon" and goes "through the city" (*astu*) before he meets Hektor at the city wall in Book 6. Both prepositional directions associated with Pergamon ("down from," *kata* with genitive; "climb up to," *eisanabasa*) and its epithet "high" (*akrē*) clearly imply that the term in Homer is restricted to the citadel of Troy and suggests the walled citadels (hence *purgos*) characteristic of the Mycenaean era. But such terminology for Troy is less typical in Homer than the proper names and general words for city which designate the entire urban complex, that is, in Blegen's words "the actual city."

Polis, Ptoliethron, Astu

Of the three words for city—*polis* (*ptolis*), *ptoliethron,* and *astu*—*polis* is by far the most common, a preference that suggests a vision of the city as a schematic whole.

Contrary to the Linear B tablets and contrary to Hesiod, there is no word in Homer to designate "village."[9] It is inevitable, then, that some Homeric usages of *polis* or *astu* refer to hamlet or village settlements.[10] Consider, for example, the home of the priest Khryses, a polis called Khryse in the Troad (*Il.* 1.37). Similarly some of the twenty-three poleis that Achilles sacked before the ninth year of the war may also be better described as villages. But in Homer all are elevated to the status of polis, and whenever one, such as Thebes, figures prominently in the narrative, its monumentality rivals Troy's.

These three terms for city in Homer are generally synonyms for the city as a whole, including citadel, town, dwellings, and streets. The word *ptoliethron,* which is lengthened from the Cypriot and Mycenaean form for polis (*ptolis*), appears to be a residue from an earlier period in epic Greek poetry, when *polis,* or *ptolis,* like *Pergamon,* referred to the upper citadel, but its use in Homer is not restricted to the citadel area alone. In the Mycenaean period, *polis* and *astu* referred to distinct areas of the city; the former meant "citadel" where the royal palace was located (in later Greek history, the acropolis area), whereas the latter meant "the lower residential town" outside the walled citadel, a designation frequently retained throughout Greek history.[11] But in Homer both words are used with little distinction. In describing this change, one critic remarks: "The small fortified settlements of Ionia have the appearance of a *polis*, but have in addition the functions of an *astu*, so that the original denotative distinctions between *astu* and *polis* are obliterated. Only connotative differences survive in epic diction: *astu* is the object of more personal feelings, while *polis* is more public and heroic."[12] Edmond Lévy elaborates by observing that *polis* in Homer typically refers to a city as seen from the exterior, often in conjunction with the city wall, and may thus evoke, like an ideogram, an image of the city as a whole (for example, when Priam went out into the Troad to ransom Hektor's body, he "descended from the polis," 24.329), whereas with *astu* the city is viewed from within with a focus upon its inhabitants and most commonly therefore upon its women.[13] This reading concurs with what we saw above: in a rush to leave his home, Hektor "crossed through the great astu" to the city gate; similarly Paris rushed "through the astu" on his way to the gate; the handmaidens of Hekabe gathered the women of Troy "down through the astu".

The term *polis* in Homer may, on very rare occasions, even imply the classical use of the word when it connotes a political, more than a topographical, definition of state which encompasses city and countryside. Glaukos may be using the word in this sense when, rebuking Hektor, he says: "Consider now how you may save the polis and the astu" (*Il.* 17.144), that is, "consider how you may save the state and the city." But Glaukos could just as well mean "save the citadel and town," although the latter two are hardly separable for Homeric Troy. In a more probable example from the *Odyssey*, Odysseus asks Nausikaa to show him the astu since he does not know anyone else who inhabits this polis and land (6.177–78). As one scholar has suggested, *polis* here may imply "the existence of a social structure combining an urban center with rural lands, and the use of the word acknowledges the growth of an institution no Bronze Age hero could have known."[14]

Preferences of the names Ilios and Troy over Pergamon, and of *polis* over *astu* or *ptoliethron*, both in their way suggest an image of a city as a whole, simplified as we have seen to its most essential forms.[15] In accord with these distinctions, strangers are asked to identify themselves by their polis, not their astu, and on the Shield of Achilles the two mortal cities, noble edifices within the landscape of sun and stars, fields and mountains, are not *astea*, but *poleis*. Not infrequently, the circuit wall by itself stands as an ideogram for the city, expressing a civic order set apart from natural forms and hostile forces.

Troy and Its Environs

Characteristic of a preindustrial city-state agrarian economy, there was in ancient Greece an essential symbiosis between polis and surrounding rural territory. Although the archaeological record of the classical period shows that there was extensive religious activity as well as small settlements and land husbandry in the space between the city and the mountains, literary representations of cityscapes from Athenian tragedy, for example, foreshorten the liminal, suburban space, fiercely juxtaposing polis and *apolis,* city and mountain. In the Mycenaean pictorial tradition, as on the Silver Rhyton Vase, one finds something of the same radical simplification of representation as landscape and city are reduced to essential characteristics—enclosed city, city wall, and fighting forces (with a few trees here and there). Extraneous detail of Mycenaean lower town or extended farm land is excluded to heighten dramatic confrontation between citadel defender and citadel attacker.

A similar foreshortening is also found in Homer, though here *Iliad* and *Odyssey* differ somewhat in their representations of extra-polis space. For the *Odyssey,* Pierre Vidal-Naquet, in particular, has splendidly mapped out the complex topography that symbolizes that gradual transition from civilized to wild, from man as cultivator to hunter to shepherd to savage.[16] But even in this poem, comparatively little is said about the cultivated fields or human architecture immediately outside the city. Although Pylos, Sparta, Ithaca, and even Scheria belong to the "grain-giving earth," with the exception of Ithaca, there are few references in the description of these cities to their arable lands. We may hear that fortified Scheria is distinct from its fields: "city and country," *polin kai gaian* (6.177, 191; also 6.3: "land and city," *dēmon te polin te*), and that the city founder is said to have distributed farming land (6.10) when building the city,[17] but even for this city set far from the dangers of war little is made of that cultivated area outside the wall. Descriptions instead tend to focus on the city proper and the city wall: "Odysseus marveled at the ships and harbors, the meeting places of men, and the city walls, long, lofty, fitted with palisades, a wonder to behold" (7.44–45; cf. 6.9 and 262–67). Even Alkinoos' rather magical garden is found within that wall: "great garden outside the courtyard, near the double doors (of his palace), fenced [*herkos*] all around" (7.112–13).[18]

But in the *Iliad,* the contrast between Troy and its environs is drawn even more sharply. Wartime conditions only partially explain such pointed juxtapositions. The present world of war and death appears to have shattered the former peacetime, agarian economy of the Trojan plain and its surrounding hills. In recalling military actions from early years of the war, the poem reveals that such radical divisions did not always exist: for example, we hear that Isos and Antiphos, both sons of Priam, were watching sheep in the valleys of Mount Ida when they were seized by Achilles (11.104–6). Similarly, when he had been "away from his cattle," Aeneas was chased by Achilles under the hills of Ida but escaped to Lyrnessos, where Achilles sacked the city without capturing his elusive prey (20.188–94). On yet a third occasion in the wartime past, we hear, Achilles caught Lykaon while the latter was cutting branches from a fig tree in his father's orchard (21.37–38). As with Isos and Antiphos, Achilles captured, then ransomed Lykaon. But in the present action of the poem, there is as little room for cattle herding, watching sheep, or cutting branches in the orchard as there is for supplication and ransom. This new reality is perhaps most poignantly expressed in the death of Simoeisios, one of the first to die in the poem. In the contrast between this lad's birth "beside the banks of Simoeis when his mother came down from Mount Ida following her mother and father to tend sheep flocks" (4.474–76) and his death while he is still unmarried and in the bloom of youth (4.474), we witness, as Seth Schein has observed, the brutal cost of war in a promising life cut short and the violation of a landscape once peaceful and nurturing.[19] There is little in the narrative of present events to soften the contrast between a world of war and uncultivated nature outside Troy, and a human world huddled within the walls of Troy.

What do we find, then, in the Trojan plain? Clearly, it cannot be equated with the "wild"; its great river, the Skamandros, is sacred to Troy and once tries vainly to rescue the people of its city from Achilles' savage onslaught. Besides this river, called the Skamandros by people but the Xanthos, or Yellow River, by the gods, a companion river, the Simoeis, also lies between Ilios and the Greek camp. Both have their headwaters on Mount Ida. The larger Skamandros is praised for its lush natural beauty: along its banks, meadows bloomed (2.467) and marshlands flowered with lotus and apium, food for the Greek horses when returning from battle (2.775–77); great elms, willows, tamarisk shrubs, lotus, reeds, and galingale grew in abundance (see 21.350–52 and 10.466–67). This is a picture of fertility, but not a fertility of human making.[20]

"Outside the polis, far out in the plain," the *Iliad* says, "there was a steep hill [*aipeia kolōnē*] with open ground on every side, which men call Batieia, or Thorn Hill, but the immortals know as the tomb of dancing Myrine" (2.811–15).[21] The Trojans and their allies use this landmark as a rallying place to form up in battle order. Another hill near the Simoeis, called the Kallikolone, or Beautiful Hill, is used by Ares to encourage the Trojans in war (20.51–53). Confident while Achilles was out of the battle, the Trojans, "far from their walls," made camp by this hill in the ninth year of the war.[22]

Somewhere between the city and the Greek camp, there is old Aisyetes' tomb, of great height, used by the Trojan Polites, Priam's son, as a watchtower to spy the first sign of a sortie from the Achaean ships (2.791–94). The fourth marker in the plain, somewhere between the Greek camp and the Skamandros, is the burial mound of Ilos, crowned with a pillar and conspicuous to the eye. This point figures frequently in accounts of the fighting and in Greek or Trojan movements across the plain.[23]

In addition to these hills (often burial mounds) and rivers, a lofty and very beautiful oak tree (phēgos), sacred to Zeus, grew somewhere near the Skaian Gate. On this tree, Athena and Apollo in the shape of vultures enjoyed the spectacle of battle (7.58–60); and nearby, Apollo encouraged Agenor in his confrontation with Achilles (21.547–49). When wounded, Sarpedon was placed under this tree (5.692–93) and once, near this marker, Hektor and Agamemnon, in the fury of battle, awaited each other (11.170–71).

We hear little of human activity other than burial taking place in the plain. Springs formerly used for washing still stand outside the walls, as well as a cart track that is mentioned once (22.146), and we are told that the Trojans, having gathered their wagons in front of the city (astu), "for nine days gathered vast amounts of wood" in preparation for Hektor's funerary pyre (24.784). Examining the terrain in terms of nature, we find the city of Troy with its houses, temples, wide streets, and "agora" on one side of the city wall, a landscape of flowering meadows, hills, and sacred rivers on the other. From a human perspective, on one side of the wall stands the city pregnant with life, housing women and children, on the other the lonely burial mounds of the dead. When Priam, descending from the city (polios kateban), reaches the plain, those following him turn back into Ilios, "wailing incessantly as though he were going to his death" (24.328–29).

One misses, that is, in the description of the land outside Troy, references to wheat-bearing acres, orchards with fruit trees, and lands for herding—the very three land uses that Diomedes mentions in the context of his father, who resides in Argos (Il. 14.122–24). Although the Trojan plain is frequently called "fertile," only once in the action of the poem does the narrator describe Troy's "wheat-bearing fields" and then as Achilles races through them in haste after Agenor (21.602).[24] Achilles himself once refers to the plowlands and orchards that the Trojans will give to Aeneas on the condition that Aeneas kill Achilles (that is, fertility in a Troy free from war; 20.184–86). In wartime, Troy's plowlands have ironic resonance: Agamemnon fears that Menelaos will die at Troy and that his bones will rot in the tilled land (4.174). Similarly Thetis, grieving at Achilles' early doom, foresees her son's death "in fertile Troy" (24.85–86).

At Troy, as elsewhere in Homer, the symbolic space frequently separating polis from nonpolis is the city spring. Troy's springs are described only once and in particularly striking terms when Achilles and Hektor finally meet in combat:

> But they dashed by the watch tower and wind-beaten fig tree
> always along the wall, on the cart track
> until they reached the two beautifully flowing springs,
> where the twin sources of the eddying Skamandros bubble up,
> for the one flows with lukewarm water, from which clouds
> of steam arise as from a burning fire;
> the other runs forth in summer like hail,
> or cold snow, or as from frozen water.
>
> (*Il.* 22.145–52)

Close by stood troughs of stone, wide and very beautiful, where the wives and daughters of the city used to wash their clothes in the days of peace before the Achaeans came (22.153–56). Simultaneously of nature and "institutionalized" by the city, and peculiarly running with hot and cold water, these springs suggest that liminal space between human and natural order and between war and remembered peace; they function therefore as an ideal meeting point for the final encounter between Hektor and savage Achilles.

In the *Odyssey,* too, the spring often serves as the point of transition between polis and *agros* ("tilled land"), or the even more antithetical *agrios* ("the wild"). Among the faraway Laestrygonians, Odysseus' crew know they are approaching a polis when they come upon a spring where the women of the city draw water (10.103–8). On the road from the sea to Scheria, Odysseus comes to a spring in front of the town "the same distance as a shout would carry" (6.291–94). At Ithaca, Odysseus and Eumaios are said to come near the city (*asteos eggus*) when they arrive at a spring, with a stone altar nearby, where the

people of the town (*politai*) draw water (17.205–11). There they encounter the bullying Melanthos as he leads goats from the country to
Odysseus' oikos. Alongside the springs at both Ithaca and Scheria,
there is a sacred grove (*alsos*) of poplars or a constructed altar (*bōmos*)
where those on the road (*hoditai*), passing between city and country,
make offerings. These are clearly religious shrines protecting passage.
So when Hektor runs by the hot and cold springs in his futile flight,
like a dove from an eagle, we are reminded of civilization's mortality as
the "monstrous" Achilles is about to slay the city defender and obliter-
ate sacred civilized order.

A Definition of the Homeric Polis

One of the most widely accepted definitions of the fifth-century polis
is that of Victor Ehrenberg, for whom it is a "community, self-ab-
sorbed, closely united in its narrow space and permeated by a strong
political and spiritual intensity that led to a kind of special culture of
every Polis."[25] For Ehrenberg, the essential feature of the city-state is
neither its territory nor any abstract concept (politeia), but the free men
who live within it—"a state of its citizens" as Thucydides defines a polis:
andres gar polis (7.77.7), "it is the men that are the polis." Carol Thomas,
citing Aristotle's claim that a territory as well as a citizen body is an
essential constituent of the polis, expands upon Ehrenberg's definition
in the following way: Though "an ancient Greek *polis* was not necessarily recognized by its degree of urbanization or its size, . . . [it may be
defined as] a community of people and of place. It was a unified body of
individuals among whom purely individual interests or family matters
had been superseded by a larger, common concern. The Greek *polis* was
also and equally the area where people with common interests resided
for it was the particular features of the territory that influenced and
directed the nature of the politically-organized body of people and
served to perpetuate the intense exclusiveness of the independent
states."[26]

Both definitions differ radically from George Calhoun's succinct
interpretation of the Homeric polis: "simply a town, an aggregation of
buildings, often fortified, on a hill or other easily defensible positions."[27] Clearly missing in Calhoun's definition is a sense in the Homeric polis of a political community or of a constructive principle of
nomos, norms sacred and profane, written and unwritten, which re-
flected the intense political and spiritual unity of the polis. But one

must be careful not to mistake the ideal for the real. One has only to mention the careers of Alcibiades, or that of his Spartan rival Lysander, to realize that the fifth-century polis, guided by its nomos, was not in actuality such a unified body of individuals as to compel all individual interests to bow before the pressure of public concern. I discuss these issues more fully in subsequent chapters.

I prefer to define the Homeric polis according to a different set of coordinates. Although not a political community, it is still a group of co-inhabitants, an aggregate of oikoi, the sum of its parts qualitatively different from each part perceived independently. This collective body comprises a paradoxical unit of inherently self-contradictory components, paradoxes that were as typical of the Homeric polis as they were of the polis in the classical period. The human city is immortally and mortally constructed as well as divinely and humanly defended; it is at once part of the natural world and yet a world of humankind that defies natural order and law; and although the place of male domination, it partakes in form and spirit of the female order. The movement of people from the slopes of Mount Ida into the walled space on the open plain, initiated by the will of Zeus, suggests that, although once of nature, humankind through architecture and community has transcended its natural origins. In the glory of technology, geometric order, and the protection of the weak and the loved, the city aspires toward a selfhood and continuity both *hieros* (holy) and *arrēktos* (unbreakable). Although it supports life and provides continuity in a world of change, it is defended by the male whose *ēthos* can only imperfectly be correlated with the domestic, the female, and continuity. In the convergence of earth and sky, the city is suspended, like the offspring of Erichthonios' mares, between two worlds; it partakes of both but has its identity in neither. The limitations of the city thus define the city. It is both closed to the whole and open to the whole, and it is these pretenses that are, of course, its noble lie.[28]

CHAPTER 2

The Sacred Polis

The Homeric polis is a paradoxical unit of inherently self-contradictory components: it is immortally and mortally constructed as well as divinely and humanly defended. In its union of temples and sacred *agora* on the one hand and urban dwellings and humankind on the other, the polis holds within its embrace the holy and the earthbound. Yet in spite of this apparent contradiction, the Homeric polis in its entirety is deemed sacred.

Of all the city and place epithets in Homer, none are more commonly employed than those that refer to this aspect of the polis. For a full list of places, enclosures, and dwellings called sacred in Homer we must mention islands, territories, sanctuaries, groves, threshing floor, glens, and cave (see Appendix 2), but the most frequent Homeric references to sacred places are to cities themselves (poleis): Troy, Pylos, Thebes, and so on. In addition to the polis at large, the walls of the polis, as its temples and agora, are also called sacred.

The frequency with which Homeric cities are called sacred is striking: forty-six instances for both poems, far ahead of the second most common epithet for cities, "steep" (*aipus, aipeinē*), which occurs no more than twenty-three times in the two epics. Even when one discounts the happy use of "sacred Ilios" (*Ilios hirē*) at the end of the hexameter line (eighteen times), reference to the city's sanctity holds a commanding lead over all other epithetical descriptions of the polis in Homer.

Our understanding of the relation between polis and sanctity is clearly fundamental to an overall sense of the motivating tensions of Homeric society and, with a narrower view, to our reading of the war waged around Troy in the *Iliad*. Yet, despite the obvious importance of this aspect of the polis in Homer, the subject of polis sacredness in Homer, or in later Greek literature and culture, has been virtually ignored by all modern scholars of ancient Greek religion. Martin Nilsson in *Geschichte der griechischen Religion* (1941) and Walter Burkert in *Griechische Religion der archaischen und klassischen Epoche* (1977; English trans. *Greek Religion*, 1985) are equally silent concerning this issue. Although both works examine hieros and polis separately, each ignores hieros in relation to polis.

The meaning of "sacred polis" in Homer is anything but self-evident. In the first place, we observe that the polis contrasts with the oikos and (human) domos, which are *never* called sacred in Homer (or in later Greek literature so far as I have been able to ascertain). This lexical observation does not mean, of course, that the house or family estate was not sacred in some sense or was without divine protection. Clearly, it was both. But its sanctity was focused on the *hestia*, already personified in Hesiod as the Guardian Goddess of hearth and home. In the *Odyssey*, the hearth's sanctity is evident in an oath by which people swear: "Zeus be my witness, and this table of my host and hearth of famous Odysseus."[1] Divine protection of the house in Homer is also implied by the altar of Zeus Herkeios, or Zeus of the Enclosure, found within Odysseus' courtyard (see *Od.* 22.335; a cult title frequently attested by later authors). But the house, whether by that term we mean the abode (domos and oikos) or the larger concept of estate (the oikos), in its entirety was *not* considered sacred. Or, at least, this is what the lexical testimony suggests. Why *hierē polis*, but not *hieros domos* (or *oikos*)? Or, slightly rephrased, why is the aggregate of houses, that is, the polis, in Homer called sacred when the individual house is not? The answer must lie in the contrast between public and private space.

If the human house is not called sacred, the "house of the god," the city temple, is (see *hieros domos*, *Il.* 6.89). We understand the temple as sacred because it houses the god,[2] but divine residence does not suffice as an explanation for the sacredness of the whole city. Surely, the matter must be more complicated than J. T. Hooker would have us believe (in the most recent study of hieros in archaic Greek): "It is not hard to discern the meaning of 'holy' in the epithet *hi(e)ros* which Homer attaches to places such as Pylos and Troy, since these may very well have been regarded as the abodes of divinities."[3]

A limitation of Hooker's thesis is immediately evident when we consider that the "circle" of the city agora is also sacred (see *Il.* 18.504). Of the many appearances of this epithet in Homer, Hooker finds this one to be "the hardest to account for." For him, "the entire emphasis is thrown on the massivity of the circle."[4] If we may cite fifth-century Greek beliefs for comparison, sacredness refers here, however, not to the mass of circle or that of the polished stone seats upon which the elders sit, but to the enclosed civic space where public, quasi-juridicial activity takes place.

Like the Propylaia, which set human space apart from divine in classical Athens, boundary stones and holy water basins, similar to those at the entrance to sanctuaries, set the agora apart from the rest of the city. Laws similarly forbade any with unclean hands from entering the agora and thereby bringing harm to the community. Both stones and lustral stoups must, most reasonably, be interpreted as markers of a religious nature, serving notice that one was about to enter purified space within the city. To quote from *The Athenian Agora* issued by the American School of Classical Studies at Athens: "The open square of the Agora was dedicated to the community life and, as such, was as sacred as any temple precinct."[5]

If areas of a religious and/or communal nature within the polis were set apart from the rest of the city and designated as sacred, why was the polis in its paradoxical union of sacred and profane also sacred? A brief comparison with Roman beliefs about sacred space will reveal the essence of this difficulty, as well as the shortcomings of Hooker's explanation. Although Rome, like the Homeric polis, was temple-oriented, under divine protection, and housed within its boundaries sacred spaces (*templa*) of a civic nature, it was not *sacra, sancta,* or *sacrosancta.* The Senate House (as a *templum*) and the juridical and political designations of state, *civitas* or *res publica,* under divine protection, were considered holy, but neither Rome nor any other Roman *urbs* was in its physical whole ever called sacred. *Sacra Roma* is alien to Roman beliefs. The reasons for this contrast between sacred temple, Senate House, and res publica on the one hand, and "nonsacred" urban vessel on the other, are not hard to determine.

In the intermixture of humanity and "sacredness," the inevitable impurity of humankind introduced an element of the profane within the sacred enclosure. Insofar as the augury rites defining the boundaries of the urbs could be considered, at least rhetorically, the same as those delimiting the space of the templum (see Cicero, *In Catilinam Oratio* 1.33), the urbs in the complexity of its composition fails to qualify in its entirety as a sacred templum. As Plutarch explains the Roman *amburbium* founding ritual (*Roman Questions* 27), the city founder lifted the plow marking the sacred boundary of the city at the points where future city gates would be placed because corpses must necessarily be removed from the city. "Making *sacer* consisted," in Émile Benveniste's words, "in making a kind of entrenchment, of putting something outside the human domain by attribution to the divine."[6]

In its admixture of temples, agora (or forum), urban dwellings, and mortal people, the city of mortals holds within its embrace the sacred and the profane; but only in Greek thought, as studied here in the context of Homer, can the polis with this paradoxical mixture be considered in its multiplicity *hierē*. Why in Greek culture can the city vessel be considered holy, while in the Roman it cannot?

Before we proceed further, we need to take a closer look at the four epithets in Homer that signify the sacredness of the polis: *hieros* (*hirē*), *ēgatheos, zatheos, dios*. Do these epithets vary significantly in meaning? Do they apply universally to all cities? Are some cities sacred, but others not? Are some more sacred than others?

Of the four, *hieros* is by far the most frequent both in its general application to persons and things of the natural world (rivers, dusk, day, fish, olive trees, wheat) and in its particular application to place (polis, islands, sanctuaries, house of the god, [circle of the] agora, threshing floor, Kirke's glens). In his study, Burkert writes of this word: "For the Greeks *hieros* was without doubt the decisive concept for demarcating the sphere of the religious from Mycenaean times. . . . [It is defined] as that which belongs to a god or sanctuary in an irrevocable way. The opposite is *bebēlos,* profane. Man consecrates something, some possession, in that he takes it away from his own disposal and surrenders it to the god."[7]

If the Greek/English dictionary (*LSJ*) broadly translates the word to signify that person or thing "filled with or manifesting divine power," when used to refer to a place, it signifies an area that is "hallowed" or "under divine protection." Benveniste's and Burkert's explanations are more lively; for Benveniste, *hieros* signifies a property or state of being, "sometimes permanent and sometimes incidental which can result from an infusion of the divine, from some divine circumstance or intervention."[8] For Burkert, in its "irreducible factor," *hieros* signifies a special relation to the gods: it "is as it were the shadow cast by divinity."[9]

Ēgatheos and *zatheos,* on the other hand, derive from *theos,* meaning "divine," each augmented by an intensive. Both words are found most often in archaic hexameters, especially in Homer and Hesiod, although each has found its way into Pindar and the tragedians. Unlike *hieros,* they are never used of persons. In Homer, they *only* qualify named places, usually poleis (Killa, Pylos, Phera, Krisa, and Nisa) but also islands (Lemnos, Kythera) and sanctuaries (Pytho, Mount Nysa). Occasionally in other authors they also qualify things in the natural world thought to possess something of the divine (for example, streams and a hill). *LSJ* offers the following translations: "very divine, most holy, sacred" and "immediately under divine protection." Burkert does not discuss these adjectives, but the noun *theos,* which he says is used almost like a predicate, he writes: "*Theos* is the annunciation and marvelling designation of *someone* present. . . . Speaking of *theos* or *theoi,* one posits an absolute and insurmountable point of reference for everything that has impact, validity, and *permanence*" (emphasis mine).[10]

Dios, like *hieros,* is applied widely to people and things: for instance, the sea, rivers, horses, goddesses, men, women, offspring, collective bodies of people (such as the Achaeans), as well as to cities and territories. The adjective derives from the oblique cases of Zeus (*Di-*), although over time the word has devalued and displaced by *theos.* The meaning of *dios* ranges from "divine" and "bright" to "illustrious," "noble," and "awful," a semantic shift that shows that its derivation predates the identity of Zeus as we have come to know him; Zeus etymologically is "brightness (of day)."

The application of both *hieros* and *theios* to a common object, in this case *polis* and *astu* (see *astu . . . theion* in Pindar), bridges the normally distinct boundary between "sacred" and "divine," defying what Benveniste claims are normal categories in Greek religion: "There is no term for 'god' which, whether in Greek or elsewhere, can be attached to the family of *hieros.* These are two distinct ideas. The adjective meaning divine in Greek is '*theios*', which is never confused with *hieros* sacred; nor in Latin is *divinus* ever confused with *sacer.*"[11] A similar blurring is seen in reference to the city walls: one finds both *hiera krēdemna* and *hiera teichea,* "sacred veil" and "sacred wall," of the wall at Boiotian Thebes and *theios purgos* and *theodmētoi purgoi,* "divine tower" and "divinely built towers," of Troy's fortification. This unlikely blend of religious terms which we find in Homer continues to echo in the literature of the fifth century. The blurring of conventional distinctions helps isolate the peculiar status of the polis: it is uniquely of the divine and the sacred, both as it were very much with the divine and cast under the shadow of divinity. The unlikely blend of religious terms describing the city clearly suggests that no single category is capable of capturing the full complexity or range of the ancient Greek association of city and sanctity.

Do these epithets describe something that is generic to Homer's view of the polis? Peter Wülfing–von Martitz argues that places in Homer are sacred according to one of three classifications: the site of cult or oracle; a celebrated state that plays a central role in myth; or an extensive territory mentioned in myth.[12] But his classifications require excessive special pleading, a fault that is especially evident in the arbitrary listings of the first category. There is little in Homer, or in the archaeological record, to support the contention that Phera (also "well-founded" in Homer) in Messenia, Krisa in Phocis, or Ismaros, ptoliethron of the Kikones in the *Odyssey,* are unusually cultic or oracular in nature.

Wülfing's second category also seems weak in that many Homeric cities important in myth are not called sacred. Mycenae, Tiryns, Athens, Ithaca, immediately come to mind (though Tiryns is *hirē* in Hesiod's *Theogony,* 292).

The sacredness of a few islands and territories is intriguing and perhaps deserves special classification, but it does not seem accidental that the islands (Lemnos and Lesbos) and territory (Elis) called sacred are also, like many poleis, *euktimenos,* "well-founded." As with cities, the sacredness of these extended spaces may well be identifiable with human habitation and its attendant ordering of place.

Against Wülfing's restricted view, the evidence in Homer suggests that sanctity is a generic attribute of the polis. This, clearly, was Eustathius' position in the twelfth century A.D.: "Not only is Thebes (in the Troad) called sacred [*hierē*], but so is every polis, as it guards those within, which [act of guarding], indeed, is divine [*theion*]" (at *Il.* 1.366). Again, we notice the intermixing of "sacred" and "divine" with the city. Like Homer, Eustathius concerns himself with the sanctity of the city itself, and less with that of extended territories or islands; the reference to polis is here clearly to the walled city proper.

The generic names of cities in the Homeric catalogues especially support Eustathius' view. Of the seven poleis offered by Agamemnon to Achilles, the names of three stand out as invented and suited to any polis: "grassy Hire, meadowed Antheia, beautiful Aipeia" or, translating the proper names, "grassy Sacred, meadowed Blooming, and beautiful Steepness" (*Il.* 9.150–52). "Grassy," "deep in meadows," and "beautiful" are common city epithets in the catalogues of Book 2 (see Appendix 1). Two of the proper names in this group themselves derive from the two most frequent city epithets in Homer: Sacred and Steep. The third proper name, Blooming, echoes the substance of its own epithet, *anthemoeis* itself being an epithet in the Greek Catalogue of Ships in Book 2. In such examples, common epithets become elevated to proper names, indicative of a generic trait. The epithet *dios* itself becomes a proper noun when it appears as the name of an island north of Crete where Dionysus rescued the abandoned Ariadne (*Od.* 11.325).

Elsewhere in the Greek Catalogue, two other common city epithets unite to form epithet and proper name, *euktiton aipu,* which might equally be considered "well-built Steep" or "steep Well-Built" (*Il.* 2.592) depending on which adjective is read as the proper noun. A similar ambiguity appears when Paris tells Helen that he has never loved her so much, not even when they lay "on the island Rocky," or, equally plausible, "on the rocky island" (*Il.* 3.445). Sacredness is no less part of the generic picture of the city than is its steepness or its well-built structures; a "sacred city" is no more "particularized" than is an Aegean rocky island. It should come as little surprise, then, that another of the cities that Agamemnon offers Achilles is called "very divine Phera" (*zatheai Phērai,* 9.151), the epithet continuing the generic quality of the catalogues. Sacredness is a condition of Homeric cities.

The double spellings of *hieros* and *hiros* invite comment but offer less than conclusive evidence in terms of Ionian perspectives about the sacred city. Both forms appear to be quite old; *hieros* is attested in Mycenaean Greek while the contracted *hiros* is mostly likely an Aeolic innovation, perhaps originating in Old Lesbian, slipping over into Ionic. The contracted *hiros* is peculiarly localized to Asia Minor (in both the Aeolic and Ionic dialects) and in Homer predominates in formulas involving Ilios, suggesting to some an ancient formula describing "sacred Wilusa/Ilios."[13] If we assume that *hieros,* modifying "cities," dates back perhaps to Mycenaean days, we might conjecture for the sake of argument that the Mycenaean acropolis was called sacred. (What term for sanctity, if any, might the people of the Greek Dark Age have used for their meager settlements?) But if the Mycenaean acropolis, often walled in the late period, enclosing the palace of the Mycenaean king and, on occasion, a small temple complex near the perimeter wall was considered sacred, the Mycenaean *astu,* or lower town outside the wall spreading down toward the plain, undoubtedly was not.[14]

But as the city grew to enclose polis and astu within a single wall, so the term "sacred" appears to expand with the new city so that in Homer not only the upper acropolis but the entire city is *hieros* and *hiros.* This vision of inclusive urban sanctity suggests an eighth-century polis like Old Smyrna more than a Mycenaean walled citadel. The family affiliation of Athena's priestess at Troy in the *Iliad* as well suggests that the sanctity of the Homeric polis is *communal* in nature rather than restricted to the king's domain. As the daughter of Kisseus, king of Thrace, and as wife of Antenor, who is an inhabitant of the polis (politēs) and an important counsellor of the Trojans but not of the royal family, Theano, is not linked by blood to the royal family.

The two large temples, or *nēoi*, to Athena and Apollo which stand at the height of Troy's acropolis equally suggest Ionian, not Mycenaean, conditions. The archaeological evidence for freestanding temples is unstable at this time, but most clues still point, as we shall see in a later chapter, to the large freestanding temple as an invention of the eighth century. Similarly, the Homeric form for temple, *nēos*, is Ionian, a reshaping perhaps of the common Greek form *naos*, which could certainly have existed for centuries in epic. Homer's description of an agora as a "sacred circle" under the care of Zeus where justice is dispensed, enclosed within polis walls, again can only date from the Ionian period and further suggests that the Homeric portrait of a walled city holding within an entire population is essentially an Ionian vision.[15]

Troy

Of the cities in Homer none is more frequently called holy than Troy. Temple oriented, of ancient origin, rich in foundation myths, Troy is endowed with unquestioned sanctity, but also unquestioned doom. That terrifying juxtaposition resounds throughout the *Iliad* but is never more starkly expressed than in the proem of the *Odyssey:* "he who wandered much from the time after he had destroyed the holy city of Troy [*epei Troiēs hieron ptoliethron eperse*]" (1.2). But first, what of Troy's sanctity?

Some scholars, such as Hooker and others, have suggested that the Homeric city in general, and Troy in particular, are sacred because we find therein the temples of the gods and the cult centers of many deities.[16] So T. E. Shaw seems to have thought; consider his translation of the *Odyssey's* proem cited above: "O Divine Poesy, goddess-daughter of Zeus, sustain for me this song of the various-minded man who after he had plundered, *the innermost citadel of hallowed Troy . . .* " (emphasis mine).[17] Placing undue stress upon the word *ptoliethron*, Shaw appears to identify Troy's sanctity explicitly with its templed acropolis.

Others consider its sanctity to stem from the divine construction of Troy's walls.[18] Consider the version of the *Odyssey's* proem by Alexander Pope: the man "who, when his arms had wrought the destined fall / of sacred Troy, and razed her heaven-built wall." His completion of the couplet, "and razed her heaven-built wall," is a gloss on "sacred Troy"; the rhyme of "fall" and "wall" nicely sharpens the juxtaposition between city destruction and god-built defense.

Perhaps because of the strangeness of the concept of sanctity to the modern mind, Fitzgerald, oddly, bypasses the issue altogether in his translation of *The Odyssey* (New York, 1961): "the wanderer, harried for years on end, / after he plundered the stronghold / on the proud height of Troy."

Still others, the scholia suggest, feel that Troy in particular, and poleis in general, are holy because it is from the city that mortals reach the Olympians through sacrifice (i.e., cities are hieros because in them people are "pious").[19] Hermes complains of traveling to Kalypso's Ogygia at the navel of the sea because, in his words, it is far from the poleis of men where sacrifices and chosen hekatombs are performed for the gods (*Od.* 5.101–2). No city is more honored than the city of Troy, Zeus says in the *Iliad* (4.44–49), for there, because of the devotion of Priam and the people of Priam, his altars are never wanting. As the place of such propitiation, the city acquires favors from the gods, fragile as those favors may be. Sacrifice, however, does not appear to be the ultimate reason why a polis should be called sacred. The hallowed nature of the walls, for instance, is not directly linked to regular sacrifice. Nor does sacrifice help us understand the sacred nature of the agora where the old men of the city preside over public quarrels. Rather, it seems that sacrifice intensifies an established sanctity and is a means by which mortals may bring into focus, or preserve, an Olympian attention already imprinted upon the sacred city.

So these four arguments—temples, divine walls, proud height, piety—seem insufficient in explaining the nature of Troy's sacredness. Analysis should begin by considering the four Olympians who especially identify themselves with the building of Troy or securing its well-being: Zeus, Poseidon, Athena, and to a lesser extent Apollo. Zeus himself sets in motion the chain of events that will lead to the founding of Troy, as assuredly he stimulates the founding of all Greek cities. The Olympians oversee all that is praised in the world; so it must be that those things which are most highly esteemed of human creations are said to derive from the supreme ruler of the gods. Aeneas describes Zeus' role in the founding of Troy as follows:

> First of all Zeus who gathers the clouds had a son, Dardanos,
> who founded Dardania, since there was yet no sacred Ilios

that had been citied [*pepolisto*] in the plain to be a city of mortal men,
but they still lived [*ōikeon*] in the underhills of Mount Ida with her
many springs.

(*Il.* 20.215–18)[20]

Troy's wall is not explicitly mentioned but is clearly implied, as elsewhere Zeus is directly responsible for the walls of Tiryns when he
orders the Kyklopes to make a circuit around that city (see Bacchylides, *Ode* 9.55–58 and 69–81). In archaic Greek thought the two
acts appear to be simultaneous and both find their origin in Zeus.

The intervention of Zeus is crucial in this passage for the transition
from undefined habitation (*ōikeon*) in the folds of the mountain to city
construct (20.218). No longer integrated with nature's forms, man of
the polis, out on the plain, separates himself from the wild and larger
world which surrounds him. Although once of nature, man coming
down from Mount Ida has transcended that original state through
architecture and community. From the human point of view this transition is analogous to the separation of earth from sky and day from
night at the world's beginning. Having initiated the founding of the
polis or the building of its walls, Zeus for the Greeks completes the
process, begun in some accounts by Prometheus, of leading human
beings to civilization.[21] By separating himself in the walled polis from
nature's randomness, man of the polis occupies for the first time a
space that can be called exclusively human. The city, in short, springs
from that human desire for presence, for stability and distinction in a
world of undifferentiated mutability and sameness. The spirit of enclosure and the conferring of a human identity define the sacral essence
of the Homeric polis and are the reasons Zeus initiates its creation.

Such achievement is only possible in the collective enclosure of a
(walled) polis, and not in the individual oikos, or household, of an
extended family estate. It is this unique capacity of the polis which
must explain why the polis but never the oikos is called hieros. We may
perhaps, then, extend Aristotle's definition of man as "by nature a
creature of the polis" (*Pol.* 1253a) to Homeric description in the following way: in the movement from oikos to polis, the human definition
changes. The collective force of man, organized around a civic rather
than a domestic perspective (sacred agora rather than the megaron),
surpasses the daily requirements of the oikos. Lewis Mumford bril-
liantly captures the spirit of this new order:

The modest foundations of the village had been laid in the earth, but the city reversed the village's values, and turned the peasant's universe upside down, by placing the foundations in the heavens. All eyes now turned skywards. Belief in the eternal and the infinite, the omniscient and the omnipotent succeeded, over the millennia, in exalting the very possibilities of human existence. Those who made the most of the city were not chagrined by the animal limitations of human existence; they sought deliberately, by a concentrated act of will, to transcend them.[22]

Sacred Troy rising from the plain deserves its epithet precisely because the polis, inspired by Zeus, leads man toward the uniquely human. The act of civilization itself is sacred and partakes of the divine. The polis, even more than a "political" community, is a religious one, separated as it is from nature (itself sacred, but for different reasons), the place of shelter guarding those within. This view, we recall, coincides with what Eustathius said of Thebes' sacredness: "every *polis* is *hieros* as it guards the people within, which [act], indeed, is divine [*theion*]."[23]

In Homer the role of the supreme Olympian in a city's defense is manifest repeatedly: Achilles urges the Achaeans to return home, "since," he says, "you shall not find the mark [*tekmōr*] of steep Ilios. For all-seeing Zeus has stretched out a loving hand over it and the people are in good heart" (*Il.* 9.418–20 = 685–87). Arguing over the fate of Troy with Hera, Zeus himself states that "of all the cities mortals inhabit under the sun and starry sky, sacred Ilios is by far the one most dear to my heart" (*Il.* 4.45–46).

We might further refine this concept of sacredness of communal space by contrasting Troy with the Achaean camp. In many regards that camp is like a city: it encloses a body of people who are governed by laws (*themistes*) and ruled by one who is "more kingly" (*Il.* 9.160; cf. 1.281). Like Troy, it has an agora and is surrounded by a wall, at one point called *arrēktos* (*Il.* 14.56). But no one ever considers the camp sacred. Solely defensive in design ("guarding ships and fighting men," see 7.338, 437; 12.5–8; 14.56, and so forth), the Achaean wall perverts the higher necessity of the polis to "defend women and children" (see 8.53–57, 265; 10.421–22; 22.110, for example). In short, a defensive wall by itself does not define a polis. The Achaean wall, neither nurturing life nor sheltering a human community, is particularly abhorrent to the gods. The protected camp is an aggregate of parts which never transcends its multiplicity into a unifying singleness; the city of Troy, as an aggregate of oikoi, by contrast is a unified whole defined by its embrace of the young and the vulnerable. Poseidon and Apollo, who as we shall see shortly have special jurisdiction over Troy's walls, particularly despise the Achaean wall, but Zeus is equally eager to see it obliterated.

Even if loathed by the gods, the wall once built can only be destroyed definitively by a terrific display of supernatural might. Pope's translation is particularly poignant as he describes the insult of such engineering on the natural landscape:

> Without the gods, how short a period stands
> The proudest monument of mortal hands!
> This stood while Hector and Achilles raged,
> While sacred Troy the warring hosts engaged;
> But when her sons were slain, her city burn'd,
> And what survived of Greece to Greece return'd;
> Then Neptune and Apollo shook the shore,
> Then Ida's summits pour'd their watery store,
> Rhesus and Rhodius then unite their rills,
> Caresus roaring down the stony hills,
> Aesepus, Granicus, with mingled force,
> And Xanthus foaming from his fruitful source;
> And gulfy Simois, rolling to the main
> Helmets and shields, and godlike heroes slain:
> These, turn'd by Phoebus from their wonted ways,
> Deluged the rampire nine continual days;
> The weight of waters saps the yielding wall,
> And to the sea the floating bulwarks fall.
> Incessant cataracts the Thunderer pours,
> And half the skies descend in sluicy showers.
> The god of ocean, marching stern before,
> With his huge trident wounds the trembling shore,
> Vast stones and piles from their foundation heaves,
> And whelms the smoky ruin in the waves.
> Now smooth'd with sand, and levell'd by the flood,
> No fragment tells where once the wonder stood;
> In their old bounds the rivers roll again,
> Sine 'twixt the hills, or wander o'er the plain.
>
> (*Il.* 12.8–33; 7.461–63)

By strangely reversing the order of appearance of Apollo and Zeus, Pope makes it seem as if the younger god were responsible for making the walls into flotsam.

In celebrating the restored order of nature defiled, Pope's last four lines press beyond the Homeric original: "He made smooth the shore by the fast-flowing Hellespont and covered once again the great beach with sand, having levelled the wall. He turned the rivers back into their channels down which the beautifully flowing water ran before" in Homer (12.30–33). Pope's "wonder," not in Homer, undoubtedly refers to more than defensive walls. Although he introduces a melancholy not found in Homer, Pope still preserves an ancient sense of nature's power to reclaim its own. Zeus leads humankind to the city whose circuit walls are deemed sacred, but he cannot permit such abhorred engineering as the Achaean wall to define the natural landscape.

A brief account of beliefs to the east and west of Greece in regard to sacred cities will help us better understand the true sense of the Homeric hierē polis.[24] As already observed, the Homeric view of urban space differs significantly from Roman beliefs in which parts of the urbs, but not the urbs itself, were considered *sacer*. Unlike the Romans, in the Near East many cultures considered their cities "sacred" (cf. *uru-kù,* Sumerian for "pure or holy settlement"), but here again those beliefs contrast with the Homeric conception of the sacred polis.

Sumerian cities from the second millennium, like Neo-Babylonian ones two thousand years later, were divided into two highly differentiated parts. The opening lines from tablet one of the *Epic of Gilgamesh* provide a convenient illustration:

> Of ramparted Uruk, the wall he (Gilgamesh) built,
> Of hallowed Eanna, the pure [*kù*] sanctuary,
> Behold its outer wall, whose cornice is like copper,
> Peer at the inner wall, which none can equal!
> Seize upon the threshold, which is from of old!
> Draw near to Eanna, the dwelling of Ishtar,
> Which no king, no man, can equal.[25]

Both parts of the city are separately named and separately walled. The name Uruk here refers to the city where people live and work, the uru or settlement surrounded by the outer wall ("whose cornice is like copper"); the name Eanna refers to the hallowed sanctuary of Anu and Ishtar at the center of Uruk, the inner house (or *é*) of the city god as well as administrative center of the city. This precinct was built before humankind was created and is surrounded by its own massive wall ("which none can equal"). Its description "from of old" suggests an archetypal model from the mythic past. At the gates to this inner temple precinct, as the liminal space separating the "city of man" from god, the major activities of the city/state were performed: civic and legal administration, regulation of the city food supply, and the like.

Within the inner perimeter rose the massive ziggurat or stage tower, cosmic home of the tutelary deity and "pure [kù] mountain, where the water is sweet," "pure place, scoured with soap," to quote from two Sumerian hymns.[26] Rooted in the subterranean waters (*abzu*) and built according to celestial models, the temple was both local *omphalos* ("Temple, whose interior is the vital center of the country")[27] and *axis mundi* ("Temple, whose platform is suspended from heaven's midst / whose foundation fills the Abzu"),[28] linking upper world, earth, and lower depths.

Humankind was created after the cities were founded, and as in the Hebrew story of Eden, man tended a world of divine making. As he approaches the city, and more particularly the temple complex at the center, he "transcends 'profane,' heterogeneous space, and enters pure earth;"[29] that is, man moves toward pure city and primordial universe. Contrary to a tradition that stresses a pastoral paradise as the original setting of humankind where Nature existed before the onset of civilization, in this world man comes face to face with god at the urban core.[30]

Both sacred and secular texts point in the same direction. If the power of the city deity extends outward bestowing fertility and abundance on city and countryside beyond, the literature in contrary fashion trains its attention upon the inner temple complex because therein lie the locus of power and the residence of the god. The Sumerian phrase *uru-kù* refers particularly to this separately walled and separately named inner temple complex. If the texts usually identify the inner precinct as the god's house (*é*), the Sumerian *uru* may describe any permanent settlement, and there is one text that with obvious jubilation calls the inner sanctuary an uru. The hymn describes a temple precinct at Kes: "Indeed it is a city [*uru*], indeed it is a city [*uru*] / The Kes temple is indeed a city [*uru*]."[31] Even if we were to regard this last description as metaphoric, as it surely is, it points the way for our interpretation, also suggested by Jacobsen, that *uru-kù* is a general term for the "inner city" where temples are clustered.[32]

A Mesopotamian city, in short, comprises two permanent settlements. City-sanctity, generic to all cities, is predominantly if not exclusively associated with the cosmic house of the god, or the inner city, and may be understood in terms of the god's presence. The hymns repeatedly exalt this "uru" as pure and holy, while they tend to omit any such praise of the "outer city." If the city of man partakes in the temple's purity, it does so as the first outer ring that embraces the place of godhead. (For a fuller account of Mesopotamian and Anatolian beliefs about the sacred and the city, see Appendix 3.)

As with the cities to their west, Mesopotamian cities are temple oriented, of ancient origin, and richly endowed with foundation myths. The sacredness of those cities is identified with the many temples at the urban center, a view, as we saw, akin to that of those who claim that the Homeric polis is sacred because of the temples within its perimeter. The Homeric portrait of the polis, however, differs significantly from the few excerpts already quoted. In Homer we see the city portrayed as a single entity: temples, palace, people of Troy housed together around one wall. Focus is almost always on the collective city, the aggregate of oikoi, and only rarely on the temples within the city. In short, the Homeric portrait of Troy, and other cities, extends the theocentric Near Eastern notion of urban sanctity beyond the house of the god to include the city of man. The Homeric view of the sacred city is equally distant from the dualistic Roman outlook, which is simultaneously abstract and hierocentric in its designation of sacred templum and sacred civitas, but not sacred urbs.

Even if the Sumerians have a word for "sacred city" and the Romans do not, both cultures seem to share an acute differentiation between sacred and profane activity. In one, sacred city describes the urban area inhabited by the god where divinely overseen activities of state are performed. In the other, where the city of god and the city of man are less sharply delineated, a distinction is made between a nonsacer city of man and a sacred templa where religious or political activities of state are performed. The Homeric model has close affinities with the Near Eastern and Roman, but it has semantically evolved beyond those models. As the polis spreads out from the Mycenaean citadel to collective aggregate, the sacred enclosure spreads out as well to embrace the whole. The result appears startling as the sacred city is perceived less in terms of the sacred and the profane and more as a differentiation between man-made and natural forms; it is a place sacred because it is infused with divinity and divine because it is a place where humankind, approaching the manner of the gods, may exist free from necessity (to paraphrase Aristotle).[33]

A metaphor common to Sumerian, Roman, and Greek texts helps illustrate the particular nature of each. In the theocentric orientation of Sumerian urban architecture, we can easily understand the frequent identification of the ziggurat temple as "head" or "crown" of the uru. In praise of Eunir, the ziggurat of Eridu, one text exclaims: "Your prince, the great prince, a holy [kù] crown / He has placed for you upon your head! / O Eridu with a crown on your head!"[34] Similarly the Sumerian word *Esagila,* the mighty ziggurat at the center of Babylon, means House with Lofty Head, a name the Akkadians later play on in the *Enuma elish* when they describe the gods building the holy mountain: "They raised high the head of Esagila equaling Apsu" (6.62). In this imagery of the body politic, the city of man is the earthly body crowned by the godhead into whose presence humankind (and civilization) has come.

Rome's most sacred templum, the Capitolium, is also "head" of the urbs: while excavating the foundations for Jupiter's temple, the Romans unearthed a human skull, a sign they believed that the Capitolium, and by extension their city, was to be *caput rerum,* head of the universe, and *summa imperi,* seat of universal power (see Livy, 5.54.4).

The Homeric metaphor for crown, however, extends to the whole polis. With its coronation of towers and gates the polis itself is well-crowned (*eustephanos* in Homer and Hesiod; *stephanos* and *iostephanos* in later poets), and is covered with a sacred veil (*hiera krēdemna*). In a phrase unique to Homer in Greek, Zeus is described as one who "has unyoked the heads [*kateluse karēna*] of many cities and who will in the future unyoke still more" (*Il.* 2.117–18 = 9.24–5). We see this metaphor implied in another. Agamemnon praises Nestor: with more men like you, he says, "the polis of Lord Priam, captured and destroyed by the Achaeans, would soon be tottering" [*ēmuseie*]" (2.373–74 = 4.290–91). The verb "to totter" (*ēmuō*) means literally "to droop or nod," as do the heads of wheat near the time of harvest. If at one time *krēdemnon* and "head of cities" referred to the Mycenaean walled citadel (the scholia even suggest that heads of poleis refers to the *acropolis*), in the *Iliad* the images of crown, veil, and city head have expanded to include the whole urban body.[35]

City head and crown no longer exclusively designate "pure earth" with divinity at the city center. Less hierocentric or theocratic than the Mesopotamian system, Greek religion appears to bestow sanctity on the entire arena that sets humankind apart from nature. We see further support for this view in the evolution of the city's name from the singular to the plural. The appearance of certain important place names in the plural in Greece (Athenae, Mycenae), both Leonard Muellner and Gregory Nagy explain as a function of political expansion: "The plural form of Athene (attested in the singular at *Od.* 7.81) means 'Athens and its environs.' "[36] The presence of the goddess has extended from her acropolis sanctuary outward.

Troy's walls, like the polis itself, are called *hieros* and *theios*. If we are to consider *hieros* a generic epithet suitable for all city walls, *theios* is more restrictive. Undoubtedly it derives from the fact that Poseidon (with Apollo) constructed Troy's circuit defense, an aspect of the Trojan wall rarely referred to in Homer (see *Il.* 8.519 and 21.526ff.) and then usually by Poseidon himself.

For him, enclosing Troy within a wall acquires the greatest significance. The building of Troy's wall "citied" Troy (*polissamen,* 7.453; the same verb, in its only other occurrence, is used to describe Zeus' founding of Troy, see 20.217). Its purpose, he says, was to make the polis "unbreakable" (*arrēktos*): "Then I built a wall for the Trojans about their city, / wide, and very splendid, in order that the city might be unbreakable" (*Il.* 21.446–47). *Arrēktos* tellingly qualifies polis and not walls, as if the polis at large, by such enclosure, could remain untouched by nature's cycles. Mumford captures this view when he sees the city wall as "both a physical rampart for defence and a spiritual boundary of even greater significance."[37]

Special as Troy's walls are, the sanctity of city walls, as noted, is not unique to Troy. In the next chapter, we shall explore further the association of the sacred with the urban wall; here it is sufficient to observe that the circuit wall may be considered an ideogram, or hieroglyph, for the city itself. The wall's sanctity, stemming from the shelter it provides for those enclosed, is to be understood as an extension of the city's sanctity; the sacred status of the community is primary, that of its walls secondary.

The preeminent tutelary deity at Troy, however, is neither Poseidon, nor Zeus, but Zeus' warrior daughter, Potnia Athena,[38] the primary defender of many cities throughout Greek history as is expressed by her post-Homeric epithets *Polias* and *Poliouchos*.[39] The interchangeable identities of this goddess and her cities can be seen in Nicole Loraux's description of Athens: "ever warlike, like the divinity that protects it, the redoubtable city, as embodied in the Athena Promachos at the entrance to the Acropolis, may be as reassuring as the Chryselephantine Virgin of the Parthenon, armed but at repose."[40] In Homer, such a city-defending Athena on the Shield of Achilles (*Il.* 18.490ff.) marches out with Ares in defense of her beseiged town. At Troy, Athena's temple (*nēos*), or sacred house (*hieros domos*), stands at the highest point in the city, a heraldic symbol to the city's enemies, human or divine, that with her figure-eight shield or her Zeus-given aegis, Potnia Athena will stand guard over the city.[41]

It is to this divine protectress that the Trojans turn when they sense that their city is in need. In hopes that she will divert the raging torrent of Diomedes from Troy, the sons of Priam order the women of Troy to supplicate the city goddess with the finest robe from the storerooms. With that offering, they pray that this seated goddess, evoked by her epithet "the rescuer of the polis" (*erusiptolis, Il.* 6.305), "will take pity on the city [*astu*] and the wives of the Trojans and the young children" (6.309–10). As noted, Athena's priestess Theano, Antenor's wife, leads the prayer for the polis.

Athena's multifaceted nature is expressive of the complex associations of the city and civic defense with the female. The Trojan women pray to her hoping that, as a female, Athena will empathize with the teeming life enclosed within city walls ("if she might pity the wives of the Trojans and the young children"), and that, as a female, she will be delighted with the delicately woven robe selected for her by the women of Troy. But it is further hoped that, as the parthenogenic daughter of Zeus, she will exercise her warrior valor in defense of the city's women and children. Fully armed and virginal, she stands as a figure of the city, particularly as it is seen from the outside: both walled city and armed Athena impregnable, unviolated, and hopefully inviolable, or, in Loraux's words, "armed but in repose." To penetrate the city walls by force is to violate the virgin goddess.[42]

The association of rape and the violation of city walls is explicitly made in the context of another metaphor, that of the *krēdemna,* or "veils," which in a complex of formulas signifies ritual purity either of married women or of the city.[43] Here again the city wall is called sacred (hieros), but not, I think, in conjunction with Athena (despite Burkert, see note 42). This metaphor, unlike the image of the city as an armed Athena, suggests the female dimension of the polis as seen from within: the wedded female, fertile and ritually pure, more like Andromache with child than like the virginal Athena. When Andromache, seeing Hektor's body dragged around the city, casts the krēdemnon from her head, a krēdemnon that had been given to her by Aphrodite on her wedding day, she signifies by that gesture the violation awaiting her and Troy when the city walls fail.[44] It is consistent with other lexical usage that the "veil" is called sacred only when it refers to the "diadem of city towers," not when it refers to the wife's headdress, as ritually pure as it may be in its own right. When Achilles prays to Zeus that he may loosen or unyoke Troy's holy diadem of towers (*hiera krēdemna luōmen, Il.* 16.100), he expresses a desire to violate the hallowed bonds of civilization but not, I suspect, a desire to rape the armed virgin goddess.

The female associations with the polis are, then, both virginal and maternal, and are linked both with the city wall and sanctity. The wall is further sanctified, as we have observed, by its association with its divine male builder. These male and female identities of the city wall converge when Poseidon is described as the guardian of Thebes' crown of towers (*Shield of Heracles* 104–5): "and the Earthshaker, receiver of bulls, / who keeps the krēdemna of Thebes and defends the polis."[45]

Although suggestive perhaps of other times and places, Homer's portrait of Athena derives essentially from Ionian practices. The roots of her worship as a polis protectress may reach back, however, into the Mycenaean period. Recently, archaeologists have discovered small temples and shrines, independent of the palace, within the circuitry of Mycenaean strongholds.[46] George Mylonas believes that three female deities were venerated at Mycenae's cult center: a goddess of trees and civilization, a goddess of family life (the Mycenaean Hera), and a goddess of war (the Mycenaean Athena), who, like a Palladion (an image of Athena fallen from heaven which magically protected Troy as long as it remained in the city), was represented by a figure-eight shield protecting humankind and "state."[47]

So far, no architectural evidence supports Martin Nilsson's thesis that the public cult of Athena Polias may derive from a household goddess who protected the Mycenaean wanax.[48] Yet absence of temple remains does not categorically undermine Nilsson's claim. Criticisms of Nilsson, archaeological in orientation, ignore events narrated in the Homeric texts. One cannot rule out the possibility that a memory of such cult worship may have survived in the *Odyssey* (7.81), where it is said that Athena went to "Athens of the wide ways" (Athens in the singular for the only time in Homer) and entered the strong house (*pukinon domon*) of Erechtheus. These details certainly cannot apply to any moment in the Ionian period. Nonetheless, Homer's Lady Mykene, "well-crowned" (*Od.* 2.120), was probably once an eponymous defender, of city or king's megaron, at Mycenae in the Mycenaean Age.

An armed city goddess is also common to the peoples of the Near East, whether in the form of Ishtar, Anat in Ugarit,[49] or the Hittite/Phrygian mother goddess Kybele who was worshiped not only as goddess of mountains, fertility, and the wealth of nature but also a giver of city walls and defender of urban enclosure. Counterpart to Inanna/Ishtar among the Sumerian/Babylonians and to the Hittite Sun-Goddess of Arinna, as fierce city defender the Phrygian Kybele wears a crown of battlements on her head.[50]

Whatever bearing these figures may have on the Homeric portrait of

Athena, the Homeric Athena at Troy and her temple in that polis are principally inspired by the new civic religion emerging in Ionia, and on the mainland of Greece, shortly after 800 B.C. The goddess's freestanding temple at the crest of Troy suggests the new public temples and common cults first seen in Greece about this time. As noted before, the Homeric form for temple, nēos, is itself Ionian and indicates relatively contemporary Ionian practices. A similar Athena is evident in the Catalogue of Ships, in what must be a late intrusion into that segment of the *Iliad,* where, now at "well-founded Athens," the goddess has her own "rich *nēos,*" a statue of Erechtheus being in place nearby (*Il.* 2.546–49). These references all point to the new Athena Polias, archetypal protectress, heart and spirit of the budding Greek polis. Of the thirteen major Ionian cities, eight may have worshiped this figure.[51]

In addition to Athena's nēos, the *Iliad* says that Apollo too has a temple (*nēos*) in "holy Pergamon" on the height of Troy (*Il.* 5.446). Within the temple, there is an inner sanctuary (*aduton,* "great and rich," 5.448 and 512, mentioned only in this passage in Homer) where Leto and Artemis wondrously heal the wounded Aeneas. If the city as a whole is sacred, clearly Apollo's and Athena's temple sites mark Troy's most sacred areas, which are, not accidentally, those places in the city where miracles occur and to which city-inhabitants repair in time of civic stress.

Neither Zeus nor Poseidon but Apollo is Troy's great male defender. If frequently associated with the building of city walls by music and song in later Greek literature,[52] in Homer he tended sheep while Poseidon labored building the walls. Although maltreated like Poseidon (see *Il.* 21.440–45), Apollo remains an untiring enemy of the Greeks and frequently stands on the walls of Troy in a desperate effort to prevent the city from falling before its appointed day. Why this loyalty? Despite the fact that it has now been proven that the name "Apollo" cannot be derived from a Lycian divine name, there are still many remarkable connections between Lycia and his cult site at Delos and between him and the Semitic god Resep and the Hittite Guardian God, particularly in regard to his association with the stage, his role as god of the plague, and his weapon the bow.[53] And in Homer two of his epithets, *Smintheus* and *Chrusaoros,* refer to cult rituals found only in Asia Minor.[54] One wonders whether these cult links with the Troad explain Apollo's "surprising" loyalty to Troy.

Similarly Aphrodite, and not Athena in spite of her temple at Troy, is that city's most loyal female protectress, "she who loves the Trojans so dearly," as Athena says with scorn (*Il.* 5.423). This Homeric Aphrodite is not the great goddess of Asia Minor, both earth figure and city protector, the all-powerful Aphrodite/Astarte portrayed on occasion like the Phrygian Kybele with a crown of towers on her head,[55] but the Aphrodite of Helen and Alexander, a goddess without civic presence or military might. She is also, however, the Aphrodite of Mount Ida and, like Apollo, clearly associated with the land of Troy. As portrayed in the Homeric *Hymn to Aphrodite,* she is the primary goddess of the Troad: deity of the wild beasts and of men, of sea and mountain, where in union with the mortal Anchises she, in Zeus-like manner, creates civilization.[56] In Homer, it is these regional deities, more than the civic Athena Polias (or Zeus Polieus), who cast the benevolence of their divinity over the Trojans and the walled polis of Troy. Not surprisingly, only Apollo and Aphrodite protect Hektor's body from Achilles' ravages (23.189–91; cf. 24.18–21).

But why does the sacred city fall? And where are the gods in the story of Troy's demise? And what of humankind? Is the destruction of the sacred city an act of sacrilege? Does Odysseus travel with impunity after having "destroyed the holy city of Troy"?

Archaeology suggests that the Mycenaeans helped defend their citadels with cosmo-magical practices similar to those used in the Near East. The latest excavations at Tiryns confirm that the Mycenaeans did place cult niches in the city walls, just as the animal figures in the Lion's Gate at Mycenae attest to Mycenaean belief in apotropaic figures of defense at city gates.[57] Similar practices, as we have seen, are widespread throughout the Near East and the Mediterranean and continue in Greece well into the classical period.[58]

In Homer, as in later Greek literature, however, references to cosmo-magical defense tend to be either ignored or suppressed; Homeric description favors naturalistic accounting over magical, fantastical, and supernatural interventions. Troy's mysterious *tekmōr,* "mark," which Achilles equates with the city's security (*Il.* 9.418–20), gives way more commonly than not to anthropomorphized explanations of city defense. Hektor, rather than the Palladion, keeps Troy safe. Both characters in the poem and the narrator more frequently refer to Troy's walls as well-built rather than as divinely built or Poseidon-built (the latter fact mentioned only by Poseidon himself).

In Homer, latent references to magical tales are often detected. Knight, for example, saw in the story of the Trojan Horse latent imagery of Greek horse magic set against Troy's strong horse magic,[59] and Burkert sees the fall of Troy linked, in long-lost cultic ritual, to the sacrifice of a horse by means of a spear.[60] Latent imagery of supernatural/magical defense is evident again when the two combatants circle Troy three times: Achilles has in effect countered the magic of Troy by enclosing it within a larger circle.[61]

Other Homeric episodes also appear to conceal stories of apotropaic magic and countermagic. When Achilles stands on the Achaean rampart, fire burning above him, for example, he gives a great shout: "There Achilles stood and cried aloud while in the distance Pallas Athena raised the war cry too. The Trojans were utterly confounded. His cry was as piercing as the trumpet call that rings out when a city is beset by murderous enemies" (18.217–20). Like the trumpets before the walls of Jericho, Achilles' shout in some other telling may have carried magical force, more efficacious than the warrior's prowess, his war cry a trumpet blast to counter the music often identified with the building of city walls.[62] The skeletal remains of magic rites, forgotten or suppressed, survive concealed in metaphor.

Both the *Iliad* and the *Odyssey* similarly fail to mention that Troy's fate was secure as long as Athena's wooden image, or Palladion, remained within the city, although the removal of this object is crucial for a later poet of the epic tradition when he explains the fall of Troy (see *Iliou Persis* 1.1ff.). Such beliefs are clearly analogous to Near Eastern and Roman practices of *evocatio,* or calling the tutelary deity out of the city by the enemy before they destroy it.[63] For the Sumerians in an earlier age, the tutelary deity voluntarily, even if with great reluctance, abandoned house (and city) when it became clear that the city's fate was sealed.[64]

Finding it difficult to explain how the god-built walls of Troy were overrun, Pindar offers the following interpretation: Poseidon and Apollo employed the help of a mortal, a certain Aiakos, and it was there where he worked that the wall was breached. The scholia state the obvious: this point in the wall marks the city's mortal vulnerability (*Olympian* 8.40ff.).

If these, usually older, magical or cultic elements commonly give way in Homer to more naturalistic and heroic explanations of city defense, we should not overstress Homeric tendencies to purge all superstitious or magical elements. As the antagonists within the poem recognize, Greek or Trojan *aretē* depends on Zeus, and the fate of Troy ultimately lies in his hands. As the frequently uttered phrase testifies, "if Zeus may grant us to destroy the well-walled city of Ilios," victory depends on more than warrior might. The greatest degree of magic, however, is seen in the context of Achilles, and especially between

Books 18 and 22 of the *Iliad,* as he prepares to duel with Troy's chief defender. Consider the fire that comes out of his head and the supernatural force of his voice (18.203–31); or his diet of nectar and ambrosia (19.340–54); or Hephaistos' armor, which like wings lifts up Achilles (19.386); or Achilles' flame, which with Hephaistos' aid causes Troy's rivers, once they have jumped their banks, to boil (21.211–384); or the divine horses with human speech which foretell his doom (19.407–24).[65] As I show in greater detail in the final chapter, Achilles has attracted to himself the full share of supernatural power more traditionally associated with magic.

Destruction of a sacred city does not, in and of itself, imply sacrilege. Greek impiety in the taking of Troy, an impiety evident from the many disasters that occurred during the army's return or once home, stemmed more from the wanton devastation of Athena's temple rather than from the sacking of the city itself. Such sacrilege, evident in many Greek texts, is also implied in a sixth-century vase that shows the Palladion on one side and the rape of Cassandra on the other.[66]

But the Trojans must assume some responsibility for their own ruin. Although Zeus singles out Troy as the city most dear to his heart because of the many sacrifices that Priam and his people have prepared for him (*Il.* 4.44–49; cf. 24.66–70), the people of Troy have also, with surprising regularity, offended the gods. The most obvious offense, of course, is Alexander's violation of the sacred code of hospitality and his criminal passion for Helen. His immorality implicates the whole polis; so Menelaos boasts over the slain body of Peisander as if all Trojans were guilty of Alexander's disgrace: "You insolent Trojans, never satiated of terrible war, nor are you lacking in other forms of outrage [*lōbē*] and shame [*aiskhos*] which you have already committed against me, evil dogs. Nor have you feared in your heart at all the harsh wrath [*mēnis*] of far-thundering Zeus, guardian of our codes of hospitality [*xeinios*], who will soon utterly destroy your steep polis, you who went away taking my wedded wife and many possessions while she treated you with hospitality" (*Il.* 13.621–27; cf. 6.55–62 and 24.27–28). Menelaos has in mind the same Zeus who punishes men with torrential rain when "by force they deliver crooked judgments in the agora and drive out justice" (*Il.* 16.387–88; cf. Hesiod, *Works and Days,* 256–60). Because of Alexander's actions, city walls collapse.

Even in its efforts to propitiate the city gods, Troy seems incapable of escaping from the consequences of its past. The prized cloth with which the women of Troy chose to honor their tutelary goddess in the hope that she would rescue the city from Diomedes is the very piece that Alexander picked up in Sidonia on his return from Sparta with Helen in hand (see 6.289–92). But behind that violation lies the even greater impiety of Troy when Laomedon astonishingly refused to pay Poseidon (and Apollo) for their construction of the city wall. As Virgil says, thinking how this impiety affects present-day Rome: "Long enough have we paid in our blood for the promise Laomedon broke at Troy" (*Georg.* 1.501–2).[67]

The Trojans (and their allies) continue to reenact their religious violation early on in the poem when Pandaros, a Lykian commander, breaks the truce after the aborted duel between Alexander and Menelaos (see 4.66–220).[68] Speaking to his wounded brother, Agamemnon says in part: "The Olympian may postpone the penalty, but he exacts it in the end, and the transgressors pay a heavy price, with their own heads, and with their wives and their children. For I know well in my heart and midriff that the day will come when holy Ilios will be destroyed, and Priam and the people of Priam, who is skilled with the ash-spear. Zeus himself, son of Kronos, from his high seat in the aether, will shake his dark aegis over them all in his anger [*koteōn*] at their unfair dealing [*apatēs*]. These things will not be unaccomplished" (4.160–68). In Troy's agora and in a sense speaking for the assembled Trojans, Antenor invites Alexander to give back Helen and all her property, reminding the Trojans that "we now fight having perjured ourselves" (*hopkia pista pseusamenoi,* 7.351–52). Although Alexander agrees to return her property, he will not think of giving up Helen. When the Greeks are confronted with this choice, Diomedes, rejecting all offers, speaks the Greek sentiment: "Know, as any fool can see, that the Trojans' doom is sealed" (literally, that the cords of destruction are fastened upon the Trojans, 7.401–2). Again, Troy with its women and children will pay for past and present crimes.

Impiety of a few, however, cannot be the ultimate reason for Troy's fall. Such failings must be considered part of a larger story. Each of the three gods most identified with Troy's foundation and city worship—Zeus, Poseidon, and Athena—is instrumental in its destruction. As already mentioned (see *Il.* 21.450–52), Poseidon may have special grievances. We may conjecture that, like Hera, Athena wishes to punish the Trojans for Alexander's blindness (*atē, Il.* 24.28, others read *archē;* cf. 21.414).[69] Perhaps she shares Hera's resentment at Alexander's preference for Aphrodite, elliptically alluded to only once (24.29–30). Her pitiless indifference to Troy, however, is never explained. In contrast to the extended descriptions of supplication and sacrifice as the Trojans try in vain to invoke their goddess in Book 6

(6.87–94, repeated 269–75, and again 286–311), her denial comprises one-half of one hexameter line and is unflinching: "but the goddess shook her head" (6.311). Why does the city goddess so mercilessly turn her back on Troy? An answer cannot be separated from her father's willingness to see Troy destroyed.

Far from "hating sacred Ilios," as the narrator claims once in a disputed line (8.551), Zeus himself says that he has a surpassing affection for Troy: "Dear Hera, what great evils can Priam and the sons of Priam have done to you so that you are raging to destroy Ilios, the well-founded city?" (4.25–49). "Deeply troubled" (okhthēsas) as he is, Zeus allies himself with Athena, to see the city fall. He prophesies: "In anger for Patroklos, brilliant Achilles will kill Hektor. / Then I will cause the war to retreat from the ships / always and continuously, until the Achaeans / take steep Ilios through the designs of Athena" (Il. 15.68–71). The two greatest defenders of cities turn city-destroyers. They work together again when Achilles "sacked [Lyrnessos] with Athena and father Zeus" (20.192).

City destruction is nothing new. Zeus has destroyed the heads of many cities in the past and will continue to do so in the future, Agamemnon plaintively remarks (2.115–17 and 9.23–25). The polis, as communal space, may be hieros, but it is also, as the epithets tell us, "the city of mortal men" (polis meropōn anthrōpōn). These two city-epithets, straining against each other, stand side-by-side ("sacred Ilios had not yet been made in the plain to be a city of mortal men"), each expressing a universal truth. When a city is cast within the frame of the cosmic setting, as Zeus casts Troy in his appeal, and acquiescence, to Hera ("of all the cities that men who dwell on the earth inhabit beneath the sun and starry heavens, sacred Ilios is most dear to me," Il. 4.44–47), city walls become insubstantial divisions of natural space (see Chapter 8). Seen from this (Olympian) perspective where the polis is set within the frame of sun and stars, we sense that Troy may be doomed because of its (endless) impieties, but that behind that particular truth lies a deeper reality. The polis of mortals, for all its sanctity, is doomed and part of a tragic paradox in which the human artifice, divine as it may be, is cast within the context of a greater divinity that dwarfs the polis. This generic proposition that all cities (Pope's "wonder" [?])—and not Troy alone—are holy but doomed is brought home by Hera when she coolly gives up for ruin the three cities she most cherishes. As she says to Zeus: "Of all the cities, three are dearest to my heart: / Argos, Sparta, and Mykenai of the wide ways. All these, / whenever they become hateful to your heart, sack utterly" (Il. 4.51–53).[70]

CHAPTER 3

The Walled Polis

A statistical approach might indicate that the city wall is relatively insignificant in the Homeric description of cities. Only nine cities in the *Iliad* are said to be walled: Troy (Ilios), Thebes, and Lyrnessos in the Troad; Thebes in Egypt; Thebes in Boiotia; Tiryns in the Argolid; Kalydon in Aitolia; Phaia on the border of Pylos; and Gortyna in Crete. When we realize that the walls for five of these nine cities are mentioned only once or only in the Greek catalogue of Book 2,[1] a list of walled *poleis* in the *Iliad* begins to look rather small indeed. Odyssean descriptions do little to alter this picture. Except for passing references to the walls of Troy and Boiotian Thebes, only the walls of faraway Scheria are cited in the *Odyssey*. No mention is made of walls in regard to Ithaca, Pylos, or Lakedaimon.

This list of Homeric walled poleis conforms with the archaeological record of Mycenaean walled citadels (except for Gortyna, which was probably not walled until Late Helladic IIIC), but it certainly does not exhaust that record. Most notably, Homer says nothing about the walls at Mycenae or Athens,[2] a silence which reminds us yet again that he neither reveals all that he knows nor is compelled to express every component at every instance. Furthermore, even if Homeric wall cities correspond with Mycenaean reality, this fact need not imply that Homer's vision of the city wall, or of the polis itself, derives primarily from inherited descriptions.

But if only a few poleis are said to be walled, no single feature contributes more to the definition of the Homeric polis than the city wall. Athens' walls are never described because Athens itself is of little narrative significance. The same may be said of Mycenae. For Ithaca,

41

which was never walled, a rather similar point may be made: the polis, as opposed to the island, of Ithaca is qualified only once in the entire *Odyssey,* and that in Book 24 when a throng of angered city inhabitants gather "outside the city with its spacious dancing floors" (24.468). As Paolo Vivante has argued, epithets arrest the narrative, adding weight to a noun as they bring it momentarily to the foreground;[3] the gravitational center of this poem lies in the island of Ithaca and in the *house* of the returning hero, not in his polis.

In the *Iliad,* by contrast, the importance of the city wall is easily demonstrated. All dramatic scenes that concern the welfare of Troy are staged either upon the wall or at the city gates, not within the city at Priam's palace or Athena's temple. The great encounter between Helen, Priam, and the city elders (the *teikhoskopia* of Book 3), the final meeting between Hektor and Andromache (Book 6), the dialogue/soliloquy with Priam, Hekabe, and Hektor as he awaits Achilles (Book 22), and the *thrēnos,* or wailing, that arises from the Trojans when Hektor's body is dragged around Troy—all take place upon the Skaian Gate. In her fear that Hektor has been killed, Andromache runs to the tower (22.447–65), and it is from the city wall that she fears Astyanax will be thrown when the city is captured (24.727–38).

These scenes move typically from enclosed interior scenes within Troy to the open wall. When Hektor returns from the battlefield to Troy in Book 6, for example, he finds his mother and Helen in their homes and expects to find his wife in hers as well. But he learns that Andromache has gone to the city gate where, after much delay, husband and wife finally meet. The first two domestic scenes prepare for this surprise encounter at the city perimeter. As Marilyn Arthur has pointed out, in the divided world of male warfare outside the city and of female domestic activity within the house, both Hektor and his wife are dislocated as "each partially entered the world of the other."[4] It is equally important to see how the domestic intimacies of husband, wife, and child have been cast within the frame of the public, how the walls which embrace the family are not those of the house but the outer membrane of the polis.

In Book 22, circumstances are reversed, but the movement from house to city wall parallels that of Book 6: Hekabe, Helen, and the women of Troy are on the walls of Troy while Andromache is at home, quietly preparing a bath for her returning husband. When she hears the piercing screams of the Trojan women from the city wall, Andromache rushes with bacchant frenzy from the house to the city-overview to see Hektor dragged behind Achilles' chariot. Like the earlier one in

Book 6, this scene is designed to intensify the "meeting" of Hektor and Andromache at the polis wall where personal destiny is simultaneously perceived in the context of collective welfare.

The *teikhoskopia* of Book 3 follows a similar movement from house to polis wall. The scene begins with Helen in her palace chambers: revealing her majestic and terrifying capacity to distance herself from the horrors suffered on her account, she is at work weaving scenes from the war.[5] When Helen, inspired by Iris, feels a sudden longing to see her former husband, her parents, and the city that she had abandoned, she leaves the weaving and goes to the city wall hoping to catch a glimpse of Menelaos out in the plain. There on the tower over the Skaian Gate, Priam and the elders of the city (*dēmogerontes,* 149) are already perched, waiting for the outcome of the duel about to take place between Menelaos and Alexander that will decide Helen's fate and save Troy from further bloodshed.[6] As these elders watch the Spartan beauty approach, in a twist of emotions they admire Helen but want her to sail home "lest she be left as suffering for ourselves and our children after us" (3.160). Once again, an urban scene at Troy reaches its dramatic climax at the polis wall where Troy's security and fate are most poignantly felt. At the end of Book 3, Aphrodite compels Helen to retrace her steps, moving back from "the lofty tower" to Alexander's bedroom, victim once again of the goddess's irresistible force; such retracing, from tower to palace, where the cause of the war will be symbolically recapitulated, has no parallel in the poem.

In only a few instances do scenes from Troy not culminate at the wall or gate. One involves the end of Book 3, just mentioned. Deviation from the norm in this case requires no explanation. Another instance occurs in Book 5 when, as discussed earlier, Aeneas is miraculously healed in Apollo's temple "on Pergamon." A third occurs in Book 7 when Antenor, speaking for the Trojans and reiterating the sentiments of the city elders expressed in Book 3, proposes in public assembly that Helen be sent back to the Greeks. This "agora of Trojans" takes place at night on the acropolis (*Iliou en polei akrēi,* 7.345) in front of Priam's palace. The "political" effort to lift the siege unfolds appropriately in public debate before Priam's palace;[7] the more characteristic military alternative, just as appropriately, when considered from within the city is dramatized at the outer rim of Troy.

In one sense, Hektor's final return reverses the movement of his wife from house to wall as his body is first mourned at the city gate after Priam has retrieved it from the Achaean camp, but the ritualized lamentation (thrēnos) for the fallen warrior is delayed until the corpse is taken to Priam's palace. Even from within those chambers, however, the city wall is remembered as Andromache considers the fate of her son: "And you, my child, will go with me to labor for some pitiless master; or some Achaean will seize you by the arm and hurl you from the city tower to a cruel death" (24.732–35). The general rule holds: the city wall at the Skaian Gate, more than palace or city temple, is the single most prominent feature of Homeric Troy.

Only once does a Homeric character gaze from within the city to the world beyond. "Having climbed to the top of Pergamon" (*Pergamon eisanabasa*, 24.700), Cassandra spies her father coming across the Trojan plain with her brother's body in a mule wagon. In all other scenes from the *Iliad,* the wall of Troy marks an absolute barrier between city and plain.[8] When Iris, for example, in Book 3 says to Helen "Come here, dear sister, in order to see how strangely the Achaeans and Trojans are behaving" (3.130–31), Helen goes out from her bedroom and walks through the city to the tower over the Skaian Gate. When Andromache, in Book 6, hears that the Trojans are being worn down and that the Greeks have won a great victory, "she rushes to the great tower of Ilios" (6.386). Similarly in Book 22, Andromache does not look out from her palace window (as happens, for example, in Mycenaean art), or peer form the acropolis (where her house is located), but runs through Troy to the city wall. This Homeric emphasis on the view from the tower may more closely reflect an Ionian walled city, founded on relatively level ground and permitting no view over the wall, rather than Mycenaean conditions. What concerns us here, however, is not the presence or absence of historical anachronism, but the way in which architectural design serves dramatic purpose.

While action from *within* Troy tends to move outward from enclosed house to city wall, the action *outside* the city moves toward Troy but does not reach it. In this regard, Homer's depiction in the *Iliad* of the siege of Troy is unlike any such scene in the Mycenaean visual arts and has no parallel even in Homer's own description of the siege at Kalydon (*Il.* 9.529ff.). The Achaean force, in numbers like the leaves of the forest or the sands of the sea, is said to have mustered over the plain "in order to fight at the city wall" (*makhēsomenoi proti astu*, 2.801),[9] but except for Patroklos, who scaled an angle of the lofty wall at 16.702, the Achaeans never touch, let alone scale, Troy's fortification.[10] And the Trojans, in spite of the military advice of Andromache (6.431–39) and of Poulydamas (18.254–83), never fight from their wall. If such narrative strategy appears to diminish the military significance of Troy's fortification, it enhances the wall's symbolic value, encouraging us to read the circuit wall, untouched by war, as the boundary between war and peace, between the wild (nature) and culture, between the life-taking and the life-sustaining. Homeric narration dramatizes the city's welfare at the point of greatest tension—the point where Troy feels simultaneously exposed and invincible. Although the wall of Troy may be secure within the frame of the *Iliad,* we are equally aware from the stories of other walled cities that have fallen, from the failure of the Achaean wall to withstand Trojan aggression, and from the many prefigurations of Troy's own fall, that this boundary between civilization and its annihilation is a fragile one.

When Virgil recasts one of these Homeric scenes, the change in setting significantly alters the dramatic tension. In his remaking of the Priam, Hekabe, and Hektor exchange at the beginning of Book 22, he places Latinus, Amata, Lavinia, and Turnus in a secluded, even enclosed space *(rapidusque in tecta recessit,* 12.81). Latinus, Amata, and Lavinia are no more successful in persuading Turnus not to face Aeneas than Priam and Hekabe were in begging Hektor to come within the Skaian Gate to face Achilles another day. But what Homer places out in the open at the city wall for all to see, Virgil removes from public spectacle. In this new, more intimate setting, Virgil can explore more carefully than Homer the inner forces that eat with cancerous fury at the heart of Turnus. Inner forces are hardly alien to the Homeric scene. They fuel Hektor's oddly private soliloquy in response to his parents' pleas, but this glimpse of interiority strongly contrasts with its context. In his adaptation, Virgil eschews the grandeur of Homeric public themes and turns truly inward. In so doing, he loses the Homeric counterpoint of public safety and individual danger, of lofty walled enclosure and exposed hero, that so magnificently characterizes Hektor's unwillingness to dry his sweat and quench his thirst with the other Trojans who "like fawns" have taken refuge behind the battlements (22.1ff.).

The Odyssean Scheria is hardly a model for the Iliadic Troy and barely resembles it in most details.[11] Nor are scenes from Scheria staged at the city perimeter. But even for this city so removed from the threat of war, the city wall is crucial in all descriptions of the city. Three portraits of Scheria show the wall's integral place in urban definition.

When moving his people away from the savage Kyklopes in the previous generation, Nausithoos founded Scheria: "He drove a wall around the polis, built houses [*oikoi*], constructed temples [*nēoi*] of the gods, and divided out the plowlands" (6.9–10). W. B. Stanford's commentary is worth quoting (at 6.9): "Note the order in founding a

settlement: first walls for protection from attack, then houses for shelter, then shrines for the gods, then divisions of tillage." As Stanford
implies in this paraphrase, the city wall is integral to any colonizing
enterprise, a fact that is all the more noteworthy since the need for
defense here is slight. But his retelling needs to be modified in one
important respect. Context strongly suggests that *nēoi* should not be
translated as "shrines," but rather as "temples," contemporary Ionian
temples or places of public cult which bind the people in a common
loyalty to city gods.[12]

Nausikaa's description closely follows the previous account:

> But when we come upon the polis surrounded by its lofty
> tower and with beautiful harbors on either of the polis,
> with a narrow way in . . . [more description of ships] . . .
> and nearby a beautiful precinct of Poseidon, there is an agora,
> fitted with deep-embedded stones quarried from the earth.
>
> (6.262–67)

Sensitive to Odysseus' interests, Nausikaa emphasizes ships and harbor; nonetheless, her portrait is sketched primarily with three bold
strokes: walls, ships, agora (with adjacent sacred precinct, understand
temenos, of Poseidon).

Of the three, Odysseus' impression is the most striking:

> But Odysseus now marvelled at the harbors and balanced ships,
> the meeting places [*agorai*] of heroes and the city walls, long,
> lofty, fitted with palisades, a marvel to behold.
>
> (7.43–45)

Wonder pervades his vision of the polis (*thaumazen d'Oduseus* and
thauma idesthai, 7.43 and 45), a feeling most strongly realized in the
viewing of the walls themselves, a marvel to behold. As with the other
two descriptions, Odysseus' impression is drawn from three strokes:
harbors, agora, walls. From these three strokes there emerge both
unity of image and complexity of movement. Scheria is simultaneously
open and enclosed: the harbors and ships permit "men to cross the seas
and visit the cities of other men," to quote from Odysseus' criticism of
the ship-lacking Kyklopes (*Od.* 9.128–29); the agora allows social and
political life within to unfold in an orderly manner; and the walls
provide definition, distinguishing the order within from the world
outside. As one scholar said of Homer in another context: "The *Iliad*
and *Odyssey* depend crucially on vision, on allowing the words to build
a visible world in which the inner events of the epic suddenly ap-

pear."[13] So here, visual image (ships, agora, walls) lend themselves to abstract representation (social order, communication with the outside, stability). The three strokes establish the paradoxical dimensions of the whole: the polis is open toward the outside yet inwardly focused, protected and exposed, with the wall as the boundary between the two worlds providing definition to both spheres. As in a Giotto fresco, extraneous detail and ornate embellishment are kept to a minimum, allowing crucial details to reveal essential form.

A comparison of Homer's vision of Scheria to Wordsworth's view of London in "Composed upon Westminster Bridge, September 3, 1802," further accentuates the significance of the wall in the Homeric description:

> Earth has not anything to show more fair:
> Dull would he be of soul who could pass by
> A sight so touching in its majesty:
> This city now doth, like a garment, wear
> The beauty of the morning; silent, bare,
> Ships, towers, domes, theatres and temples lie
> Open unto the fields and to the sky;
> All bright and glittering in the smokeless air.

The wonder that touched Odysseus in first seeing Scheria is also apparent in Wordsworth, expressed here as a feeling of majesty that moves the viewer's soul. But even though the two visions have much in common, they are essentially at odds. Just as Wordsworth erases the conventional division between quatrains by running the first into the second in the strong enjambment, "wear / The beauty of the morning," so he elides the sharp Homeric distinction between city and noncity. Such an opening out may be said to be the poem's special achievement, and it is distinctly un-Homeric. The radiance is still perceived in architectural forms, but the Giottesque simplicity of detail is gone. The melancholic nineteenth-century dream of an urban pastoral where city opens out to fields and up to sky loses the strictness of Homeric urban order, made spatially coherent by the vision of the all-defining circuit wall.

Whether a polis be at war or at peace, whether it be "Ionian" or "Mycenaean" in design, no single feature contributes more to the definition of a Homeric city than its city wall. For Homer, the polis is essentially a spatial and architectural entity, that place which nurtures, by enclosing, civilization with its prize of women and children.

A circuit wall (*teikhos*) can make a polis linguistically (*polizō*) as well as architecturally: "in building the wall I citied Troy," as Poseidon phrases it; or, in Lattimore's translation, "the wall which I and Phoibos Apollo / built with our hard work for the hero Laomedon's city" (*Il.* 7.452–53).[14] The Odyssean description of the founding of Boiotian Thebes makes a similar equation, though with different verbs:

> ———Antiope,
> Asopos' daughter, said that she lay in the arms of Zeus.
> She begot two children, Amphion and Zethos,
> who first founded [*ektisan*] the seat of Thebes, seven-gated,
> and towered [*purgōsan*] it since they were not able,
> without a tower, to inhabit Thebes of the broad dancing
> place, although they were mighty.
>
> (*Od.* 11.260–65)

The double verbs *ktizō* and *purgoō* ("to found" and "to tower with a wall") illustrate again how polis and circuit wall may be considered synonymous and, accordingly, how the city wall is part of the generic image of "the polis."

A study of Homeric formulas will offer a more detailed understanding of walls in the Homeric rendition of cities. Of all city epithets, those describing polis-fortifications are second only to *hieros,* and related words. Furthermore, every city prominently featured in the *Iliad* and *Odyssey* is described as walled, whether that city is under attack or far from danger. The presence of a city wall, moreover, is a sine qua non in any Homeric description of polis under attack (whether a siege is ongoing, as at Troy or at Kalydon, or whether a city has already been destroyed, as at Thebes and Lyrnessos in the Troad, and Thebes in Boiotia). Lyrnessos' walls, for example, are mentioned only once in the *Iliad,* when Achilles speaks of having won Briseis as a reward for city-destroying prowess: "having won her by my own hand, sacking the well-walled polis" (16.57; cf. the generalizing phrase by Nestor, 4.308). Under such conditions, walls, towers, or city gates may stand metonymically for the polis itself: for example, "they destroyed Lyrnessos and the walls of Thebes" (2.691); "fleeing the Trojans reached the Skaian Gate" (said three times).

Homeric epithets describing the circuit wall fall into two major categories according to whether they describe the wall's excellent craftsmanship and construction or its sacred nature. The strength of a city's defense thus derives from human and divine sources where neither explanation denies the importance of the other. As with the more often remarked double motivation in Homer where both human and divine will "explain" human action, so both human and supernatural power contribute to the impressive strength of the urban fortification system. We shall consider each of the wall's strengths separately without straining, we trust, their normal complementarity.

Euteikheos

The many epithets referring to a city's fortifications prefixed with *eu-* denote construction performed with engineering skill, knowledge, and ability. City towers are "well-made" (*eudmētos*); gates are commonly "well-fitted" (*eu araruiai*) or "well-made" (*eu poiētai*), less frequently just "made" (*poiētai*). Like their towers, the whole city is "well-made" (*eudmētos*) and "well-walled" (*euteikheos*), "well-crowned" (*eustephanos*), "well-towered" (*eupurgos*). All these epithets celebrate the elegance and skill of the walls' human construction. Other epithets similarly accent strength through technology. City gates are "solid" (*puka*) and "compact" (*stibaros*), as well as "doubled." The city wall "constructed" (*tetugmenon*), "steep," "wide," "long," "a wonder to behold."

The most common of these epithets—"well-walled," "well-towered" and "well-made," and "lofty-gated" (*husipulos*)—do not merely describe durable technology. Since it is almost always the Greeks, and not the narrator or the Trojans, who describe Troy in this manner, the epithets evoke a view of the city as it is seen from the eyes of the besieger, defining Troy by its height and stalwart defense.

The same technology inspires the Trojans with a sense of security. Listen to Poulydamas when he advises his companions to return to their city before Achilles reenters battle: Don't dally by the ships, he pleads. Let the Trojans husband their strength in the agora while "Troy's towers, / its lofty gates, and the tall, well-polished doors / that are set therein, bolted fast, shall defend the city" (18.274–76). Again such description of walls and construction clearly carries emotional weight. When, a few books later, Achilles has finally routed the Trojans and they are forced to take refuge behind city wall, the bearing of that technology upon the human psyche becomes explicit: "So throughout the city, the Trojans, fleeing like fawns, / dried the sweat from their bodies, drank, and slaked their thirst, / leaning on the beautiful battlements" (22.1–3). Within the embrace of the walls, warriors have become young and helpless, refreshed and suckled, as it were, by the city's restorative juices (the mother/infant associations here are unmistakable and will be considered in more detail in the next chapter). It would be very difficult to regard the use of *kalos* ("beautiful") in this instance as conventional or irrelevant to context. Of its ten occurrences in the *Iliad,* this is the only time that *epalxeis* (breastworks of planks or battlements) are modified by an epithet, and in only one other example does *kalos* modify a word referring to city defenses: "I built the walls wide and *very beautiful* [*mala kalon*] in order that the city of Troy be *unbreakable*" (21.446–47). These three passages from Books 18, 21, and 22, illustrate, among other examples, how references to Troy's fortification become ever more explicit, and urgent, as the final confrontation between Achilles and Hektor draws near.

Like all objects of human workmanship, the man-made Trojan wall has inevitable points of weakness. Pindar explains the Greek success at Troy in precisely these terms, as we have noted earlier: although divinely constructed in most areas, the wall fell where the mortal Aiakos aided the gods (*Olympian* 8.40ff.). In the *Iliad,* Andromache is equally concerned that Troy will fall where the wall is weak. In fear for her husband's life and in terror that the enemy may learn, either through prophecy or through the lust of battle, that the city is not uniformly secure, she advises her husband that the Trojan troops should pull back from the plain and defend the city at that point, by the wild fig tree, where the wall is especially capable of being scaled (*ambatos,* 6.434) and the city is most open to assault (*epidromos,* 6.434).[15] Human defense, she hopes, will suffice where skilled engineering has failed.

Hiera Teikhea

Although only two cities are said to have sacred walls, Troy and Boiotian Thebes, all city walls are divinely protected if not actually divinely built.[16] The sanctity of a Homeric city wall stems from the fact that it shelters civilization within. Not only a physical boundary, the city wall is also a spiritual barrier, preserving the divinely sanctioned enclosed order from a profane world encircling the city. Mircea Eliade explains such boundaries in terms of kratophany and hierophany: "Long before they were military erections, the city walls were a magic defense, for they marked out from the midst of a 'chaotic' space . . . a place that was organized, made cosmic, provided with a 'centre'. . . . The 'magic circle' in so many magico-religious rituals is intended to set up a partition between the two areas of different kinds."[17]

Magical explanations may be rare in Homer, but religious explanations are certainly not altogether absent. Richard Wycherley claims that the city walls "were not sacred objects" intrinsically but were made sacred through cults and shrines frequently attached to them.[18] I disagree. It is true that shrines have been discovered in the walls of Mycenaean Tiryns and in the walls of later Greek cities, and it must be admitted that, although Homer makes no reference to such worship in the poems, we cannot argue from this silence that the sacred city wall in Homer was not understood in the context of such wall-shrines. It is more natural, however, to understand the sacred dimension of the city wall as an extension of the sacredness of the polis itself, the object of divine interest by virtue of its enclosure of the polis, and its women and children. Cult ritual merely augments an intrinsic sanctity.

Such matters are merely speculative. More specific testimony exists in Homer for the divine construction of Troy's wall.[19] Poseidon acknowledges that it took great effort for him and Apollo (*athlēsante*, 7.453; cf. 21.442–44) to build Troy's defense, an effort similar in nature, it seems, to that which the Achaeans needed to build their own wall (*mogeontes Akhaioi*, 12.29). Poseidon is also jealous of that wall, fearing that the Greek effort will diminish the glory of his own creation (see 7.446–63 and 12.9–36). If in the later tradition Apollo is more frequently identified with the constructing or remaking of city walls than is Poseidon, the situation is reversed in Homer, where the earth-shaker and hard labor, and not Apollo's magical lyre, account for the divine strength of Troy's circuit defense.

Poseidon's bellicose nature and fiery spirit have often seemed antithetical to urban aspirations. We are more prone to think of the earth-shaker and sea god (tidal waves in this context) as a destroyer of cities and urban walls, and it is in this capacity that we typically identify the Homeric Poseidon, eager in his anger to devastate the Achaian wall, to destroy Troy, and to hurl a mountain over the city harbor at Scheria. In L. R. Farnell's words: "Poseidon is not normally associated with mental, higher aspects which Greek religion occasionally displays or with the higher artistic life of Hellas."[20]

But as divine beings reveal themselves in positive or negative form (e.g., Apollo either sends the plague or drives it away), Poseidon is occasionally associated throughout Greek history with the building, or defense, of city walls. A particularly strong identification is to be found with his jurisdiction over the walls of Boiotian Thebes.[21] A passage from the *Shield of Heracles* (104–5) neatly juxtaposes the double nature of this powerful deity as the first line pits the god's stormy side against his protective concern for city veil (wall) and polis in the second line: "The earth-shaker, receiver of bulls, / who keeps the veil of Thebes and defends the polis."[22] At Delos, sacrifices were offered to Poseidon *themelioukhos*, "Poseidon, holder of [city] foundation walls,"[23] an attribute perhaps implied by the name of one of his sons, Eurypylos, Wide-Gate (see Pindar, *Pythian* 4.33). In the Trozen, he was worshiped more generally as *polioukhos*, "holder of the city," and as *basileus*, "king,"[24] although Jackson Knight argues that Athena came to be known as the goddess who defended the whole citadel whereas Poseidon had special jurisdiction over city walls alone.[25]

Apollo's association with city foundations in the later tradition is just the reverse of the Homeric account. In the *Iliad*, Poseidon says at one point that he built Troy's fortification while Apollo looked after the shambling cattle on the many ridges of Mount Ida (see 21.446–49). But Stephanus counts at least twenty-five sites where Apollo was honored as the leader (*hēgemon*) or founder (*ktistēs*) of a settlement; many of these settlements were probably indebted to him for his Delphic guidance. Farnell again: "for most of the Greek states, [Apollo was] preeminently a patron deity of the *Polis*, ranking in this respect by the side of Zeus and Athena."[26]

Apollo's contribution to a wall's strength came not from a Poseidon-like physical exertion but from the magic of music, the charm of his lyre weaving a divine thread through the structure of stone. Callimachus speaks as if Apollo's musical aid in construction was part of any restoration of old city walls: "Let not youths keep the lyre silent if . . . the wall is to stand upon old foundations [*themethlois*]" (*Hymn to Apollo* 12ff.). In the same hymn, the Hellenistic poet says that mortals follow Phoebus when they map out cities (*polias diemetrēsanto*) because the god delights in the founding of cities (*ktizomenēis'*) and weaves (*huphainei*) their foundations (*themeilia*).[27] In the much earlier Theognis (773–74), the god is hailed as having towered (*epurgōsas*) the polis of Megara as a favor to the son of Pelops; in a fragment from Hesiod, it will be recalled, lyres (with no mention of Apollo in the fragment) built the walls of Thebes.

In the *Iliad* references to Troy's divinely constructed wall are scarce until the last lines of Book 21, where they appear in a flurry as Achilles presses ever more dangerously against the city. The sudden interest in this aspect of Troy's wall corresponds to an increased proliferation of references to the skilled craftsmanship of Troy's walls at this point in the narrative. The narrator notes that Priam, standing "on the divine tower," saw the "monstrous Achilles" rushing toward his city. It hardly seems accidental that the only reference to the city's wall, tower, or gate as *theios* (21.526, but see 8.519) should come at a time when divine defense is needed to help the city withstand the thrust of a wrathful superhuman force. A few lines earlier Apollo is said by the narrator to have "entered holy Ilios / for the wall of the well-built polis was a concern to him, / lest the Danaians destroy it on that day before its time" (21.515–17); and just before that Poseidon describes how he had built the fortification wall of Troy in order that the polis be unbreakable (*arrēktos,* 21.447).[28]

These references to Troy's wall and its divine construction, as the "de-structive Achilles" (21.536) nears the city, pit two elemental forces against each other. Casting human events in "magical/superstitious" terms may appear to violate Homeric tendencies, but at this point in the story the poem has already begun to break out of its own conventions. The change is evident in the middle of Book 21 when Achilles' battle-rage transforms heroic warfare into a duel between fire (Achilles and Hephaistos) and water (the Skamandros river), not only anthropomorphizing nature but casting war as a clash of primeval elements (21.212–384). Achilles' force, "beyond what is just for man" (*peri d'aisula . . . andrōn,* 21.214–15) as Skamandros describes it, is now brought against Troy itself. "Standing on the divine tower," Priam orders that the gates quickly be opened for the men of Troy and then just as quickly be barred "for I fear that this destructive man [*oulos anēr*] will leap the city fortification" (21.536). *Oulos* is an epithet associated elsewhere only with Ares. In Priam's surrealistic fear that Achilles will leap the city wall (*es teikhos halētai*), proleptic in its anticipation of the Trojan horse, Homer strongly sets Achilles' inhumanity against the polis order, the city wall deservedly "divine" for its protective, if tragic, embrace of civilization.

CHAPTER 4

The People
of the Polis

In Homer's *Iliad*, the polis is tripartite, an interlocking earthly trinity of enclosing wall, divine presence, and city inhabitants. This structure can be seen in three types of epithets commonly used to describe Troy: "if the gods grant to us to destroy the *great city of Priam*" (9.136); "if ever Zeus grants to us to destroy utterly *Troy, the well-walled polis*" (1.128–29); "the day will come when *holy Ilios / and Priam and the people [laoi] of Priam* will be destroyed" (6.448–49). I discuss these epithets more fully in the next chapter, but here it is fitting to observe that the Homeric polis is not an abstract entity with an autonomous existence independent of the inhabitants within, but a community of people, "a city of mortal men" (*polis meropōn anthrōpōn*).

Describing a polis by describing its inhabitants is not as obvious or tautological a procedure as might first appear. The fifth-century polis, for example, is commonly conceived of as an independent being, transcending (or suppressing) the human plurality from which it is derived.[1] Nicole Loraux, in particular, has discussed the significance of such a politicized perspective for fifth-century Athenian funeral oratory, in which the people of the city are subsumed in a kind of hypnotic praise of *hē polis*. Pericles sees the people who died for Athens in terms of democracy, individual and artistic freedoms, state festivals (Thuc. 2.36ff.).[2]

As the polis in Homer is defined less politically, so the motives for warfare are less abstracted: Greek and Trojan alike fight around Troy for the women and children of the city. For the Greeks, the women of Troy are the *geras* (prize) that gives "fame" (*kleos*).[3] For the Trojans, and their allied troops, "driven by stern necessity to fight for their wives and children" (8.57), the people of the city provide no less a stimulus for war. Hektor feels this "necessity," when exhorting his allied captains:

> Hear me, countless tribes of neighboring allies,
> Not desiring, nor needing, a multitude did I
> gather each of you here from your *poleis,*
> but in order that you might zealously defend for me
> Trojans' wives and feeble children from warring Greeks.
>
> (17.220–24)

And so does Agenor, when facing Achilles in Book 21: "My lord Achilles, no doubt you thought that you were going to sack the proud city of Troy this very day. That was a foolish error. Troy will survive to witness much hard fighting yet. While we are there, she has plenty of stalwart sons to fight her battles under the eyes of their parents and their wives and children."[4] Periclean motives, by comparison, look deflected, sophisticated, and political, and far from the Homeric perspective in which heroes fight for the polis because it is filled with vulnerable human life.

"The City of Priam and Other Trojans"

Even though it is possible to perceive in the *Iliad* and *Odyssey* the early signs of a polis ideology, an *Etat populaire* and *l'idée de l'Etat comme d'une communauté d'hommes libres,*[5] or a *certain sentiment communautaire,*[6] "political" perceptions are still rudimentary. Members of the Homeric *dēmos* cannot quite be called citizens; nor are they exactly subjects, conscripted and taxed, of a definable state system.[7] The prepolitical nature of the Homeric state is evident in a word like *etēs* which in the classical period describes one's public status (i.e., a townsman, neighbor or, more narrowly, private citizen) but in Homer describes distant blood relations (i.e., clansmen) and is always found in the plural.[8]

The Homeric *politēs* is particularly interesting as it derives from polis and is therefore in a sense subordinated to the concept of *polis.*[9] Although some have argued that it, like the Homeric *laoi,* refers to "the defenders of the fortress, neither more nor less,"[10] the textual evidence is far from conclusive. Examples refuting this narrow definition of *laos* are too common to note in detail (e.g., *Il.* 24.715). *Politai* is worth closer examination.

When Iris, in the likeness of Priam's son Polites, encouraging the Trojan leaders to prepare for battle, "sets the *politas* in order" (2.806), the word (in its only "Herodotean" spelling in Homer) unquestionably refers to Troy's fighting force. The name Polites itself reenforces such an interpretation: Priam's son,[11] posted as a lookout in the plain, appears to personify the garrison defense of Troy.

But the sense of the more frequent form *politai* is less certain.[12] Referring to those members of the polis who go down to the communal spring to draw water (7.131; 17.206), Odyssean usage surely includes the women of the polis. Iliadic examples, although less obviously, also seem to refer to all free inhabitants of the city: "Priam wept (for Hektor) and [*de*] beside him the politai mourned / and [*or: but*] [*de*] Hekabe led the women of Troy in heavy lament" (22.429–30). If the second *de* were adversative, *politai* might denote the young men of Troy, but it is more reasonable to regard the connective as copulative. This unique phrase *epi de stenakhonto politai* ("beside him the politai mourned") further suggests the more common formula *epi de stenakhonto gunaikes* ("and nearby the women mourned") which describes Hekabe leading Trojan women in mourning for Hektor.[13] The one other use of this word points in the same direction. When Hektor says that the Achaeans may "capture steep Ilios and destroy her *politas*" (15.558), we are reminded less of Troy's fighting contingent than of the city's women and children, who are frequently associated with the compulsions of war. Contrasted then with the exclusively male and politically oriented meaning of *politēs* in the classical period, Homeric usage is striking, as it refers to the plurality of people who collectively inhabit the city. Homeric *politai* suggests a collective "body polis" rather than a "body politic," defined by no more (and by no less) than its shared communal identity.[14]

Rather than *Iliou polis*, "the city of Ilios" (attested only once), Homer prefers to call Troy (Ilios) either "the city of Priam" or "the city of the Trojans." Of the two expressions, the "city of Priam" predominates by a margin of two to one (twenty occurrences versus ten), in a variety of formulaic phrases distributed throughout the line:[15]

Position	Phrase	Number of occurrences
Beginning of line	*astu peri Priamoio*	2
	astu mega Priamoio	2
Middle of first foot	*Priamoio anaktos . . . polis*	1
Beginning of second foot	*astu mega Priamou*	1

Middle of second foot	*Priamoio polis*	2
	Priamoio polin	3
Beginning of third	*astu mega Priamou*	1
foot	*astu mega Priamoio*	1
	astu mega Priamoio anaktos	3
Middle of third foot	*Priamou polin*	1
"Weak caesura"	*polis Priamoio anaktos*	3
	TOTAL	20

Add to this list the many references to Priam and the sons of Priam, and it often seems in the *Iliad* as if the Achaeans were waging war against a single oikos rather than a collective polis. For example, the narrator speaks of a Trojan ally, Amphios from Paisos, whom fate led to help "both Priam and his sons [*huias*]" (5.614). Hera, similarly, in her hatred for Troy centers her desired vengeance squarely on one family: "bringing evils to Priam and his children" (4.28). Andromache thinks that the death of Hektor will bring evils "for the children of Priam" (*Priamoio tekessin*, 22.453) as if there were no others in Troy. Ares addresses the entire army of Trojans and allies (*Trōas stichas*) as if they were an extension of Priam's house: "Oh sons of Priam [*huieis Priamoio*], divinely nurtured king" (5.464).[16]

But behind this emphasis, it is not difficult to discover the aggregate of many oikoi and to see an oikos-centered problem reach out and absorb an entire polis. Frequently, reference to Priam and his children in one line precedes mention of the other Trojans enjambed in the next line: that is, "Now Priam and the children of Priam might be happy, / and the other Trojans might rejoice in their hearts" (2.255–56; cf. 2.304, 4.35–36, 6.283). Achilles expresses one interpretation of the hierarchical relationship between these two parts when he states that he will bring death "for all the Trojans, but especially for Priam's sons" (*kai pantōn Trōōn, peri d'au Priamoio ge paidōn*, 21.105).[17] The relation may also be formulated along slightly different lines: angry that Hektor's body has not been returned to Troy, Apollo rebukes the other gods:

> Now you do not dare to save him, though a corpse,
> so that wife, mother, and child might see him,
> and Priam, his father, and the people [*laoi*] . . .
>
> (24.35–37)

In the syntactic extension of line 36 to line 37, we find the union of two worlds, the oikos of Priam and the polis of Priam, private and public, the female defended and male defenders.

Hektor

In the Greek classical period, men and not walls were said, in a familiar *topos,* to be the true bulwark of a polis. Cities were not built from stone but existed wherever men knew how to defend themselves. So claimed Alcaeus already in the sixth century. "There," he said, "you will find a *city* and a *wall.*" When asked whether the Spartans should fortify their city, Lycurgus reportedly said that no city is without walls (*ateikhistos*) if it is crowned (*estephanotai*) not with bricks but with a body of men (Plutarch, *Lycurgus* 19). In this phrasing, even the metaphoric language of polis as "crown" has been appropriated by the male fighting force. In the words of the Persian messenger reporting back to his queen: "Athens has a secure bulwark [*herkos*], so long as she has men" (Aeschylus, *Persians* 349; cf. Herodotus 8.61). "Men," in short, "are the warlike tower of a city" (*polis purgos areuios*).[18]

It was a commonplace in the classical period to believe that the use of city fortifications made city dwellers effeminate.[19] Plato explains that a fortification wall invites the city people "to seek refuge within it instead of repelling the enemy; instead of securing their safety by keeping watch night and day, it tempts them to believe that their safety is ensured if they are fenced in with walls and gates and go to sleep, like men born to shirk toil, whereas a new crop of toils is the inevitable outcome, as I think, of dishonorable ease and sloth."[20] Quoting a poet's "well-turned sentiment," Plato advocates the use of soldiers rather than man-made fortifications: "city walls [*ta teicha*] ought to be bronze and iron [i.e., weapons] rather than earth [i.e., fortifications]" (*Laws* 778d).

Such beliefs are deeply rooted in Homer, where both Achaean and Trojan are compared to city fortifications. Standing strong against a wild Hektor, raging like a mountain fire, furious like Ares, Zeus-backed, the Achaeans appropriate the symbolic strength of a wall: they stand "firm, fitted close like a rampart [*purgēdon arērotes*], moving no more than a great beetling cliff that lies close by the sea, standing against the wind" (15.617–20). Against Hektor rushing forward, on another occasion, like a boulder set free by a river that has burst its banks, the Greeks make "a dense guard of men [*pukinēis . . . phalagxin*]," while Hektor shouts that they will not hold him back for long, "not even if they close themselves in like a rampart [*purgēdon . . . artunantes*]" (13.136–54). The Greeks yet again "close themselves in like a rampart" (12.40–46) in an effort to stop Hektor, who is bursting forth like a whirlwind, like a wild boar, and like a lion turning this way and that among hounds and huntsmen. In the metaphorical language of these middle books, the Achaeans become like an urban wall trying to withstand a force of uncontrolled natural might; in later books the Trojans, facing an even greater manifestation of natural might, will literally close themselves in behind the ramparts of their city wall.

On two occasions, minor characters stand like a rampart or tower (purgos): as if part of the Greek wall itself, "the tower of great-hearted Menestheus" stands on the wall, warding off the Lydians who are attacking like a storm cloud (12.373); the Trojan Echepolos falls like a "tower" (4.462). The great tower-like warrior, however, is Ajax, whose body-shield "like a tower" (11.485; 17.128) "girds around his skin."[21] As a "bulwark" of the Achaeans (herkos),[22] he appropriately reminds the Greeks that they can rely on no stronger wall than themselves (15.733–41).

Even more than Ajax, Hektor typifies the transference of defense from the physical rampart to an individual, and is commonly portrayed as the very soul of the city-holding defense.[23] Seneca makes the equation explicit: *tu murus eras umerisque tuis / stetit illa decem fulta per annos,* "[Hektor] you are the city wall and supported on your shoulders she stood for ten years" (*Troades* 126–27). Homer is hardly less baroque. Priam laments that although he had fifty sons when the Achaeans arrived, "there was one alone for me and he by himself guarded the city (*hos de moi oios eēn, eiruto de astu kai autos*), / [who now has been] killed while defending his country, / Hektor" (24.499–501). (Others read *autous* for *autos* in l. 499: "he guarded the city and its people.") Having raced around the walls of his city three times (22.165), Hektor has in effect encircled in his fatal run the fate of all Troy within. (Seneca, when he has Hektor's death occur on Troy's final day, again makes explicit what Homer leaves implicit [*Troades* 128–29; cf. 188–89].) When Hektor is dragged around by Achilles, the people of Troy wail "as if all frowning Ilios had been burning top to bottom in fire" (22.410–11; cf. 12.10–11).

Hektor's name, which means "the one who holds," is undoubtedly an abbreviation from Hekhepolis, "the one who holds the polis."[24] In its reverse form, *polioukhos,* his name becomes an epithet ("protecting the city") which, like Polieus and Polias, always describes the guardian deity of a city.[25] In some traditions, then, it is with little surprise that we see Hektor himself equated with that tutelary figure. Stesichorus, for example, endows Hektor with divine power by making him the son of Apollo (fragment 224 Page *PMG*), and the *Iliad* itself may obliquely suggest the same when Priam claims that his son was "a god among men" (24.258) or when Poseidon says that Hektor boasts of being the son of Zeus (13.54).[26] But, normally, the poem is at pains to deny such elevations for Hektor. Poseidon's claim appears rhetorical, even sarcastic, for it is said while he tries to rouse the two Aiantes to stand against Hektor. Nor is Hektor's power ever thought to derive from divine lineage. Quite the contrary. Agamemnon is astonished by the carnage Hektor can accomplish in one day, "although he is called the son of neither a god nor goddess" (10.47–50). Hera, with equal indignation, explicitly contrasts the mortal Hektor (*thnētos*), suckled at the breast of a woman, with Achilles, "the child of a goddess." It is not right, she says, that they should be honored equally (24.56–63). Hektor is, then, protector of the city, but a mortal tutelary figure.

In a *figura etymologica* of his name, Andromache states this double truth outright:

> My husband, you were lost young from life, and have left me
> a widow in your house, and the boy is only a baby
> who was born to you and me, the wretched child. He will never, I
>   think,
> come of age, for before then head to heel this city
> will be sacked, for you, its defender, are gone, you who guarded
> the city, her wives, and her innocent children.
>
> (24.725–30)

In Hektor's own words: "The best of all omens is to fight in defense of your country" (12.243).

Although "holder of the city," Hektor claims in Book 6 that he is motivated less by a sense of responsibility for Troy, or even for his parents, than by fear of his wife's potential enslavement. So to Andromache, he says: "Deep in my heart I know the day is coming when holy Ilios will be destroyed, and Priam and the people of Priam of the good ash spear. Yet I am not so much distressed by the thought of what the Trojans will suffer, or Hekabe herself, or King Priam, or all my gallant brothers whom the enemy will fling down in the dust, as by the thought of you dragged off in tears by some Achaean man-at-arms to slavery" (6.444–49).

If he confesses, like Meleager, that his impulse to war is domestic rather than civic, house oriented rather than city motivated, he is also conscious, as was Kleopatra (cf. 9.587–96), that the defense of the house lies in the security and well-being of the city. The city wall defines the whole and binds all Troy within its common circumference. When he fights for Andromache, by necessity he fights for the city. If the motivations for war for the city-defender germinate from impulses planted deep within the oikos, those stimuli naturally meta-morphize so that the hero also fights expressively for the polis itself:

> Patroklos, you thought perhaps of devastating *my polis*,
> of stripping from the Trojan *women* the day of their freedom,
> dragging them to the land of your fathers.
> Fool! When my swift-running horses fought
> in front of Troy and when I with my own spear
> am conspicuous among the Trojans, I will beat off
> their day of necessity.
>
> (16.830–36)[27]

The people of Troy also understand this double motivation—in fight-ing for Andromache their defender must fight for Troy—as they indi-cate by the name they choose for Hektor's and Andromache's only child. The son named Skamandrios by his parents is renamed by the people of Troy as Astyanax, "ruler of the city."[28] This public name fuses the bond between Andromache's freedom and Troy's liberty. The narrator makes explicit that the son has been renamed after his father's essential nature: "because Hektor alone guarded Ilios" (*oios gar erueto Ilion Hektōr*, 6.403).

Priam . . . Hektor . . . Astyanax

Much like the technological and sacred dimensions of a city wall, the Homeric city, both "sacred" and "of mortal men" (*polis meropōn an-thrōpōn*), is a paradoxical union of divinity and mortality; its omnipo-tence is ephemeral, its belief in the eternal illusory. As in Aeneas' description of Troy's origins—"since not yet had sacred Ilios been made a polis in the plain, a polis of mortal men" (*epei ou pō Ilios hirē/en pediōi pepolisto, polis meropōn anthrōpōn, Il.* 20.216–17)—these two con-trasting elements are inherent and stand side by side, each expressing a universal truth. That "ephemeral immortality" is nowhere more viv-idly expressed in the *Iliad* than in Aeneas' continued account of Troy's history (20.219ff.).

Zeus, Aeneas says, sired Dardanos, who founded Dardania because Troy had not yet been built. Dardanos in turn begat Erichthonios, the owner of three thousand mares and from whom the Trojan line proper begins.[29] Erichthonios in turn begat Tros, from whom the district of Troy and its people are named; Tros fathered Ilos (for whom Ilios was named),[30] Assarakos, and Ganymedes. Of these three, Ilos begat Laomedon, and Assarakos begat Kapys, while Ganymedes, "the most beautiful of mortal men," was lifted up to Olympus to live among the immortals. Laomedon, in turn, begat Tithonos,[31] Priam, Lampos, Klytios, and Hiketaon, while Kapys begat Anchises, from whom Aeneas came, and Priam begat godlike Hektor. Except for Priam's many brothers, Ganymedes is the only one of these many offspring not to beget his own offspring and further the line of Troy.[32] By virtue of the fact that the people moved down from the slopes of Mount Ida to the plain and lived in a walled world of their own making, it is possible to provide in the city an orderly, peaceful transmission of authority in unbroken sequence from father to "only" son and from son to grandson.

In the *Iliad,* where the identification of the city lies with the genealogy of one house and one family, the stability, if not immortality, of the city rests, literally and dramatically, in the unbroken line of that family. In its focus on Hektor, the *Iliad* thus concentrates on one link in the succession and on that hero's efforts to pass the rule of his city from his father to his son. Hektor's identity within the family as "the son of Priam" (*Priamoio pais* and *Priamidēn*) and as "the father of Astyanax" (*Hektoridēn;* cf. *Il.* 6.401) corresponds with the identity of Troy as "the city of Priam" (*Priamoio polis* and *astu mega Priamoio anaktos*) and as the city of Hektor's son, evident in the name by which the Trojans elect to call Hektor's son, Astyanax, "lord of the city."

Although for the Achaeans it often seems that an active father inhibits the maturation of the son,[33] in Troy father and son are active simultaneously and indeed are mutually supportive. Priam is the unquestioned king and ruler of the city, while Hektor commands in the field. Their relation, as James Redfield describes it, "is presented as cooperative. Hector first appears on the scene in the assembly at Troy; Priam presides at this assembly, but Hector adjourns it (2.786–808). Later, when Hector arranges the duel between Paris and Menelaos, he sends for his father from the city (3.116–17). Priam and Agamemnon exchange the oath, while Hector and Odysseus make the practical arrangements (3.264–317). Hector does not ask his father's consent, but in the formal working-out of the occasion he steps down to second rank."[34] In a more immediate way than that of his Greek counterparts, Hektor's selfhood is defined by his past, as by his future. The Greek hero on the plain of Troy achieves adulthood by a series of heroic actions that demonstrate an identity independent of his father. For Hektor, the "holder" of the city, on the other hand, selfhood rests, to much greater extent, on an ability to transmit the city from one generation to the next. That difference between Hektor and the Greeks stems not from cultural differences in kinship relations, but expressly from their respective relations to the city. The defender of the city and "only" son of Priam is bound, unlike the city aggressor, in a web of time inasmuch as he is the vulnerable link between past and future.[35]

At any one moment it might appear that the contestants on the battlefield fight from an identical view of the heroic code, but the presence of the city causes a generic and fundamental difference between defense and assault. As is particularly evident in the personalities of Hektor and Achilles (to be discussed in Chapter 8), the Greek can fight with complete equanimity and purely for kleos (fame). If he dies, or if the Greeks lose, he merely brings shame upon himself. The Trojan is without such freedom. Kleos for him must always be tinged by a sense of obligation to those dependent on his success. If he dies, he knows that what he fights for dies as well.

In the Greek view of the universe, both the natural world in its ever-recurring rhythms of life and death and the divine world in the deathless and timeless nature of the gods enjoy a kind of immortality. It is for humankind alone to suffer mortality. In Homer, of all things touched by mortals, only epic song and the polis aspire to attain escape from mortal bondage: "undying" fame and "unbreakable" city. In speaking of the classical Greek city-state, Hannah Arendt equated the *bios politikos* ("the life of the citizen") with a "striving for immortality which originally had been the spring and center of the *vita activa*."[36] Differences in the social and political realities between the Homeric city and the classical city-state hardly need to be stated. Those differences notwithstanding, the Homeric polis in its unbroken line of rulers, as in its interlocking machinery of technology and Olympian overseers, seems to be something more than human, though it is also "a city of mortal men." The components of wall, people, and sanctity that set it apart from the formless world around it also set it apart from the standard laws of nature, time, and space.

That paradox of the ephemeral polis within its immortal frame is evident in Aeneas' description of Erichthonios' three thousand mares, a myth which shows a dynamic interplay between Olympian and chthonian components. Erichthonios, whose name suggests autochthonous origins,[37] is closely associated here with earth-bound forces, as are his horses pasturing "along the low grasslands" (20.221; see also 223).

While grazing, the mares excite the North Wind, who comes down from the sky and impregnates them all. The spirited copulation of horses and North Wind, as it parallels the general fertility of the royal line, culminates in a strange buoyancy of the foals

> when they would play along the grain-giving tilled land,
> they would pass along the tops of corn tassels and not break the
>   divine yield,
> and again, when they played across the sea's wide ridges
> they would run along the wave tops where it breaks on the grey salt
>   sea.
>
> (20.226–29)

The wonderful and fertile mixture of earth and sky of Erichthonios' mares echoes the double nature of the polis in its interplay of human and divine components, of technology and Olympian, of oikos and polis, respectively.

As much as the city may aspire to aspects of immortality, it is the place of fertility and propagation par excellence. A complete identification with the earth would return its inhabitants to the prepolis conditions on Mount Ida; but a total link with the divine, as in the case of Ganymedes, results in a sterile union.[38] The Homeric polis, like the foals of Erichthonios, partakes of two worlds, not bound entirely to the earth but at the same time not free of its gravitational pull either. Only in such a suspended position can there exist both the fertility that ensures the continuation of the Trojan line and the unbroken chain of succession in the line, going from Zeus to the present, that guarantees the city's permanence.

Hekabe . . . Andromache

To conclude this discussion of the people in the polis, I shall briefly sketch its identification with the female. Dominated as the polis is by males, both mortal and Olympian, who rule and defend it, the city is female in form.[39]

In one sense, the city's "femininity" suggests a virginal femininity like that of Pallas Athena, "the one who guards the city" (erusiptolis): walled or armored, virginal in the sense of being impregnable, masterful and secure in her craftsmanship (technē)—the very characteristics, it would seem, of the "cultured" but warlike "daughter of a mighty sire" (*obrimopatrē*). The female metaphors for the city wall, "holy *krēdemna*" and "well-crowned," also suggest skilled craftsmanship and religiously protected chasitity (if not virginity).

The polis form is clearly maternal as well: a mother with her young, as in the image of the mother sparrow with her eight young whose deaths foretell the fall of Troy (cf. *Il.* 2.311ff.; cf. a similar image of the destruction of Troy in Aeschylus, *Ag.* 119: the twin eagles "fed off a hare, bursting with young yet unborn"). Fertile and pregnant, much like the pregnant mares of Erichthonios, the polis is a world apart, the place of women and innocent children.[40] The offspring is invariably male. Thus at the beginning of Book 6 when Agamemnon tells Menelaos to "spare no Trojan, not even a woman pregnant with male child," he is speaking about Troy itself—the city as female container holding in its womb tomorrow's warrior:

> Dear brother, o Menelaos, are you concerned so tenderly
> for these people? Did the Trojans treat you well at
> Sparta? No, let not one of them go free of sudden
> death and our hands; not the male child that the mother carries
> still in her womb, not even he, but let all of Ilios'
> people perish, utterly blotted out, unmourned for.
>
> (6.55–60)

Agamemnon's attack against the unnamed pregnant Trojan is directed at the affirmation of life, family, and generation that the female body makes possible. The woman, we realize, doubles for the polis itself; the wall of the city forms, as it were, the thin but strong membrane that holds nascent life within.

Agamemnon's generic reference to a Trojan woman with child at the beginning of Book 6 is visualized in bodily form at the end of the same book when Andromache with her male child stands on the wall of Troy. The unspecific and generic has become the particular and historic, and each description helps interpret the other. Andromache is never simply the wife of Hektor, but, as her position on the wall suggests, she embodies something of Troy's form as well, her presence on the wall with Astyanax at her side representing the city "pregnant" with male child. As previously noted, Andromache's position at the city perimeter has been well prepared for by the poet. Homer builds on that expectation only to lend greater poignancy to the eventual encounter between husband and wife at that point where the line of demarcation between city and war, security and death, may be felt most urgently.

Her presence at the gate when Troy's defense is still a living possibility thus points to a large contrast that pervades the epic—between domesticity and battle, between civilized humanity and savagery—and her conversation in particular makes manifest what is evident in Agamemnon's command of brutality: that the city and the female in their affirmation of life are enclosing and seek enclosure. As in Kleopatra's plea before Meleager (cf. *Il.* 9.587–96), Andromache's concerns shift from Hektor to the community at large,[41] and her perspective quite naturally leads her to adopt a military strategy of transferring the war from the open plain to the protected area of the city wall, where a siege defense can be conducted.[42]

Hektor, however, cannot accept Andromache's military strategy without regressing into something like that nascent male, a possibility that becomes even more real the next time Hektor and the city intersect. In the shadow of the Skaian Gate, as a snake coiled before its hole, Hektor awaits Achilles. Both Hektor's parents standing on the wall at the city gate implore their son to come within the city. In the final appeal, Hekabe lays bare her bosom in supplication:

> So the old man spoke, and in his hands seizing the grey hairs
> tore them from his head, but could not move the spirit in Hektor.
> And side by side with him his mother in tears was mourning
> and opened the fold of her dress and with one hand held out
> a breast, and wept her tears for him, calling in winged words:
> "Hektor, my child, look upon these and obey, and take pity
> on me, if ever I gave you the breast to quiet your sorrow.
> Remember all these things, dear child, and from inside the wall
> beat off this grim man. Do not go out as champion against him,
> o hard one . . ."
>
> (22.77–86; Lattimore's translation, modified by author)

The figures of sheltering mother and protecting walls naturally merge.[43]

In contrast to the exposed and death-ridden world of war, the city appears to the returning hero as warm, full of life, supportive. The two spheres do not easily blend. Hektor, whether as parent (Book 6) or child (Book 22), is asked to make a choice between heroic action and civic embrace. He does not feel free to combine both, so to speak, by fighting from the wall. Hekabe's nurturing appeal by its very gesture inevitably subverts the virility she hopes to utilize from within the city.

Perhaps as an emblem of this city orientation, Hektor himself in his final moments contemplates a blending of this life-supporting domestic manner with the warrior spirit. But quickly he decides it is impossible to talk to Achilles gently:

> . . . (he will) kill me naked so, as if I were
> a woman, once I stripped my armor from me. There is no
> way anymore, not from tree nor from rock, to talk to him gently
> whispering like a young man and a young girl, in the way
> a young man and a young maiden whisper together.
> Better to bring on the fight . . .
>
> (22.124–29; Lattimore's translation, modified)

The masculine ethos of the city warrior struggles against a feminine ethos of the city he seeks to secure.[44] The wall, which gives the city its definition, leaches courage from the male in the face of death and makes the city a place of refuge for the weak; Homer uses the phrase "a young fawn" (22.1ff.) to describe the warrior who flees behind the wall when pursued by the likes of Achilles. Helenos makes the ambivalence explicit when he shouts to Hektor. In vulgar expression, when a warrior runs from danger into the city, he runs into the arms of women:

> Stand your ground here; visit your comrades everywhere; hold them
> fast by the gates, before they tumble into their women's
> arms, and become to our enemies a thing to delight in.
>
> (6.80–82)[45]

When Hektor does return to the city in Book 6, we see that each of the three women whom he encounters tries to hold him within Troy.[46] Hekabe: "But stay" (6.258); Helen: "But come now, come in and rest" (6.354); Andromache: "But come now, take pity on me, stay here on the rampart" (6.431). Hekabe tries to detain him by urging religious worship: "From the peak of the citadel [ex akrēs polios] lift your hands, praying / to Zeus . . . / and afterwards, if you will, drink yourself" (6.255–60). Helen, conscious that Hektor has assumed the burden of the war on account of her and Alexandrer's "sin," speaks of the "vile destiny" that shall make them the subject of song for generations to come (6.354–58). Like Hekabe, Helen, in her expressed concern for city, war, and heroic action, tries to restrain Hektor from battle and in effect by turning to conversation would transform the doer of "things of song" into a passive listener.[47] Andromache's request that Hektor fight from the city walls is most compelling and telling. Hektor's acquiescence to it would enable him to continue in battle but would effectively do away with the principles of heroic endeavor. As we have seen earlier in this chapter, Hektor's inability to accept Andromache's military advice stems from a deep-seated split in the Greek spirit: inasmuch as Hektor will fight for the city, he cannot fight from it.

When Hektor answers each—to Hekabe: "go yourself [269, 279] . . . while I go [280]"; to Helen: "but you, rouse this man [363] . . . for I am going [365]"; and most fully to Andromache: "Go therefore back to our house and take up your own work, / the loom and the distaff . . . / but the men must see to the fighting, / all men who are the people of Ilios, but I beyond others" (490–93)—he clearly separates in his mind the feminine world from the masculine. The division of genders is most explicit in his answer to Andromache: women to the loom, men to war.[48] Women and the city offer embrace; they have as their jurisdiction the privilege to shield and receive. Men, on the other hand, must engage in war on behalf of women and city in a place beyond the shelter they offer, in what ultimately must be a futile effort to triumph over death.

CHAPTER 5

City Epithets and
Homeric Poetics

More often than not, references to Troy or Ilios in Homer are without an epithet, though the omission is more common in narrative than in speeches. Examples from speech, however, are certainly frequent enough: for example, "there are many of us / who in front of our own parents, wives and children / will guard Ilios" (21.586–88). (In fact Troy in conjunction with the verb to guard [*eruomai*] is never found with epithet; cf. 24.499.) But when the subject concerns the destruction of Troy, references to the city rarely lack an epithet. I know of only five examples.[1] Conventional theories of formulaic usage cannot help us explain this Homeric phenomenon. It is also surely pertinent that twenty-six of the twenty-nine examples cited below are found in speeches.[2] Whether these stock phrases are with the verb *alapazō* ("to plunder or destroy"), *perthō* ("to sack"), *haireō* ("to seize"), or *ollumi* ("to destroy"), whether Troy is the subject or object of the sentence, and whatever may be their metrical place in the line, Troy and Ilios (but no other cities) are invariably qualified by an epithet. Those epithets usually come from one of the three categories discussed in the chapters above: the walled, peopled, or sacred city.

I list these formulaic phrases both to show their interlocking nature and to identify the narrow "contextual field" in which they are found.

With the verb (*ex*)*alapazō,* usually in the infinitive, Troy in the accusative is modified as the "great city of Priam," "Troy the well-walled city," or the "well-founded citadel of Ilios." The examples are as follows:

ei de ken aute
astu mega Priamoio theoi dōōs' alapaxai
    if hereafter the gods
permit us to destroy *the great city of Priam*

(9.135–36 = 277–78)

ai ke pothi Zeus
dōisi *polin Troiēn euteikheon* exalapaxai
    if ever Zeus shall permit us
to destroy utterly *Troy, the well-walled city*

(1.128–29; see 8.240–42)

ai ken moi dōēi Zeus t'aigiokhos kai Athēnē
Ilion exalapaxai *euktimenon ptoliethron*
    if aegis-bearing Zeus and Athena permit me
to destroy utterly Ilios, *the well-founded citadel*

(8.287–88; cf. 4.33; with variation at 5.642)

With an aorist form of the verb (*ek*)*perthō* (aorist *epersa*), Troy in the
accusative is qualified as "well-walled Ilios," the "well-founded citadel
of Ilios," the "well-inhabited citadel of Ilios," the "well-inhabited citadel of the Trojans," "your well-inhabited city," the "city of Priam,"
the "great city of Lord Priam," or the "holy citadel of Troy," as we see
in the following lines.[3]

Ilion ekpersant' *euteikheon* aponeesthai
to return home having sacked utterly *well-walled Ilios*

(2.113 = 2.288 = 5.716 = 9.20)

Ilion ekpersantes *euktimenon ptoliethron*
having destroyed Ilios *the well-founded citadel*

(21.433)

Iliou ekpersai *eu naiomenon ptoliethron*
to sack utterly *the well-inhabited citadel of Ilios*

(2.133)

Trōōn ekpersōs' *eu naiomemon ptoliethron*
[the Achaeans] may sack utterly *the well-inhabited citadel of the Trojans*

(1.164)

hoi de takh' ekpersous' *eu naiomenēn polin humēn*
[they] will soon sack utterly *your well-inhabited city*

(5.489; cf. 13.380)

humin men theoi doien Olumpia dōmat' ekhontes
ekpersai *Priamoio polin,* eu d'oikad'hikesthai
may the gods who have their homes on Olympus permit to you
to sack utterly the *polis of Priam,* and to reach home safely

(1.18–19)

astu mega *Priamoio anaktos*
ekpersei
[Achilles] will sack . . . *the great city of Lord Priam*

(21.309–10)

With the verb *perthō,* again, Troy now in the nominative is the "city of Priam" (in the narrative, 12.15);[4] in related formulas with the participial form *perthomenē,* Troy in the nominative is the "city of lord Priam" and "your well-inhabited city" (three times, all in speeches).[5]

There is a certain metrical economy in the use of these formulas: *euteikheon,* whether preceded by *polin Troiēn* or *Ilion . . . ,* always comes after the strong caesura in the third foot (six times); *euktimenon ptoliethron,* preceded by *Ilion,* always comes after the weak caesura in the third foot (three times); *eu naiomenon ptoliethron,* and once *eu naiomenēn polin humēn,* always comes after the strong caesura in the third foot (four times); *astu mega Priamoio (anaktos)* occurs either at the beginning of the line (twice) or after the second foot; and *Priamoio polin* occurs once after the strong caesura in the second foot. Each epithet may be said to occupy a "fixed" place in the line, but the persistence of epithetical usage in this contextual field needs further explanation. When used with other cities, the epithets *eu naiomenos* and *euktimenos* may be found in other contexts and in speech or narrative (cf. 5.543, 6.13, 16.572, 21.40), but when modifying Troy they *always* appear with the verbs *alapazō* or *perthō* and almost exclusively in speech. Similarly, *euteikheos,* which modifies Troy or Ilios, on six of its seven occurrences always occurs after *alapazō* or *perthō* and only in speech.[6] Other examples support the same conclusions.

In the accusative after the verb *haireō* (aorist *heilon* or *helon*), Troy is the "great city of Priam," "holy Ilios," "steep Ilios," and "lofty-gated Troy."

. . . eis ho ken *astu mega Priamoio* helōmen
. . . until we may take *the great city of Priam*

(2.332)

Trōas dēiōsōsin helōsi te *Ilion hirēn*
cut up the Trojans and take *holy Ilios*

(4.416)

kat'akrēs
Ilion aipeinēn heleein ktasthai te politas
utterly
they will take *steep Ilios* and kill her inhabitants

(15.557–58)

In the narrative, it is said that if Apollo had not intervened:

entha ken *hupsipulon Troiēn* helon . . .
then the Greeks would have taken *lofty-gated Troy* . . .

(16.698)

As subject of the verb *ollumi*, Troy is "holy Ilios":

essetai ēmar hot' an pot' olōlēi *Ilios hirē*
kai Priamos kai laos eummeliō Priamoio
The day will come when sacred Ilios, Priam
and the people of Priam will be destroyed

(4.164–65 = 6.448–49)

Once again a comparison of these diverse formulas reveals a remarkable uniformity of context. The interlacing of these epithets suggests a
cross-weave pattern of holy Ilios, lofty-gated Troy, and the great city of
Priam making up the fabric and design of Homer's Troy. In certain
constructions the tightness of the weave is evident, as for example, in
the formulaic line "and Priam and the people of Priam" which follows
"sacred Ilios" in the fifth and sixth foot of the preceding line. Sacred
Troy, its ruler, and its people (*laos*) are formulaically part of a uniform
tapestry.

What may account for this closely woven texture of verbs and epithets? And why so predominantly in speech? A closer study of Homeric usage will help define the limited contextual fields in which
Homer employs these epithets.

In recent studies, Paolo Vivante has significantly advanced our understanding of the aesthetics of the Homeric qualifying epithet beyond
what Milmann Parry would allow in his brilliant formulations, now a
half-century old. Arguing that an epithet is visual and concrete in
nature, and thereby evocative of an essential and generic quality of its

noun, Vivante sees it as isolating an object in the mind's eye, bringing that object momentarily to the foreground. Instead of asking the conventional Parryian question, whether an epithet is particular or ornamental in function, he asks why epithets appear in one instance but not in another, and more often in the nominative than in oblique cases. In response to his own question, he observes that epithets appear where and when they do because they serve to add weight to, or highlight, a noun already syntactically prominent in the sentence: "The problem of the epithets seems to crystallize at a sensitive point much that is pertinent to the appreciation of art. It is the problem of why and how an object of perception is singled out, mentioned, exposed. By highlighting the slightest object in its moment of emergence, an epithet impresses upon the occasion a sense of general existence."[7]

Vivante is especially good at describing the slight pause in the rapid flow of narration, or analyzing the way our attention is fixed for a moment by an epithet's image-making power to "crystallize" a generic quality of a noun. His aesthetic reevaluation further gives us a way to understand epithets as a resource of power and a medium of signification in their own right. Highly visual, concrete, and expressive of essential character (e.g., hero "swift of foot," "deep-waisted" women, "swift" ships, mountains or cities "windy"), epithets awaken a latent *dunamis,* infusing with life-force objects perceived.

In extreme loyalty to the view that poetry embodies timeless being and to the belief that an epithet is "so intimately bound to a certain noun as to form with it one sole image,"[8] Vivante insists that the epithet "is irrelevant to the narrative occasion" and "without any pointed connection of meaning with the context."[9] In so insisting, he fences himself out of major areas of analysis of Homeric poetics. The most serious of these is an epithet's "contextual field." As Anne Amory Parry has demonstrated so effectively, it is necessary to study all occurrences of an epithet, in each of its contexts, before its final semantic range and force can be determined. After such an undertaking, she writes, "one is impressed by how precise and subtle, and by how severely restricted in meaning, Homer's words usually are; even the commonest words and most obviously formulaic phrases are significant and exactly definable. . . . The study of epithet and formula lies not in its particular usage as much as in its cumulative use and variation. . . . The meaning and appropriateness of these repetitions are acquired during the process of composition and ultimately through repetition and its subsequent variations."[10] Following Amory's lead, we discover that, although some epithets appear to be used loosely without any clearly definable narrative occasion, others are obviously magnetized around a relatively narrow contextual field.

These observations by Paolo Vivante and Anne Amory Parry bear emphatically upon our study of an epithet like *euteikheos* ("well-walled") as it both brings the image of Troy into focus, crystallizing a generic quality of the polis, and is clearly part of a specific and identifiable contextual field. This Iliadic epithet is used almost exclusively with Troy (six of seven times), always in speech, and always by the Greeks (and once by Hera, echoing Greek sentiments).[11] There are two formulaic phrases: "to go home after having utterly destroyed well-walled Ilios" (*Ilion ekpersant' euteikheon aponeesthai*), and "if Zeus / grants us" (or "desiring") "to sack well-walled Troy" (*dōisi polin* [or *hiemenos*] *Troiēn euteikheon exalapaxai*). Thus it *always* appears in a context where desire (human or divine) plays against the seemingly impregnable defense of the city. Even more than highlighting a general sense of Troy's existence, the epithet with almost verbal energy of its own struggles against the sentence's actual verb, thwarting its telos. It takes Zeus as the father of gods and men to tip the scales in favor of one side or the other. Counterpoint between verb and epithet not only is forceful but appears intentional as it sustains much of the dramatic tension within the line. When we recognize that all these examples occur only in the speeches by the Achaeans, it is hard to deny that the epithet carries emotional weight.

Consider Agamemnon, frustrated because of Zeus' failed promises, as he laments (characteristically) before the Achaeans:

> My dear heroes, Danaans, companions of Ares,
> Zeus the great son of Cronos has bound me in rash ruin.
> He is hard, who swore and *promised* to me before that I should
> return home *having destroyed utterly well-walled Ilios,*
>   [*Ilion* ekpersant' *euteikheon* aponeesthai]
> but now he has planned an evil deception . . .
>
>   (2.110–14)

Similar context may be found at 2.284–90, 5.714–17, and 9.19–21, the last two again with reference to gods who have not lived up to their promises.

The context is similar in another speech by Agamemnon:

> but on all your altars I burned the fat and thighs of oxen
> desiring *to sack utterly well-walled Troy.*

Ah, Zeus, *accomplish this very wish* for me!
Let us escape with our lives, if nothing else.
(8.240–43; cf. 1.128–29)

Here praying directly to Zeus, Agamemnon asks that the Achaeans be
granted the power to storm the strongly fenced city. As in the first
example, only Zeus can arbitrate between the Greek will and the city
defense. He is invoked either because he is perceived as having broken
promises in the past (2.112–13 and 9.20–21; cf. 5.714–17) or because it
is hoped that he will fulfill long-delayed dreams in the future (1.128–29
and 8.240–42). In each of these examples, there is a triangular tension
between (1) promises (usually from Zeus) and Greek desires, (2) the
verb, which signifies destruction or plunder, and (3) the city of Troy,
epithetically described. The epithet marks one point of that triangula-
tion and must be considered equal in weight to the verb and Zeus.

Of the epithets in this "contextual field," *euktimenos* does not explicitly refer to city fortifications but instead suggests the well-structured settlement of a city. The epithet occurs fifteen times with cities in
the *Iliad*,[12] of which three refer to Troy. All three occur in speeches: *Ilion
exalapaxai* (or *ekpersantes*) *euktimenon ptoliethron* ("to sack utterly" [or
"having utterly destroyed"] "Ilios the well-founded citadel"). Identical
to the contextual field of phrases with *euteikheos*, epithet and verb appear
contrapuntal, desire and frustration set the tone, and ultimate authority
lies with Zeus. In one example, Zeus asks Hera what Priam may have
done to her so that she desires "to destroy utterly the well-founded
citadel of Ilios" (4.33); in another, Agamemnon says that if Zeus and
Athena will grant to him "to destroy utterly the well-founded citadel of
Ilios," he will give the first prize of honor after his own to Teucer (8.288;
cf. 21.433).[13]

The pattern is seen yet again with the epithet *aipienē,* or *aipus*
("steep"), when applied to Troy in the *Iliad,* where it is found only in
speeches and only in the context of the city's security. Zeus is usually at
the center of the storm. Menelaos, for example, rebukes the Trojans for
not fearing the harsh wrath of Zeus, defender of the laws of hospitality,
"who some day will utterly sack your steep *polis,*" (. . . *diaphthersei
polin aipēn,* at the end of the line, 13.625). The verb differs here from the
previous examples, but context is thoroughly familiar. Later Zeus himself refers to the day when the Achaeans "will take steep Ilios through
the designs of Athena" (*Ilion aipu helōsin . . . ,* 15.71). In one instance
polin aipēn appears at the end of the line, in the other *Ilion aipu* occurs at

the beginning. If the variety of formulaic phrases and positions is arresting, equally noteworthy is the uniformity of setting.

The phrasing of *Iliad* 9.418–20 = 685–87 retains the combination of epithet and "contextual field" in a most unusual way: return home, Achilles advises the Greeks, "since you shall not find the mark / of steep Ilios (*Iliou aipeinēs*). For all-seeing Zeus has stretched out a loving hand over the city and its people have taken heart." The appearance of *Ilios aipeinē* at the beginning of the line is common enough whether in the nominative (13.773), the accusative (15.558), or the genitive (9.419 and 15.215), even if the wording "find the mark of" from the preceding line is unique. More surprising is the reference to Zeus, who in typical fashion is mentioned in the context of Troy's welfare but is syntactically separated from the formula "steep Ilios." In short, while the phrasing with the epithet is unparalleled, the larger setting or contextual field in which the epithet appears is perfectly consistent with other examples of this epithet with Ilios. In another variation of conventional patterning, Apollo questions Aeneas: "How could you mortals, even against the gods, defend / steep Ilios?" (*kai huper theon eirussaisthe / Ilion aipeinēn*) (17.327–28).[14] In spite of the variation, the epithet again appears in the context of city destruction; as in the Homeric usage of *euteikheos,* we sense in *aipeinos,* when used of Troy, a kind of *dunamis,* the epithet evoking an image not only of lift but also of insurmountable obstacle.

The most striking of these descriptive phrases is particularly hard to translate. Scolding Alexander for being woman-crazed, Hektor equates Alexander's fall with Troy's ruin: *nun ōleto pasa kat' akrēs / Ilios aipeinē, nun toi sōs aipus olethros* ("Now wholly destroyed is all / steep Ilios. Now your destruction is utter," 13.772–73). I also offer Rieu's prose translation: "This is indeed the end of Ilium: its topmost towers are down. There is nothing for you now but death." In Homer, the parallel placement of *nun,* the chiastic order of *Ilios aipeinē* and *aipus olethros* in line 773, as well as the chiasm of *ōleto* and *olethros* in 772–73 are artful. The *figura etymologica* between the verb *ōleto* and the noun *olethros,* and the juxtaposition between the literal use of *aipeinō* (steep) for Ilios and its metaphoric use (sheer or utter) for destruction, are equally striking.[15] We find here a paradox of Troy that has been often seen before: if Troy's epithets describe a city that appears almost impregnable to hostile forces because of its rocky height and mighty wall, context describes a city that it is equally vulnerable. Here elements of that paradox are linked through the double use of *aipus.*

In only one instance does a *city-defender* refer to the city's well-crafted fortifications. Again the will of Zeus looms behind the scene. Speaking to Trojans and Achaeans alike, Hektor says that now that the truce has been broken Zeus will keep them all suffering "until that day when you [the Greeks] storm well-towered Troy [*Troiēn eupurgon helēte*] or that day when you yourselves are broken beside your seafaring vessels" (7.71–72). Hektor's epithet *eupurgon* is unique, but the context resembles those outlined above.[16]

All but two of the passages cited above occur in speeches and before Book 16 of the *Iliad*. But between Books 16 and 22, references to Troy's destruction are increasingly recorded in the narrative. Twice within the space of these books characters make striking reference to the city wall (Poulydamas, 18.254ff.; and Poseidon, 21.446–47), but for the first time the narrator himself brings attention to the walls: "All these Patroklos slew; but the others turned their minds to flight. There and then the sons of the Achaeans would have taken lofty-gated Troy [*hupsipulon Troiēn helon*] by the hand of Patroklos, if Apollo had not stood on the well-built tower [*eudmēton purgon*]" (16.697–701). "The Trojans fled straight for the city and the lofty wall [*teikheos hupsēloio*], parched by thirst and covered with dust. But Achilles in his haste followed them with his spear. An overmastering lust of battle always gripped his heart and he yearned to win glory. There and then the sons of the Achaeans would have taken lofty-gated Troy, if Apollo had not inspired Agenor, Antenor's noble son" (21.540–46). Twenty lines before, in the only other use of *eudmēton* with Ilios or its circuit, the narrator says: Apollo "entered holy Ilios. For he had come to the wall of the well-built city [*teikhos eudmētoio poleos*] lest the Danaans destroy it that day" (21.515–17); "Priam, the old man, stood on the divine tower [*theiou epi purgou*] and recognized the monstrous Achilles" (21.526–27). Finally, with their thirst quenched, the Trojan army "leaned on the beautiful battlements" (22.3). This shift of Troy's epithets from speech to narrative corresponds with a transition from hypothetical action to the narrator's description of imminent danger.

The Homeric use of epithets for Troy in speech and narrative stands apart from what many consider typical Homeric formulaic usage. In a recent study of formulas related to three verbs of joy in Homer, for example, M. Finkelberg has observed that "formulae proper" (i.e., in their unmodified form) occur predominantly in the narrative but that the unusual phrase (i.e., a "modified formula" or an "isolated expression") is characteristically found in direct speech.[17] Of epithets for Troy the evidence is almost reversed as the isolated expression or modified phrase (e.g., *theiou epi purgou* or *hupsipulon Troiēn helon*) is located in the narrative and most standard formulaic patterns are part of direct discourse. Paolo Vivante, before Finkelberg, also regards the epithet as more at home in the narrative: "When the object is mentioned in a speech and in the accompanying representation, it often happens that it has an epithet in the latter but not in the former";[18] when in speech, "the epithets reflect the speaker's stand point, though not his mood. They are most at home when things are perceived, remembered. . . . The opposite is the case when the speaker's overriding interest sets in."[19] The cumulative evidence of our data conforms to neither of Vivante's rules: (1) epithets for Troy are more often in speeches than in narrative; (2) they appear, it seems to me, precisely when interest sets in, and they reflect mood. To summarize the eight epithets we have examined so far, four are found in speech (*euteikheos, eupurgos, euktimenos, aipienos* or *aipus*) and four more in the narrative (*eudmētos* for both *purgos* and *polis, hupsipulos, hupsēlos, theios*). While there is little difference in the signification of epithets from either set (*hupsēlos* is not markedly different from *aipeinos* or *eupurgos, eudmētos* resembles *euktimenos* and *euteikheos*), there is considerable variation in frequency of usage and in distribution throughout the *Iliad*. Those in speech far outnumber their narrative counterparts and are found throughout the epic, usually in the mouths of the Achaeans, while those in the narrative are almost exclusively restricted to the later stages of the poem when the war begins to press threateningly against holy Ilios. The force of epithets in both categories resonates in contrapuntal fashion against the verb, revealing the strength of Troy.

Unlike the other epithets discussed in this chapter, the last epithet I consider is found in both speech and narrative. While the contrapuntal tension is not evident in any of the examples from the narrative, "holy" used in speeches often has considerable force. Of the twenty-six occurrences of *hieros* and *hirē* with Troy, Ilios, and Pergamon (twenty-three of them in the *Iliad*), thirteen are in the narrative, mostly from a single mold after the prepositions *eis* ("to, into") and *proti* ("to, toward").[20] Three occurrences in speeches are also in such prepositional contructions.[21] The remaining ten occur in contextual fields resembling those with *euteikheos,* and company, where resonance between epithet, verb, and Zeus is poignantly felt. For example, Agamemnon imagines the day when "Zeus will destroy sacred Ilios, / Priam and the people of Priam" (4.164–65; cf. 4.416, 6.448–49, 16.100, *Od.* 1.2). The most evocative expression occurs in Book 4: asking his wife why "she desires / to destroy utterly the well-founded city of Ilios" (4.32–33), having gone through the gate and strong walls and devoured raw

Priam, the sons of Priam, and the other Trojans, Zeus expresses his reluctance to honor Hera's wishes while at the same time acquiescing to her will with the following phrasing:

> Of all the cities under the sun and starry
> heavens which mortal men inhabit,
> none is more esteemed in my heart than sacred Ilios
> and Priam and the people of Priam of the good ash spear.
> My altar was never lacking its due share of wine and fat.

(4.44–48)

In this conflicted speech, the many components of Troy's epithetical "language" come together: the well-founded city, its majestic gate and walls, its sanctity and people, all resting in the hands of Zeus.

The evidence culled from the Homeric application of all these epithets makes it impossible, I believe, to ignore context when considering formulaic usage. What D. G. Miller says about formulaic usage in general applies in principle to the subset of epithets for Troy: "Formulas attach to and are triggered by the repetition of certain themes (arming, battles, counsel, dining, etc.) and speech turns (turn-taking, resumptions, introductions, greetings, etc.). These situations are facilitated by, and in turn carry with them, a number of expressions engineered for easy insertion, removal, and substitution."[22] Similarly Norman Austin, observing the Homeric use of an epithet like *polumētis* ("of many counsels"), notes that sixty-three of the sixty-five occurrences modify Odysseus as the narrator prefaces direct discourse. Austin concludes from this evidence that the phrasing with that epithet "is not a formula floating in free suspension in the repertory but a formula for only one particular situation."[23] Observations of this kind affect translation. Austin again: "It might be better to translate the formula in that context as 'thinking hard, Odysseus spoke,' or 'while his mind ranged far, Odysseus spoke.' Such translations remind us that when Odysseus speaks he is usually pleading a case, marshalling his most persuasive arguments."[24] Austin observes much the same for the Odyssean usage of *polumēkhanos* ("of many devices"): "[It] is no faded metaphor but one that proclaims that Odysseus is about to contrive, or has just contrived, some new strategem bordering on the magical."[25] Notice how Austin interprets both epithets in a verbal manner: he translates *polumētis* as a participle and *polumēkhanos* as a verb.

Applying the observations of Vivante, Austin, Miller, and others, we may understand the epithets for Troy in Homer as a medium of

signification in their own right. Many of these, such as *euteikheos,*
eupurgos, and *aipus,* are in typical Homeric fashion not only highly
visual and concrete in nature but also expressive of verbal energy evoking an image of lift and insurmountable obstacle, reenacting visible
phenomena, bestowing life-force upon the object perceived, rendering
thing into action. Accumulating throughout the epic, these epithets
hold before our eyes the drama in its widest dimension: not the wrath
of individual heroes on the battlefield, but siege warfare where men
and gods strive to plunder cities well-towered, well-inhabited, and
sacred.

CHAPTER 6

History and Composition

Eternity is in love with the productions of time.
                                    —Blake, "Proverbs of Hell"

History and the Homeric Polis

In the beginning of this book, I suggested that the semantic range of polis in the Homeric poems—a range from Mycenaean acropolis to eighth-century Ionian city-state—afforded difficulty as well as opportunity. Opportunity resides in the capacity of the word *polis* to bridge the cultural diversity of the various eras, presenting in the poems a single, unified image of the city. To study the city in Homer is to examine continuity across discontinuity, the preserving power of tradition. Accordingly, this chapter examines in some detail the particular historical milieux from which the poems and the epic tradition drew sustenance. No attempt is made to applaud the poems for their mimetic representations, whether of Mycenae or eighth-century Ionia. Such an exercise in literalism is best left for the tourist. I propose, rather, to show the unifying work of the poems by examining the disparate images of the historical polis.

I shall be considering history, therefore, to make what is finally an ahistorical argument, using diachronic analysis, if you will, to draw a synchronic conclusion. The Mycenaean and Ionian versions of the polis pass through each other in a double exposure (or a triple exposure, if you include the imprint from the Greek Dark Ages) to constitute the Homeric image. To change the metaphor, I could propose playfully the model of autobiography, especially that of romantic autobiography, to exemplify unification emerging from diversity and severence. As in Wordsworth's Moebius strip formulation "the child is the father to the man," romantic autobiography, by which I mean

81

testimonials like Rousseau's *Confessions* and Wordsworth's *Intimations Ode* and *Prelude,* privileging childhood, looks back to the past, finding there the sources and resources of adult spiritual life. To push the metaphor a little further, autobiography imposes a structure of linear narrative on inchoate events; by this linear telos, it constructs a unity of self out of the fragments of origin, evolution, and the time of reflection. So the Homeric poems may be viewed as a kind of cultural autobiography in that, while privileging the Mycenaean past, they *fuse* widely divergent eras into coherent unity. While retaining Wordsworth's formulation, I would, however, invert the relation between past and present. If the past engenders the present, it is equally true, and more accurate in this instance, to say that the present brings the past to light: through the evolution of the Homeric poems, the contemporary eighth-century world was giving birth to its own past.

The social and political characteristics of Homeric cities often reflect ninth-century conditions when aristocracies and oikoi were the pre-eminent centers of power, but the physical portrait of Homeric walled cities can only derive from poetic memories of a remote Mycenaean past (1400–1100 B.C.) or reflect eighth-century conditions of the emerging city-state. For most of the period in between, according to Antony Snodgrass, "there can have been no city life, mainly because the settlements were so small and few."[1]

Mycenaean and Ionian city-types, however, differ dramatically in form and content. Mycenaean "cities" (poleis), more properly called citadels, crowned steep hills which, at the edge of a plain and often ten to fifteen kilometers from the sea, overlooked the territory stretching below. These citadels served as the palace centers of the Mycenaean wanax, who, as king of a highly bureaucratic and hierarchical society, was responsible for the organization of the state in almost all spheres of life: social, economic, political, military, and religious.[2] If the citadels were walled, as a sizable number were in the thirteenth century, the fortification housed only the megaron of the wanax, a shrine of the citadel's protecting goddess, and storerooms, whereas the vast majority of houses, trading centers, markets, shops, and the like were located outside the massive walls in a lower town (astu) on the slopes of the acropolis or spread out onto the plain. That sharp division between polis and astu begins to blur only in the last phase of Mycenaean civilization, when in a few instances the walled citadels grew to enclose a limited portion of the more extended community.[3] In addition, many satellite settlements of village-like agglomerations existed in an array resembling spokes of an opened umbrella joined to the center staff by a radiating bureaucracy administered from the palace center.[4]

All major activities of state were concentrated around, and intimately linked to, the royal palace;[5] as seen in Mycenaean art, the palace, portrayed in relief from a distance, may almost be read as an ideogram for the society at large. The popular subject of storming walled hill towns in Mycenaean palace frescoes, pottery, and silver vases testifies to a Mycenaean fascination with this theme and to the citadel's symbolic significance as an image of the kingdom itself.[6]

Unlike their Mycenaean counterparts, the newly formed Ionian cities of the eighth century tend to be located on low-lying peninsulas, ideally situated for maritime trade and for defense from a less-than-friendly indigenous, inland population. With a protecting wall at the neck of its peninsula or with an enclosing circuit fortification, the secured area of an Ionian city shelters the vast majority, if not all, of its people. By 750 B.C., Old Smyrna, densely built up with four or five hundred houses of mud brick and stone foundations, held approximately two thousand people, with perhaps half that many off the peninsula along the coast.[7] Although no historical records from the period survive to confirm it, the urban design of these new cities—houses, communal agora, and often city temple within a common defensive system—suggests that these communities were considerably less stratified, and monarchical, than the Mycenaean kingdoms. If the Ionians had abandoned the visual and symbolic manifestations of Mycenaean majesty, exclusive walls, aristocratic height, and palace-centered economies, they gained a new spirit of collective urbanization.

With the decay of Mycenaean civilization, as with the decay of a tree stump, the center was the first to wither. In the aftermath of such catastrophic devastation, life continued in village-like settlements, but even these were greatly reduced in number and size compared with their Mycenaean counterparts. In this sense, there was little or no possibility of continuity between Mycenaean acropolis and Ionian polis. Although the following quote by Moses Finley is extreme when considered in a larger cultural context, it serves admirably when we narrow the lense and compare Mycenae to eighth-century Ionia in terms of urban design:

What happened after the fall of the Mycenaean civilization was not merely a decline within the existing social framework but a decline and a change in character altogether. Then as the new Greek society emerged from these new beginnings, it moved in a very different direction, so that the kind of world which had existed before 1200 B.C. never again appeared in ancient Greece proper. In that sense, the break was complete and permanent.[8]

The Submycenaean culture (c. 1125–1050 B.C.)[9] in this period of rupture and upheaval was sadly impoverished. In the wake of destruction (first 1200, then 1125 B.C.), mainland Greece, the heart of Mycenaean civilization, was emptied of its people. In some regions, numbers of known *sites* declined by at least 90 percent:[10] class stratification was radically simplified;[11] specialization decreased; trading networks dried up;[12] agricultural areas shrank.

In the absence of the Mycenaean monumental citadel, people of the post-Mycenaean era lived in small and relatively isolated communities. According to one recent count (1982), cited by Carol Thomas: "in Greece, we know of three hundred twenty sites for the thirteenth century, one hundred thirty for the twelfth century and only forty for the eleventh century."[13] Although little is known at present about the internal design of settlements, density of population appears to have been greater in the Cyclades and Crete than on the mainland where most settlements consisted, Ian Morris says, "of clusters of houses separated by open spaces."[14] Morris in particular has been most generous when calculating population figures for this period: "the major Dark Age sites are likely to have had a few thousand inhabitants."[15] Generally, views are more pessimistic. Jeffrey Hurwit, for example, writes that "Dark Age Greece was a land of small communities that barely qualified as communities;"[16] others see communities of fifteen inhabitants in the eleventh century rising to twenty-five in the next.[17]

The architectural remains from this period are, as one might expect, extremely meager. There is not one fortification wall. Mycenaean technology both of large-scale Kyklopean masonry and of domestic timber and stone construction appears to have disappeared totally.[18]

In the eighth century, with a profound change in social structure, the polis arose "out of a mass of competing world views," according to Morris.[19] City institutions emerged, suggesting that the oikos had begun to lose its central hold, and farming had become more prominent than animal husbandry. Most startling of all, the population from 800 to 700 B.C. multiplied, Oswyn Murray states, "by a factor of six. . . . Within the period 800–750 the population of Attica . . . quadrupled, and almost doubled again in the next fifty years: a half-empty landscape was repeopled."[20] The consequences of these changes seem equally dramatic. New settlements sprang up both in mainland Greece and in areas to the east and west of Greece not explored by the Greeks since the Mycenaean era.[21]

The archaeological remains indicate that these new communities were little more than clusters of villages,[22] where communities tended to grow around the old Mycenaean citadels. Excavations at Athens, Corinth, and Eretria, for example, indicate that "poleis" here during the eighth century were little more than hamlets, unfortified and loosely grouped. At Argos there is some evidence that its population was coagulating during this period into something of a village community near the site of its later agora, but there is no evidence of a concentrated urban center at any one of these three locations.[23]

It is the Greeks along the Asia Minor coast—where Mycenaean emigrants had been settling for generations, in waves of migration since 1050 B.C.—who showed the most enterprise in building new and more ambitious cities. Or so the archaeological record would suggest. N. G. L. Hammond speaks of these unique conditions as follows:

> On the Asiatic coast, each settlement was isolated, so that its settlers formed a single and self-contained entity; and they only maintained their hold by concentrating round a defensible city and staving off their enemies. Under such conditions in Asia Minor a series of small city-states sprang into being, incapable at the outset of linking together and incapable, as the event proved, of conquering the hinterland to form a larger and unified state. For each settlement the defensible centre . . . took on a new significance: it became the focus of social and political life.[24]

The quotation is, of course, pertinent both to the development of the polis and to the portrait of the polis in Homer.

The first walled communities since the Mycenaean era are to be found among these Ionian settlements. At Old Smyrna, the modern Baykali near Izmir, the first circuit walls are to be dated circa 850 B.C. At Iasos, in Caria to the south of Old Smyrna, the city walls were no later than 800 B.C. Other complete circuit walls were built at Melie, also in Caria and at Emporio on Chios, an island just off the Asia Minor coast and not far from Old Smyrna. Both Melie and Emporio were small acropolis sites, similar in form to the ancient Mycenaean citadels, but their walls, especially at Emporio, were hastily thrown up in rough rubble construction. A massive wall was also constructed across the peninsula's neck at Zagora (founded before 800 B.C.) on the island of Andros. By the end of the Late Geometric period (circa 700

B.C.), Phaistos on Crete and Ayios Andreas on Siphnos were also refurbished with protecting "urban" walls.[25] By contrast, the first examples of polis walls on the Greek mainland occur in the seventh century.

Of the city walls that were built for settlements along the Asia Minor coast, or on the islands nearby, none rivaled those at Old Smyrna in scale or technological method. The inspiration for such sophisticated engineering still remains something of a mystery. About that technological know-how John Coldstream writes:

> Such precocity can hardly be explained by eastern influence, since Ionia had very little communication with Phrygia or the Levant before the end of the eighth century. It has been suggested that the first Ionian settlers might have brought with them some skill in monumental masonry inherited from the Mycenaean tradition, which they would then have adapted and transformed throughout the Dark Ages; alternatively, a native Anatolian tradition of fine masonry, as seen in the final walls of Troy VI (i.e., 1250 B.C.), may not have been entirely forgotten. Even so, we have no positive evidence of any such skill among the eastern Greeks before the ninth-century circuit of Old Smyrna.[26]

He compliments their workmanship in the following way: "There was nothing hasty about the walls of Smyrna which must have been the pride of the city."[27] The first wall built from sawn ashlar blocks and the second, built one hundred years later with huge hammer-dressed blocks of approximately polygonal shape, both show a skilled stone craftsmanship unexampled since the Mycenaean era. The great thickness of Smyrna's walls, like those of old Mycenae, created an image of monumental architecture unwitnessed for over four hundred years.

Snodgrass is hesitant to identify these new settlements as poleis on the basis of circuit walls and dense populations alone. To believe that one's loyalty was bound to a larger order than the self or family estate, there must be some evidence, he argues, of public cults or public institutions. Communal walls and settlement densities in his view are less indicative of this new spirit than a temple in which a cult image of a tutelary deity might be housed. "There was no factor more important in the composition of the state than the devotion to common cults," he writes. "It shows that the god has taken over the monarchy. By this reckoning, Smyrna may have become a *polis* only after about 750 B.C."[28] Such centers would have sparked the political changes necessary to disrupt the social units previously based on kinship and tribe.

Except for an apsidal building at Lefkandi circa 1000 B.C.,[29] such structures first appear among the Greeks at the beginning of the eighth century:[30] examples include a temple of Hera Akraia at Perachora opposite Corinth, of Apollo at Eretria in Euboia, and of Hera on Samos off the coast of Asia Minor. Aside from a temple at Antissa on Lesbos, early apsidal temples were located on the Greek mainland.[31]

The great innovation in temple construction occurred in the monumental Hecatompedon (100-footed) temple, first built on Samos perhaps as early as 800 B.C., shortly after the first monumental circuit wall at Old Smyrna and shortly before a public cult site or temple attested there by archaeology. Soon after the completion of the temple at Samos, temples of similar design were built at Eretria and at Gortyna in Crete.[32] In the middle of the eighth century, a large platform was built at Old Smyrna, "comparable in height and extent with the later temple platform,"[33] upon which a grand public cult temple was built by 700 B.C. There is thus a strong likelihood that the early structure of 750 marks the date of Old Smyrna's first public temple.[34]

In addition to Old Smyrna, Oikonomos on the island of Paros exhibited many of the characteristics deemed necessary by Snodgrass to qualify as an emergent polis: located on a small peninsula with safe harborage on either side, and fortified, it had residential housing in the upper section of the peninsula, an agora with administrative and religious buildings lower down, and an isolated apsidal building, prominently placed, apparently housing a temple to the polis' protecting deity. The most recent evidence suggests that the settlement should be dated close to 700 B.C., that is, one hundred and fifty years after the construction of the first walls at Old Smyrna but only fifty years after the remodeling of Smyrna's walls, the building of its first temple, and the dense settlement of its urban area.[35]

What bearing, if any, might this historical survey have on our understanding of the Homeric portrait of poleis? To what extent might the contemporary urban picture influence Homeric image or thematic development?

Writers on the polis in Homer like to point out Homeric trappings from both periods. If Scheria in the *Odyssey* resembles a contemporary Ionian settlement on a flat peninsula with a double harbor (such as Old Smyrna and Oikonomos), then Troy in the *Iliad*, set back from the sea on a hilltop, is typically Mycenaean. (In Homer's period, such walled hilltop towns were also found at places like Emporio or Iasos; however, they were located on promontories overlooking good harbors.) But the differences between Troy and Scheria are in fact not so sharply drawn. If, in the description of Scheria, it is evident that the poet was, in the words of Spiros Iakovidis, "visualizing a coastal city such as the Ionic ones of his own day,"[36] it is also true that within that polis Alkinoos' megaron is unquestionably of a Mycenaean type. And if Homeric Troy is Mycenaean, Homer's view of a densely populated polis with all its people settled within a common wall does not derive from the old traditional remembrance but comes from the formative period of the Epic,[37] that is to say, the eighth century B.C. Of equal importance at Troy, the Homeric temples of Athena (*Il.* 6.87f.) and of Apollo (*Il.* 5.446), located on the city's crest, do not derive from an inherited memory of the tutelary Mycenaean deity perhaps housed in the megaron of the wanax but imitate contemporary architectural features of the emerging polis. That is, they are another eighth-century anachronism affixed to an imagined Mycenaean citadel. Similarly, the towers of Homeric Troy may seem "Mycenaean" in design, but the building of the Achaean wall at Troy follows Ionian methods. When speaking of that wall, the archaeologist John Cook, undoubtedly romanticizing the figure of Homer but responding to the similarity between descriptions in the Homeric poems and eighth-century Ionian wall construction, observes: "Homer describes what he unquestionably witnessed and what would be well-known to his audience."[38]

As mentioned in an earlier chapter, in the Troy of Homer the women and old men *must* go to the *wall* to see the plain, contrary to the Mycenaean depiction of besieged cities in which the women of the city often stand in palace windows to look out onto the field of battle. And as suggested before, Homer's placement of most city scenes on the wall of Troy may have been prompted by contemporary Ionian conditions, where an overview from within the city would only be possible from atop the city wall.

There are, then, at least four important parts of the Homeric portrait of Troy (and the Achaean wall at Troy) which suggest that the "Mycenaean" citadel is in fact, like Scheria, seen in the context of a contemporary Ionian city, or polis: the city enclosure of the entire city population, city temples, wall as absolute visual boundary, contemporary (eighth-century) construction. Like the Homeric description of political organizations, elements of Mycenaean cities have been threaded within the fabric of a later city organization. Each of these contemporary details intensifies the prominence of city and wall in the poems: all of civilization, sanctified by public cult, is held within the city enclosure, and the city wall, built by the most "advanced" forms of modern engineering, symbolizes the radical division between civilization and its annihilation.

Cook objects that the more spacious and well-built houses in the later seventh-century Old Smyrna, rather than the tight conditions of eighth-century Smyrna, more closely resemble the grand residences, fine masonry, and freestanding temples of Scheria in the *Odyssey*. He thinks, also, that other Ionian cities of the eighth century that were larger and commercially more advanced than Old Smyrna serve as better models for Homeric portraits of the polis.[39] Such prudent objections should caution us that no one historical model should be considered the prototype from which Homeric Scheria or any other Homeric polis was modeled. It is also worthy of mention that all walled cities in the poems, except for Gortyna in Crete, are of the Mycenaean period: Troy, the three Thebes (in Boiotia, the Troad, and Egypt), Lyrnessos, Kalydon, Pleuron, Phaia (in Elis). Even if Homer's view of the polis may be determined by the world around him, his information about walled cities, and undoubtedly much of the formulaic language about those poleis, has been inherited through the oral epic tradition.

Two points of crucial importance emerge. On the one hand, the Homeric *vision* of the polis, and even of Troy, seems in essential detail to have been deeply influenced by contemporary conditions at Old Smyrna, said in antiquity to have been his birthplace.[40] But in other respects the portrait contains a conservatism that looks back to ancient Mycenaean citadel. In part, the Homeric polis can be both old and new because the circuit wall, fundamental in Homer's portrait and common to Old Smyrna and Mycenaean citadel, neutralizes historical difference. Furthermore, the generalizing quality of epithets erases difference. So the epithets of Troy, Scheria, and other poleis tend to fashion the polis from a standard mold, cast in generalities rather than particulars, describing features that are as much Ionian as Mycenaean. Both facts are important, and, keeping them in mind, we see how the historical city of Homer's day can merge with the remembered city of myth, how a vision inspired by contemporary conditions and inherited formulas can conflate Mycenaean and Ionian features.

The social and political picture of Homeric communities suggests a society even more confusing, and perhaps less contemporary, than does the architectural portrait. But here again the portrait is not specific to any one era. Many signs indicate an archaic society of the tenth or ninth century. Although writing was in use in both the Mycenaean and Ionian eras, there is no evidence of its existence or need in the poems. Rights and claims were decided, in most instances, within the family structure, not subject to the rights and powers of outside agencies.[41] Alliances tended to form between aristocratic families and were based upon ancestry, wealth, and guest-friendships, rather than determined by "political" affiliations. Individuals were distinguished as much by aristocratic bearing as by polis habitation. The lowly Thersites, for example, was identified not by family name or polis home, but by his nonaristocratic status. Such conditions, it seems fair to say, were reminiscences and survivals, often garbled, of a Dark Age society, representative neither of the Mycenaean nor of the changing political conditions well under way near the end of the eighth century. On the other hand, the extended family of Priam, with his fifty sons and fifty daughters all residing in one palace complex, harks back to an even earlier period. Similarly in the modern Scheria, the unusual influence of Queen Arete suggests a pre-Mycenaean, mythical past.

Against this primarily Dark Age social environment of saga-heroes, with an occasional Mycenaean or earlier intrusion, one also finds an overlay of living conditions suggestive of a contemporary city aristocracy—"an aristocracy," as Werner Jaeger describes it, "which (as is shown by the description of Hector and the Trojans) already knows the organized life of the city-state."[42] A new *aidōs* ("reverence, regard, sense of shame"), defined by a common good, intrudes upon the individualistic tendencies of the oikos-bound Dark Age aristocracies. In the monumental temples of the city, as in the sacred agora, we see a consolidation of social structures built around an urban center. In Odysseus' survey of the Kyklopes' island, we see the perspective of a man, and colonist, who defines the world in terms of polis bonds and virtues.[43]

In this historical survey two points stand out: the early forms of the polis, if still rather nascent, came into existence during, if not before, the time of Homer in the latter half of the eighth century; although the world picture in both poems is a mosaic of conflicting periods within Greek history, neither the *Odyssey* nor especially the *Iliad* would exist in its present form if the ideals and manners created by the new polis had not already been taking shape. This claim is most pertinent to the dramatic setting that frames the *Iliad*. I shall conclude this synopsis, then, with three quotes supporting the argument that polis is more prominent than oikos and that the background of the poems is of contemporary derivation. First, the archaeologist John Cook:

> There is so much taken for granted in the human and social background and so much that can be shown by archaeological discoveries to belong

to Homer's own time (after the allowance has been made for anachronisms and traditional elements) we can with some confidence draw on
the poems to illuminate the general pattern of life and thought in the
Ionia of the poet's own day.[44]

Although he does not elaborate his point, I find that the comments of J.
Sarkady, a social historian, are even more responsive than Cook's to
the Homeric description of cities:

> The majority of scholars agree that Homer's world is one before the city-
> states were created. Still it seems justifiable to say that some—not unim-
> portant—remarks of Homer refer to ideals and manners created by the
> *polis*. This assumption can be extended so far as to say that the back-
> ground of Homer's work is the established and finished *polis* even if its
> concrete depiction is missing owing to his material taken from earlier
> days and to his artistic method.[45]

Lastly, remarks from the historian Oswyn Murray:

> Some features from the Homeric poems point to an earlier state; but as
> far as social and political organization are concerned, despite the impor-
> tance of the *genos* and the *oikos,* Homer and Hesiod show that the *polis*
> already existed in all essential aspects by the end of the Dark Age.
> Homer takes the same view of human nature as Aristotle: the Cyclopes
> are utterly uncivilized, not only because they ignore the rules of guest-
> friendship; "they possess neither counsel-taking assemblies nor *themistes,*
> but dwell on the tops of high hills in hollow caves, and each one utters
> judgments for his children and wives, and they take no need of one
> another" (*Odyssey* 9.112ff.).[46]

Catalogues in the *Iliad* and the Homeric Landscape

This section briefly examines the scope of the Homeric landscape
and how cities fit into that landscape in order, once again, to consider
the "historicity" of Homeric representation.

The geographic expanse of both the *Iliad* and *Odyssey* is so vast that
one might well sympathize with Strabo's impulse to begin his scientific
study with an extensive review of Homer as the founder of the science
of geography. Within the grand cosmic arrangement of sun, stars, and
river Oceanus, and of Sea, Hades, Heaven, and Earth, however, only a
relatively circumscribed horizon line is recorded with detail or preci-

sion. In the *Iliad,* Homer's geography extends, with fleeting reference, as far north as Thrace, Southern Russia, and the Lower Danube, and southward to Sidonia, the chief city of the Phoenicians, to Thebes in Egypt, and even farther south to the Pygmies and the Aithiopians at the world's end. The *Odyssey* offers more extended descriptions but is equally vague in geographic detail: we hear of Cyprus, Phoenicia, Egypt, Aithiopia, Sidonia, the Eremboi (Arabia?), and Libya in the eastern Mediterranean and Near East; to the far north, we find the Laestrygonians whose fjords and shortened nights remind one of Scandinavia and Arctic summers (10.82–94). Beyond them, the Kimmerians, covered in mist and darkness, live at the limits of Oceanus (11.3–9). About mainland Greece and the islands to the west of Greece, we hear comparatively little, and nothing of much geographical precision.

The Homeric map comes into sharpest focus when the poems describe the Aegean Sea, especially its northeastern section. Descriptions of Troy and its surrounding terrain, of Tenedos offshore, and of the sailing conditions near the Hellespont, have impressed many. In the *Iliad,* Hera's journey from Mount Olympus to Mount Ida is itself noteworthy for its accuracy: first passing over Pieria and lovely Emathia, and then the Thracian mountains and Mount Athos, she crosses the Aegean to the islands Lemnos and Imbros, finally reaching Lektos (or Lekton, a promontory on the southwest corner of the Troad) where she flies up to the ridges of Gargaros, the highest peak of Ida (14.225–30, 280–91). In the *Odyssey,* the heroes' return from Troy again shows an intimacy with the sea routes of the northern Aegean: ships travel from Tenedos to Lesbos and then either cut across the open sea, above Chios with Psyra to the left, and finally reach Euboea's southern promontory at Garaistus (safe only in the summer), or drop down between Chios and Cape Mimas on the peninsula near Erythrai, not far from Old Smyrna in Asia Minor, and then island-hop across the Aegean to the Greek mainland (see 3.159–78).

The few references to land near Old Smyrna in the *Iliad* suggest a similarly informed, if rarely expressed, familiarity with that area: i.e., Niobe's figure carved into stone on Mount Sipylus (24.614–17), and the flat watermeadows around the Cayster River, near Ephesus (2.259–63). Elsewhere the narrator of the *Iliad* speaks of a Trojan ally who lived under Mount Tmolos in the rich territory (dēmos) of Hyde by Lake Gyge (Gygaian in the Trojan catalogue, 2.865), by the rivers Hyllos and Hermos (20.385–92), itself less than one hundred kilometers inland from Old Smyrna.

But even more revealing for our purposes is the contrast between the landscape in the main body of the *Iliad* (and epithets for place therein) and that in the catalogues, especially in Book 2 of the *Iliad* (and the epithets of place found there).

In contrast to the landscape of the catalogues, the topography of the *Iliad* proper is spotted with only a few poleis, but each of these is architecturally imposing and well-defined. If such a landscape were to correspond to any historical moment, it would have to be to Homer's contemporary Ionia with its few and well-settled communities. Compare Homer's Troad to Hammond's description of the small Greek city-states on the Asiatic coast (cited in the previous section): "each settlement was isolated," its settlers forming "a single and self-contained entity," maintaining "their hold by concentrating round a defensible city . . . incapable at the outset of linking together." Hammond is referring to the twelve poleis of the original Ionian League, ranging in geography from Miletos to Klazomenai, to which Old Smyrna slightly to the north was added as the thirteenth. The thirteen varied in size and importance, but each was autonomous and self-defined, as, we may assume, were Troy and Thebes of the Homeric Troad.

In the main body of the *Iliad,* eleven cities in the Troad are named: Troy (also called Ilios and Pergamon), Khryse, Killa, Arisbe, Thebes, Lyrnessos, Zeleia, Pedasos, Pedaios, Thymbre, Dardania.[47] Only two of the eleven are mentioned with any regularity in the poem—Troy and Thebes—but most, when named, are endowed by epithet with grandeur and monumentality. Four are walled or architecturally impressive: Troy, well-walled, well-made, etc.; Thebes, lofty-gated; Arisbe, well-founded (euktimenon); Pedasos, steep. Five are sacred: Troy, Thebes, and Zeleia are hieros; Killa is zatheos and Arisbe dios.

But for most of the narrative, the Troad appears to be dominated by one city. Although other poleis or places appear here and there, as for example those mentioned above or the twelve poleis that Achilles sacked in the interior and the eleven that he destroyed along the coast (including Andromache's walled Thebes and Briseis' Lyrnessos), the impression clearly given is that few cities are to be found in the Troad landscape. In the *Iliad* proper, Troy seems to be the only city within a great distance, and all its inhabitants are comfortably housed within its great wall. Except for one mention of the springs of hot and cold water where the women used to wash long ago in a time of peace (a passage cited in the first chapter), the city seems to look inward. There are no parts of Troy outside the fortification and no smaller settlements nearby.

In the Trojan Catalogue of Book 2,[48] twelve places in the Troad are mentioned: Troy, Zeleia, Adresteia, Apaisos, Pityeia, Tereia, Perkote, Praktion, Sestos, Abydos, Arisbe, and the river Selleeis. Of the twelve, three overlap with places named in the rest of the poem: Troy, Zeleia, Arisbe. Description of those settlements in the catalogues often identifies a harmonious interplay of human dwellings and nature: for example, "those, prosperous, who lived in [enaion] Zeleia below the foot of Mount Ida and drank the dark water of Aisepos"; "those who held [eikhon] Adresteia, the countryside [dēmos] of Apaisos, and held Pityeia and the steep slopes of Tereia." Of these places mentioned here, only Arisbe shares an epithet with those found for cities in the Troad in the rest of the poem. In the main body of the Iliad, epithets for Troy and other cities of the Troad emphasize instead the construction of cities which separate the human from the natural.

The Achaean Catalogue, itself a ringing invocation of the Greek peoples, their cities and lands, unlike the sparse Troad landscape of the poem, lists one hundred and seventy five place names of settlements found throughout mainland Greece and its islands to the east and west.[49] Of these, only two are said to be walled: Tiryns and Gortyna. In addition, four others are described as "well-founded cities" (euktimenon ptoliethron): Mycenae, Athens, Thebes, and Medeon (in Boiotia), while Iolkos in Thessaly, in an abbreviated form of the phrase, is simply called euktimenē. The Kleonai, a people under Mycenae's rule, were euktimenai, and Dion, a ptoliethron in northern Euboia, was "steep" (aipu). In one instance, the name of place in Messenian seems generic euktimon aipu, either "well-founded Steep" or "steep Well-Founded."[50] But the epithets most frequently found in the catalogue are of a different type and are rarely, if ever, found in the rest of the Iliad: e.g., grassy, flowery, leaf-trembling, rocky (trēkheia), hilly, on the seashore, by the sea, with dovecotes, rich in grapes, rich in sheep, rich in goats. Of these many epithets, other than euktimenon (used for major sites), only "steep," "fertile," "lovely," and "sacred" are commonly found in both catalogues and main body of the poem. (See Appendix 1.)

A study of the landscape and epithets in the catalogues of Book 2 reveals the special quality of the topography and language of cities in the Iliad proper. If our circlings seem to bring us back once again to Old Smyrna and the Ionian eighth century, we realize as well how Homeric descriptions distort historical reality. The size of Troy and its solitary presence are not typical of Mycenaean conditions; the tendency to wall all settlements when highlighted in the narrative exceeds Ionian instances of walled communities. Neither exactly Mycenaean or Ionian, this picture certainly does not reflect the Dark Age. Rather than *réalité de géographie,* there is a drastic simplification of detail as Homer avoids the dramatically irrelevant. As in the Tuscan backgrounds in early Renaissance paintings like the Guidoriccio da Fogliano by Simone Martini, the city edifice, magnificently defined by its imposing outer wall, stands nobly against a natural landscape. Both in the work of artists of the early Italian Renaissance and in Homer, space is poetically, not descriptively, conceived; the city is an idealized vision: self-contained and stalwart in a natural world, the only place for civilization, and the only home for men, women, and children.

Poleis and the Homeric *Iliad*

About a composer who collects, collates, or weaves a number of shorter lays into a single, monumental, and dramatic structure, the *Iliad* and *Odyssey* tell us nothing. That change from episodic and discrete to interwoven and large-scale is regarded by all students of Homeric poetry to be part of the Ionic refashioning of the inherited epic tradition, contemporary with, if not unique to, these poems. The *Iliad* is distinguished by the subordination of episodic stories (relatively easily identified as the *aristeia* of Diomedes in Books 5 and 6, Agamemnon in Book 13, etc., or the individual scenes like the assembly visit to Achilles' hut in Book 9, the gathering of the Achaean forces in Book 2, the bedroom scene with Aphrodite, Helen, and Paris in Book 3, etc.) to an overarching structure. Our capacity to break the *Iliad* down into these identifiable parts suggests that the poem "retains an earlier phase of epic art," as C. M. Bowra phrases it,[51] even if in its present form once detachable parts have been woven into a discernible whole. As is well known, it was precisely that ability to mold massive amounts of material around a single, dramatic theme that distinguished "Homer" from the other poets of the archaic epic tradition and made Aristotle consider "him" divine (cf. *Poet.* 1459bff.).

As seems certain from Mycenaean art,[52] Mycenaean "epic" poetry concerned siege warfare, a poetic tradition dating back perhaps two hundred years into the fourteenth century when Ajax's tower shield and Odysseus' boar's tooth helmet were common fare and when that culture was in its prime.[53] Aspects of those stories dealing with raiding parties and great warrior exploits may well have survived, and indeed flourished, in the Dark Ages. But the central Mycenaean theme, that of citadels under siege, would have had little or no meaning, as should be clear by now, for an audience in the tenth century. As isolated villages were all that survived the fall of Mycenaean society, so in epic poetry a residue of individual *aristeiai* may have been all that survived as the Mycenaean theme of siege warfare gradually disappeared from a living reportoire.

As these oral stories change under the pressures of tenth-century realities, the centralizing Mycenaean theme would have been fractured as the complex themes of extended warfare around city walls lost their urgency. For tenth or ninth century singers, composition could well have gravitated increasingly toward short, nonurban, and relatively self-contained encounters. In brief, the age-old theme of cattle raiding would reemerge in Dark Age poetry, displacing Mycenaean preoccupations with citadel walls. Nestor's account of his fighting prowess in the cattle-raiding contests between Pylians and Epeians three generations before the Trojan war (11.669–761) may well have been typical of epic lays from that period.

May we not, then, see a causal link between this eighth-century, Ionian innovation of monumental poetry (very possibly beginning with the *Iliad*) and the reemergence of walled cities? Singers of the tenth and ninth centuries would have known about the great walled cities of the heroic "Mycenaean" age from the inherited formulaic tradition, but in a period of Greek history that lacked an urban center, or what Chester Starr calls the "polis spirit," they would have had no context in which to interpret them dramatically. The reemergence of walled cities might well have provided the context, and indeed the inspiration, in which Dark Age episodic poetry could be reinterpreted, and rewoven, around themes familiar to the old Mycenaeans. For the Ionian audiences in particular, such themes would again have had a genuine immediacy, or vividness, in their concrete detail.

The impetus that inspired the creation of the monumental form is often explained along mystical lines. James Redfield, for example, says that once this project defined itself to Homer, "the tradition lay before him where to choose. . . . He inherited the poetry and of it made The Poem."[54] Similarly, Cedric Whitman writes: "There is no evidence that the poet of the *Iliad* invented a single character or episode in his whole poem. He may not even have invented a single phrase. His invention was the *Iliad*."[55] I suggest that the invention involved reconstructing and reshifting the center of gravity around the very old and very new perspective of cities and walls. It was, in short, the urban revolution of Ionian Greece that made such innovations, and the *Iliad,* possible.

If this theory of composition overstates the case, could it be that the Ionians, by associating old themes with a new consciousness of urbanization and walled cities, discovered the means by which to distance themselves from and to reflect on their emerging world? That is, in an age already conscious "of contemporary links with the past,"[56] as J. Schafer describes the "Homeric" age, the gradual revival of the city, although in a vastly different form from that of the Mycenaean palace-citadel, makes possible for the eighth-century Ionians a new poetic and literary link with the Mycenaeans. Stefan Hiller describes that new possibility as follows:

> The discovery of the Mycenaean past, though it culminated in the second half of the eighth century, had not been reborn with Homer nor did it come overnight. It had a long prehistory of its own. During the dark years of decline, depression and isolation, the world of the heroes must have seemed to vanished forever. The more, however, the Mediterranean world was opened up again and the more prosperity grew, the more vividly the heroic past revived. Its revival actually kept pace with the increasing material base for putting its model into execution and so making identification with that heroic past possible.[57]

The unity of the *Iliad,* however defined, depends on that city culture for its deepest tragic themes. Without the women and children of Troy, the death of Hektor, and the destruction of civilization and a human community loved by Zeus, the wrath of Achilles would mean much less than it did to the Athenians of the fifth century, or than it does to us today.

Although the Mycenaean tradition is undoubtedly the most significant influence on the Ionian story of a city under siege, it may also be true that similar themes in contemporary Near Eastern art and literature were instrumental in the development of the Homeric, or Ionian, epic. The oriental influence on the formation of Greek mythology, especially in Hesiod's *Theogony* and *Works and Days,* is by now well attested. More recently, Walter Burkert has argued that eastern influence (especially Assyrian) is also evident in "the last formative stage of the Greek epic" (by which he means the narrative Homeric epic more than the didactic Hesiodic form), even if "direct contacts of Greeks with cuneiform literature, although almost unavoidable at the time, will not have been intimate."[58] Some scholars have suggested that the siege-engine, considered to be an Assyrian invention, is represented in the Greek epic cycle in the perverted form of the Trojan Horse by which the Achaeans break down the Trojan fortifications, while others have equated the rare usages of the ax in the *Iliad* to its depiction in Assyrian art where the ax-adze is used to demolish city walls. The repeated versions of siege warfare in Assyrian art since the mid-ninth century, as on the Gates of Shalmaneser III (858–25 B.C.) and on the palace walls at Dur Sharrukin (modern Khorsabad),[59] may have further inspired the ever-present theme of Troy's fate, whether boldly highlighted or quietly smoldering, in the story of the *Iliad*. The deeper reference unquestionably goes back, nevertheless, to Mycenaean sources.

In summary, the vision of the *Iliad* is deeply rooted in a city culture. A listing of many of the poem's key events illustrates that point: the meeting of Hektor, Andromache, and Astyanax at the Skaian Gate in Book 6, the building of the Achaean wall in Book 7 and its assault in Books 12–15, the final battle of the poem in the meeting between Achilles and Hektor before the gates of Troy in Book 22, and the concluding scene between Achilles and Priam in Book 24 shape the entire poem. Conflicts between male and female, between younger and older generations, between the desire for individual glory and the drive to protect humankind's richest and most sacred achievement, the "holy city," are all inescapably linked with the story of a city under siege.

Second, through the medium of traditional epic poetry, the local realities of Ionian urbanization, strained through Mycenaean mesh, have been purified of their immediate parochialisms. As always, the pouring of current reality into myth "precipitates and purifies," in George Steiner's phrasing, "the agitated, opaque elements of the immediate situation"[60] and produces something approaching eternal essence. The mythic representation retains its own inner energy, however, because, to change the metaphor, the matter of myth has been crystallized around a node of contemporary Ionian affairs.

Third, even though the competitive values of the warrior often seem dominant at the expense of cooperative values of the city, the poetry of the *Iliad* is not intended exclusively for a court audience; nor is it molded to customs, mannerisms, and pleasures of a noble elite. If it had been, the poem would never have acquired its universal appeal to the polis-civilization of Classical Greece. In the Homeric vision of heroic warfare, we cannot help seeing an underlying identity of spirit between Homer and the later Greeks. The "factor of race and nationality, which we can feel by intuition, not by logic," as Jaeger writes in *Paideia,* "continues to work with a strange immutability through all historical variations of spirit and the varying tides of fortune; but in our thought of it we must not underestimate the immeasurable effect on later Greece of Homer's creation of a complete human world."[61] Central to that human world, as illustrated on the Shield of Achilles, lies the polis in its multiple forms, the place of peace, of war, of marriage, and of death, but always centermost in the definition of the human.

CHAPTER 7

Oikos and Polis
in the Homeric Poems

The absence of political terms like "citizenship," the dominance of Priam's family at Troy, and the attention to individual achievement cause many to assume that a Dark Age aristocracy prevails in the Homeric world. Moses Finley, in his seminal work *The World of Odysseus,* printed in 1954 with second edition in 1977, has set the tone, with some modification, for subsequent generations of Homeric critics: neither the *Iliad* nor *Odyssey* "has any trace of a polis in its classical political sense. Polis in Homer means nothing more than a fortified site, a town. . . . The *oikos* was what defined a man's life, materially and psychologically."[1] Arthur Adkins, following Finley: "the unit of power, the social unit, the economic unit is the *oikos:* no effective larger unit than the *oikos* possesses any property, and hence no larger unit could provide the comer with nourishment."[2] Similarly persuaded, James Redfield writes: "inheritance secures the continuity of the household [i.e. *oikos*], which is the fundamental social institution."[3] More recently, a new wave of scholars joins in the chorus: e.g., John Halverson, "the organizational—and indeed psychological—basis of society is the *oikos.*"[4]

Arguments for the preeminence of the oikos seem particularly persuasive for the *Odyssey.* Ithaca, like Troy and Scheria, is called both polis and astu, but in little else does it resemble either of those other poleis: there are no city walls or public buildings; no public temples or local shrines; no acropolis; Odysseus' "palace," far from being majestic, has dog dung piled out in the courtyard; the polis is never called "sacred" or "well-settled"; and the list continues. Architecturally,

Ithaca the polis appears to be a small town, or even village, rather than a city of imposing dimensions.

Nor does Ithaca the polis appear to have a discernible system of government. Twenty years ago, Odysseus, as king (basileus), "ruled over the people [*laoi*] as gently as a father" (2.233–34; cf. 2.46–47), but what power, or office, if any, did the basileus exercise, institutionally, legally, or religiously, and what has become of that "office" in Odysseus' absence?⁵ The poem does little to answer these questions, nor are class relationships between ruler and ruled a subject of much concern.⁶ When leaving for Troy, Odysseus leaves his wife in charge of their family and oikos (*Od.* 18.266–70 and 19.524–31), but asks Mentor, it appears, to look after the interests of his oikos if public matters should arise (*Od.* 2.224–27).⁷ If Odysseus made any provision for the basileus "office" that he vacates, nothing is said about it, nor is there any mention of a state organization that might administer Ithaca in the absence of a ruling basileus. For reasons we cannot altogether understand, Laertes has abandoned whatever authority may have still been invested in him (*Od.* 2.225–27) and withdrawn to his garden retreat in the hills (*Od.* 11.187–96).

Standing against this mass of evidence suggesting a governmentless society of a village community at Ithaca is the extended scene in Book 2 where, at Athena's suggestion, Telemachos has called the Achaean heroes (1.272; cf. 2.7) to the agora. Unlike the agora found at the door in front of Priam's palace (*Il.* 7.345–46), this one, like the one on the Shield of Achilles (*Il.* 18.497), is at some distance from Odysseus' oikos, and near the harbor (*Od.* 2.10 and 24.420). Its placement in the polis further reminds one of the agora "of heroes" at Scheria which was by the ships with a precinct sacred to Poseidon on either side of it (*Od.* 6.266; 7.44; 8.5). In most examples, other than the one from Troy, the agora has been removed from the king's palace, and his direct control, to a place of public domain and, in the cases of Ithaca and Scheria, to a place of commercial gain.⁸ About trade and mercantile profit Homer says nothing; the agora at Ithaca, like all agorai in Homer, is a place of public meeting.

Of the physical description of Ithaca's agora, we know only that, having arrived with his dogs, Telemachos sat "in his father's seat" (*Od.* 2.14) among the old men of Ithaca.⁹ In addition to being called an agora, this event of Ithacans gathering is also called a thoōkos or "sitting" (2.26), the same word used to describe Odysseus' seat (*thōkos*) in the assembly. Although the arrangement of this assembly place and its seats at Ithaca are not specified, presumably its structure is similar to that of the Phaiakians' agora, "set firm with deep-bedded quarried stones" (6.267) and like the agora described on the Shield of Achilles: a formal space in the city "where the old men sat on polished stones, in a sacred circle" (*Il.* 18.503–4).

Admitting that as "a real institutional assembly, this agora is unique," Halverson goes on to describe the Ithacan agora as follows: "it is simply a place in town set off for any kind of meeting, something like a village square, a convenient place to get together with friends or cronies to talk. . . . There is no reason to think there is anything formal, legal, or political about it."[10] In dismissing this public assembly, Halverson writes elsewhere about Ithaca's agora: nothing more is implied than "that at least one assembly was called twenty years ago (one might well imagine that it was for the extraordinary purpose of recruiting for the Trojan expedition), and as far as the poem tells us, that may have been in turn the first in twenty years."[11] Are we to imagine that the Ithacans allocated permanent seats to distinguished members of their community and placed those seats conspicuously in the center of the polis in order to hold five public gatherings in a century? It is true that the assembly's voice was advisory rather than binding, its authority dependent on public opinion and oracular signs rather than legislative power, but this is a far cry from saying that the city's agora was without formality or public purpose. Heralds summoned the people (2.6ff.); the first question of the day was "Is this a matter about the army or some other public issue" (*ti dēmion allo*) (2.32); a speaker needed to hold a scepter in hand in order to address the crowd. Ithaca's agora is not specifically called sacred (e.g., "the sacred circle"; *Il.* 18.504), but perhaps that may be implied by Telemachos when he reminds his fellow Ithacans that Zeus and Themis (goddess of social order and of laws established by custom) "convene and disband the *agorai* of men" (2.68–69). However anomalous the *descriptions* of Ithaca may be in the *Odyssey* and however inadequate the agora may be to prevent public wrong, formal public spaces and assemblies convened and disbanded by Zeus *are* part of the Ithacan world. These "institutions" may exist in rudimentary form and the *Odyssey* may, in most instances, pass over their existence, but it is clear that, even at quiet Ithaca, structures are in place where the people of Ithaca can meet formally to deliberate issues of great concern, where a polis-oriented perspective displaces those of individual oikoi.[12]

The relative insignificance of Ithaca's polis should not be surprising since the *Odyssey* is primarily concerned with the reconstruction of a family and societal order constructed around the extended family. When Telemachos summons the Achaean heroes to the agora in Book 2, he says he has *not* called the assembly for a public matter but because of an evil that has befallen his oikos (2.44–45; cf. 2.58–59, 237–38). Although Telemachos would like to be basileus, he demands only that he "be ruler [*anax*] over his own household [*oikos*] / and servants" (1.397–98). Telemachos travels to, and departs from, "Pylos, the well-made city of Neleus" and "the steep city of Pylos,"[13] but it is the oikos and the dōmata of Nestor that concern him.[14] When coming to or leaving hollow Lakedaimon with its broad dancing place (cf. 4.1 and 15.1), Telemachos passes through the ptolis of Lakedaimon (15.183), seeking the home of Menelaos and Helen. Epithets for Pylos and Lakedaimon may draw our attention momentarily to those poleis, but we do not linger there because of Telemachos' haste to seek family news from Nestor and Menelaos. Prominence of individual oikoi in both visits reflects an aristocratic network of oikos and guest-friendship bonds important to Homer. The story of Telemachos is first and foremost the story of oikos and fatherland.

The same is true of Telemachos' father. When responding to Alkinoos' question: "Tell me your land [*gaia*], your district [*dēmos*], and your city [*polis*]" (8.555), Odysseus ignores the question about polis, choosing instead to speak about his island, locating it quite precisely on the map, not an inappropriate response for someone seeking homeward passage (9.21–28). But in continuing his reply, he speaks only of the oikos: "There is nothing sweeter than one's fatherland or parents, if indeed someone far from his rich home [*oikos*] lives in another's land, apart from his parents" (9.34–36).[15] As a more complex vision of the polis exists in the portrait of Scheria, so perhaps greater attention might have been paid to the public return of Odysseus, but those themes give way in the poem as the return of Odysseus is first a reunion with wife and family, and only secondarily a reestablishing of himself as king, or ruler, of Ithaca. As Michael Nagler has recently written: "The highpoint of order (as always, more tentative and problematic) is achieved when husband and wife meet at the center of the oikos (23.269); the restoration of the oikos, as an economically and socially functioning institution, capable of continuing to build and service the network of social bonds with other such institutions through *xenia,* is the theme of the return and the hero."[16] In this, the *Odyssey* complements, or stands in contrast to, the *Iliad.* As Nagler observes, the poems focus on two competing bases of social order, "*laoi* and *oikos,* which involve different networks of loyalty and responsibility and can involve mutually contradictory values."[17]

From a poem that is so focused on the oikos, it seems unreasonable to derive categorical statements about the Homeric polis. Thirty-four of the thirty-five epithets and adjectives that describe Ithaca in the *Odyssey* refer to Ithaca the island and not to the polis of the same name. In what is a startling statistic, the city itself is modified only once by epithet (24.468).[18] Should we be surprised that this unique instance of an epithet with the city of Ithaca occurs precisely when the polis enters prominently into the story? If we are permitted to say that epithets appear with nouns when those nouns assume thematic presence, it is equally noteworthy, by negative example, that no character in the *Odyssey* ever describes Ithaca the polis by epithet or adjective. This fact gains further relevance when we remember by contrast the many instances in which speakers bring Ithaca the island into focus by epithet or adjective. Other cities in the *Odyssey* fare much better in this regard than the polis of Ithaca; when contrasted with Iliadic tendencies, the absence of epithets for Ithaca's polis in the *Odyssey* truly catches us by surprise.

An Odyssean usage of the popular epithet "well founded" (*euktimenon*) captures some of these shifting perspectives. All sixteen occurrences of the epithet in the *Iliad* appear in conjunction with a polis, whereas in the *Odyssey* it applies more frequently to an oikos (nine times) than to a polis (six times). The "new" phrase is: "if ever you shall return to your well-founded oikos and your dear fatherland." That shift in epithetical use, I suspect, may be explained by different networks of loyalty and responsibility in the poems and the corresponding shifting emotional centers.

The Odyssean change of focus from polis to oikos is illustrated by a simple tabulation of Iliadic and Odyssean instances of words signifying "city" (*polis* and the related *ptolis, ptoliethron,* and *astu*) and household (*oikos* and *dōma*). In contrast to the 242 references (by my count) to city and the 112 to household in the *Iliad,* the *Odyssey* has 160 references to the city and a surprising 410 to the household. Contrary to the focus of the *Odyssey,* in which the reconstruction of Odysseus' house implies the restoration of order for the whole, in the *Iliad* the fate of each individual oikos is subsumed within the larger fate and welfare of the collective. The tragic scope of the poem diminishes if the pervasive social order of the polis is ignored when reading the foreground story of heroes and their individual glories. The confrontation of Achilles and Hektor in Book 22 is greater than Nestor's story of cattle raids in Book 11 precisely because we know that the welfare of Troy lies in the balance. Perhaps if Finley had titled his work *The World of Hektor,* or even *The World of Andromache,* his conclusions might have pointed in a different direction.

The most important scenes at Troy do not occur within Priam's palace, but, as already seen, at the city wall. And it is here that we should begin our examination of the city. To define the polis in terms of its political, legal, or economic organization, or in terms of inheritance, property control, and constitutional rights, measures the Homeric polis along a graph of fifth-century criteria. Using this graph, then, and arguing that the oikos, by default, is "the organizational— and indeed the psychological—basis of Homeric society," as Halverson and Finley do, undervalues the nature of Homeric representation as it obscures a truer understanding of the relation between polis and oikos.

Refining George Calhoun's definition of the polis, "an aggregate of *oikoi,*"[19] Émile Mireaux writes: "One has only to read the texts of Homer or Hesiod without preconceptions to become convinced that the Greek city is in no way, and has probably never been, a simple aggregation of clans. Besides the aristocratic lineages it includes in fact a substantial majority of men free from all conditions and who are not answerable to any *genos.*"[20] The collective nature of this "aggregate" transforms the individual identity of each household. The wall of the polis, characteristic of almost all significant Homeric poleis except for Ithaca in the *Odyssey,* encloses the community and redefines the individual oikoi.

Even if "for Homer and his audience, the polis is regarded as the typical form of human community," as John Victor Luce describes the world of Homer,[21] scholars frequently argue that the focus, in *Iliad* as well as *Odyssey,* on the individualistic warrior aristocracy prevents the polis from playing a significant dramatic role as a higher coercive power. An epic hero perceives only peripherally that communal responsibilities may modify personal desire for glory. So Wilhelm Hoffmann: "For the ruling class the state stood only on the periphery of existence."[22] More extensively, the same critic writes:

> The nobleman might frequently, within his circle, cultivate certain forms of living in which the mass of men take no part; for him there might exist a knightly code of behavior [Ethik] which is only suitable to him and to which he feels bound; however, in the end, he is unable to disassociate himself from the ground of the state, which is his homeland [Heimat]. (p 164)

As Peter Greenhalgh paraphrases this perspective, the hero, though divided in his loyalties, feels his primary "obligation is to his own prowess and his drive to victory and power."[23] Thus, the argument goes, even if the polis supersedes the oikos in Homer, its quality is somehow precivic and its sense of community spirit nonbinding.

Such descriptions of the self-seeking hero distort a more complex picture. While all Homeric warriors fight for glory (with the possible exception of the Trojan Poulydamos), the Trojan impulse to fight differs greatly from the Achaean, as the *Iliad* frequently makes clear. Greenhalgh points out what must be obvious but is too seldom expressed:

> There is one very simple reason which goes some way towards explaining why the concepts of patriotism and obligation to the community are more vocal on the Trojan side: Hector and the Trojans are fighting for the very existence of their city, whereas the Achaeans are an invading force from far away across the sea. The Achaeans are not fighting below the walls of their cities, to save them and their families inside them from destruction and enslavement.[24]

The motivation of the polis warrior to enter battle is well illustrated by both Phoinix's story of Meleager and his wife, Kleopatra, and by Hektor's conversation with Andromache in Book 6.[25] Both heroes, it is true, are moved by the thoughts and pleas of their wives (Meleager ignored the supplications of the city's leading priests, his father, sisters, mother, and comrades, 9.574–86; Hektor, in thinking of Troy's fall, is less distressed by the thought of what the Trojans will suffer, or his mother, father, or brothers, 6.450–53),[26] but each wife moves the hero by rehearsing the horrors that befall a fallen polis. Phoinix tells the story of Kleopatra's supplication:

> But even so they could not persuade the heart within him
> until, as the chamber was under assault, the Kouretes
> were mounting along the towers and set fire to the great city.
> And then at last his wife, the fair-girdled bride, supplicated
> Meleagros, in tears, and rehearsed in their numbers before him
> all the sorrows that come to men when the city [astu] is taken:
> they kill the men, and the fire leaves the city [polis] in ashes,
> and strangers lead the children away and the deep-girdled women.
> And his heart, as he listened to all this evil, was stirred within him,
> and he rose, and went, and clothed his body in shining armour.
>
> (9.587–596)

Andromache, equally, has made Hektor aware that in defending her, he must fight for the polis: "I am without father or mother. / Indeed godlike Achilles killed my father / when he destroyed utterly the city of the well-settled Cilicians / Thebes with its high gates" (6.413–16). As Meleager must fight from the city wall by necessity, Andromache begs that Hektor also fight from within the city, but, for reasons I shall explore in the next chapter, he will not or cannot.

Like Achilles, Meleager withdraws from public service because of an "excessive" individualism, "in the wrath of his heart against his mother" (9.555), and like Hektor he is persuaded to fight only by his wife's pleas, and not those of the suffering community or his family members. If the successful plea comes from the inmost recess of the oikos, Meleager's radical change of heart comes from a generic description of what happens to the polis collectively. The city-defender subordinates his individualistic impulses precisely because Kleopatra makes him realize her well-being is inseparable from that of the whole.[27] Hektor, in a sense, has already anticipated that escalation from wife to city, when earlier in his return to Troy, he said heatedly to his brother: "The people are dying, fighting around the city and steep walls. . . . Up now, Paris, lest soon the city be carried away in destructive flames" (6.327–31). Both scenes dramatize the fact that even while the hero may be defined "materially and psychologically" (to use Finley's phrase) by his wife, although not by the extended oikos, he is also motivated to act by the collective needs of a beleaguered polis.

An elegant passage finely interweaving narrative, simile, and speech (15.405–746) clarifies the differences between Achaean and Trojan wars, and defense. Interspersed between narrative description of "war and battle drawn equally on both sides" (15.413), in a verbal tug-of-war Hektor and Ajax alternately exhort their forces to victory. (See the three sets of speeches, at 15.484–514, 552–65, and 716–42). Flying swiftly from ship to ship like a skilled charioteer, shouting vehemently at the Danaans to protect ships and shelters (15.674–88), Ajax speaks primarily about *aidōs,* "an emotion," as James Redfield defines it, "provoked by the perception of one's place in the social structure and of the obligations which accompany that place."[28] "Shame [*aidōs*]" Ajax shouts, "now is the time for decision, either to be killed, or be saved and to save evil from falling on our ships" (15.502–3). In his next exhortation, he repeats the word: "Be men, let shame [*aidō*] be in your hearts / And have some regard [*aideisthe,* i.e., shame] each for another in the strong encounters."[29] Agamemnon reveals the nature of that "regard" when in an earlier book he exhorts the Achaeans:

Friends, be men and take up a bold heart,
and consider [*aideisthe*] each other in the strong encounters
since more come through alive when men consider [*aidomenōn*] one
  another
and there is no glory [*kleos*] when they give way, nor warcraft either.

(5.529–32)

In our passage, the narrator underscores the (temporary) success of
Ajax's pleas for mutual consideration: "shame and fear held the
Achaeans" (15.657–58). Supporting Ajax's efforts, Nestor bids the
Greeks be men, mindful of their aidos, while encouraging them to
"remember your children, wives, property, and parents . . . who are
not present" (15.661–66).

On the other hand, raging like an eagle on swans or cranes (15.688–
94), furious in his onset like a destructive fire, like wind and waves
beating on a rock promontory, like a great wave upon a ship, and
finally like a lion crashing in on a herd of oxen (15.605–38), Hektor
turns the battle on the Greek ships. In his exhortations to Trojans and
the city's allies, he *never* speaks of aidos, *nor* does he need to recall for
his troops memories of absent loved ones. His appeal is both less self-
directed and more concrete. In his first address, he concludes in the
following way: "It is no dishonor for one to die defending country
[*patrē*]. But your wife, children, house [*oikos*], and property will remain unharmed, if the Achaeans should withdraw with their ships to
their homeland" (15.496–99). He concludes the second address by reference to Troy itself: "If you do not kill the Achaeans, steep Ilios will
be utterly destroyed with all her people [*politas*]" (15.556–58).[30]

Hektor speaks of Troy itself, seen not as an abstracted image of state
but, as noted in chapter 4, an enclosure teeming with vulnerable life—
wives, children, *politas*. There is little one might categorize here as self-
seeking. As in the Meleager story, wife, and oikos, move a warrior to
action, but each house is cast without the context of the whole, "steep
Ilios."

When Hektor does speak of an aidos that compels him to war, it is an
aidos, or compulsion, seen in the service of Troy and therefore different in kind from that which drives the Greeks:

In truth these things are also of a concern to me, lady, yet most
  dreadfully
I shrink [*aideomai*] from the Trojan men and the women of Troy with
  their trailing garments

if like a coward I shrink back from the fighting.
Nor does my heart so instruct me; I've learned to be a good warrior
And ever to fight with the foremost of the Trojans,
Winning great fame of my father and myself.

(6.441–46; cf. 22.104–7)[31]

Hektor is held to his obligations, as Redfield says, "by his feeling for the feelings of others. . . . His virtues are the outcome of his responsiveness to society,"[32] and the people of Troy.

A simile in Book 17 illustrates how individual units (i.e., the oikoi) are subordinate to the collective whole of the (walled) community with respect to defense:

. . . and the fight that was drawn fast between them
was wild as a fire which, risen suddenly, storming a city [*polis*]
of men sets it ablaze, and houses [*oikoi*] diminish before it
in the high glare, and the force of the wind on it roars it to thunder.

(17.736–39)

The polis is distinct from its many oikoi as the singular is from the plural, as the whole is from its parts. Such a distinction is made explicitly when the narrator, in describing the birds that Zeus sent as a sign to the people of Ithaca, says that they passed "through the houses and their city" (*dia oikia kai polin autōn, Od.* 2.154). More dramatically, the relationship of the one to the many is clear in Agenor's chiding words to Achilles: "You thought no doubt that on this day / you were going to sack the polis of the proud Trojans. / Fool, indeed she [*hē polis*] will survive to witness much hard fighting yet / For she [*oi*] has many strong heroes / who under the eyes of their own parents, wives, and children / guard Ilios" (*Il.* 21.584–88). Again we see the juxtaposition of the singular and the plural. Defined by its people and perceived as the place of generation where past, present, and future reside (parents, wives, children), Troy, and only Troy as the walled aggregate of oikoi, can offer defense against Achilles. The mode of defense offered by individual oikoi and the collective aggregate is different in kind rather than in degree. From this perspective, the walled polis must supersede in importance its component parts. Having survived the sack of Thebes in the Troad, Andromache especially recognizes the relationship between the two: her first household was thoroughly lost in the destruction of her father's oikos, and a new home will be sustained—Hektor as father, mother, brother, as well as husband (6.429–

30)—only as long as the polis, through Hektor, survives. The security of her new oikos lies behind the wall of the polis, as she knows; Andromache tries, accordingly, to command Hektor's defensive strategy. But as much as Andromache may wish to unite human and stone defense of her polis, Hektor does not succeed in joining the two. Defender of Troy, as seen above, he cannot also fight from Troy, a paradox which exposes one of the great tensions of the poem.

In summation, the currently popular view, this time expressed by Luce when writing about the polis in Homer, appears to me very peculiar: "The heroes dominate the polis just as they dominate the Assembly. In the pursuit of their individual satisfaction they may even totally disregard the interests of the social group. Achilles nursing his wrath, Paris refusing to surrender Helen are cases in point. By comparison with classical Athens or Sparta, the Homeric polis seems powerless to check the wayward impulses of the leaders of society."[33] There are many strange aspects to this statement. As much as Achilles is needed in his social group, his community does not include women and children and thus it cannot be considered on a par with Troy; Paris is not in anyone's mind considered representative of a city-defender. As for the paradigmatic models of Athens or Sparta in the fifth century, Luce undoubtedly has in mind the power of Athenian society to hold in check the individualistic impulses of an Alcibiades.[34] My point here is a simple one: there is not, as many would have us believe, a single, monolithic heroic ethic in Homer. In the *Iliad*, one's outlook on war, failure, death, one's sense of aidos, one's motivation for action—in short, one's "psychology," to use Finley's word again—are shaped precisely by whether one is attacking or defending the polis (communal and walled space).

So much for relation between walled polis and oikos in times of war. As in the Iliadic accounts cited above, in the Odyssean descriptions of walled Scheria, or of the nonpoleis that Odysseus visits between Troy and Scheria (only by antithesis does he fulfill the words of the prologue: "and he visited many cities [astea] and knew the minds of many men," 1.3–4), we sense a landscape defined by the presence, or absence, of poleis. This broader picture, I believe, directs the poem's foreground attention to one man and his reintegration with wife, family, and finally extended community. In particular, the prepolis conditions of the island of the Kyklopes reveal by negative example how intrinsic the polis is to the Odyssean view of human habitation.

Underlying the surface emphasis on the lack of agriculture among those demi-gods lies the observation that these ancient creatures do not live within a settled community. Leaving everything in the hands of the immortals, the Kyklopes neither plant with their hands nor work with the plow. Furthermore:

> These people have no established customs, no meetings for counsels;
> rather they make their habitations in caverns hollowed
> among the peaks of the high mountains, and each one is the law
> for his own wives and children, and they care nothing about each
> other.
>
> (*Od.* 9.112–15)

These creatures, in short, lack every form of communal organization. Homer is expressly speaking about civilization and cultivation, and he clearly has in mind the polis and not the oikos: "established customs" (*themistes*), "meetings for counsels" (*agorai boulēphoroi*), and "care nothing about each other" (*oud' allēlōn alegousi*) invoke public concerns and community needs beyond those of the extended family.[35]

In one sense, the Kyklopes' life resembles that of the independent oikos and a primitive patriarchal order ("each one is the law / for his own wives and children"), as Plato noted.[36] But in other respects the Kyklopes' existence resembles life not in the oikos but only at the lowest level of human existence. The significant alternative to either form of existence is found in communal organization higher than the family: technology, commerce, communication, and (legal) assembly are implicit in the making of civilization. Their place is the polis:

> For the Kyklopes have no ships with cheeks of vermillion,
> nor have they builders of ships among them, who could have made
>   them
> strong-benched vessels, and these if made could have run them sailing
> to all the various cities of men [*aste' ep' anthrōpōn*], in the way that
>   people
> cross the sea by means of ships and visit each other,
> and they could have made this island a strong settlement [*euktimenēn*]
>   for them.
>
> (*Od.* 9.125–30)[37]

In conclusion, in the tension between oikos and polis, the household estate, for the most part predominant in areas like economics and property control (following Finley), exercises a prominent but not exclusive role in the determination of ethical decisions (following Adkins). But along another set of axes, the Homeric polis, whether modeled on Mycenaean or contemporary Ionian cities, or a double exposure of both, sets the household within a larger frame and one of greater importance in the poems for two reasons: its walled fortifications, which defined the collective nature of the aggregate of oikoi inside, offered a security not available in any other form, and its collective structure offered a technology, commerce, and "center" unavailable to a smaller social unit. Although the warrior code is individualized and self-seeking, it must also be remembered that the heroics are without great consequence if the polis does not exist at the core—the seat of strength and endurance over which the fight for women, children, and wealth acquires meaning and honor.

Homer's Polis and Aristotle's *Politics*

Following Plato (*pasa gar sugkeitai polis ex oikiōn,* 1253b3; cf. *The Laws* 680d–e), Aristotle believed that every polis was composed of a number of oikoi and that, in spite of this blood tie, the polis, logically prior to the oikoi, differed in kind from the household. Although the city came into being on account of life (*ginomenē men oun tou zēn heneken*), it exists in order that one live well (*ousa de tou eu zēn*) (1252b30–31). Its goal (*telos*) is to free itself from necessities (cf. 1291a17 and Plato's *Republic* 2.369b–71e), to achieve political virtue and to pursue political partnership. In the words of Hannah Arendt: "At the root of Greek political consciousness we find an unequaled clarity and articulateness in drawing the distinction. No activity that served only the purpose of making a living, of sustaining only the life process, was permitted to enter the political realm."[38] According to this view, the polis, invulnerable to time, provides a unique kind of *bios,* or life, for humankind which was absolutely free from all demands of the earth and biological definition. Such complete freedom from servitude, physical or spiritual, most closely approaches the felicity of life among the immortals; the mature polis therefore provides, as Aristotle argues in the *Protrepticus,* that environment in which the divine nature of mortals can best be realized as it aspires toward "perfect self-sufficiency" (*pasa ē autarkeia,* 1252a29ff) and aspects of immortality.[39]

Unlike the intensely politicized perception of the polis—often seen as the emblem of a mutually defining process between the individual and the political system (see Plato, *Republic* 591d, where he conceives of a politeia existing within the state and each individual)—the city in Homer has almost no concept of political definition. Study of the epithets used with polis reveals, rather, that the fortification system, the city's sanctity, and its inhabitants form a close mutually supporting conception of the city. This is not to say, however, that the later political definition cannot in some way be understood from the Homeric portrayal. The city in Homer, seen in concrete, tangible terms of wall, protection by the gods, and the place that secures human life, can in time be reinterpreted in abstracted and political terms as the place of human perfectibility, devotion to the good, and aspiration toward "perfect self-sufficiency," with aspects of immortality. The sources of the Aristotelian view of the city as somehow separate from the natural world, freed from the necessities of existence associated with the oikos, and finally the place where mortals can contemplate the infinite—these sources may be traced to their nonphilosophical and nonpolitical counterparts in the Homeric portrayal of the city as a stable and walled community of humankind set apart from the natural landscape, protected under the eyes of the Olympian gods, and in a fundamental manner hirē (holy).

CHAPTER 8

Achilles, Troy, and Hektor:
A Configuration

Even those critics who see man in Homer as a creature of the polis say that the "epic is not about the *polis,* but about the famous deeds of great men," to quote John Luce.[1] That is, although they may see the polis as central in the organization of human life, they do not see it as central in the story of the *Iliad.* Wolfgang Schadewaldt in his famous work on the psychology of Hektor[2] pays little attention to the *Polisordnung* and its influence on the hero. Similarly, Cedric Whitman puts primary emphasis on the role of Patroklos in affecting the consciousness of Achilles and pays less attention to the hero's "city-destroying" (*ptoliporthos*) prowess.[3] This concentration of attention on individual heroes, I contend, distorts the more inclusive vision presented in the poem itself. As in the first question and answer of Porphyry's *Quaestiones Homericae* ("Homer wished to show not only Achilles but also, in a way, all heroes . . . so unwilling to call it after one man, he used the name of the city, which merely suggested the name of Achilles"[4]), so the personal theme of Achilles' wrath expands throughout the poem until Achilles embodies a theme of much more generous, and general, dimensions.

The progressive escalation of theme from hero's anger to a war over Ilios in Books 1 to 4 illustrates this expansion. Quarrels between Khryses and Agamemnon and between Achilles and the Achaean leader move by the end of Book 1 to involve a quarrel on Olympus. Book 2, with its marvelous similes of waves and flocks of birds, introduces us to the dips and swells of the Achaean army responding to an inept king, to an upstart braggart of the people, and to cool-headed Odysseus, and then broadens our visions even further with the introduction of all the contingents, Greek, Trojan, and Asian allies. Both sweeping embrace of fighting forces and ringing invocation of an Aegean geography which stretches from Pylos in western Greece to the Lykians in southeastern Anatolia, from the Myrmidons west and north of Euboea to the Phrygians east of Troy, the catalogues open windows to horizons well beyond the story of one man. The effect is not unlike the expanding spatial arena which Achilles experiences when he withdraws from the Greeks: "Weeping apart from his companions he sat removed at a distance on the edge of the near grey sea, looking out over the limitless ocean" (1.349–50).

The next book introduces the two armies at war, Greeks moving forward in absolute silence, Trojans cackling like raucous cranes. But as seems appropriate to the beginning of this poem, both sides quickly agree by formal treaty to let Alexander and Menelaos decide the fate of Helen and the war in single combat. The poem then moves to the city itself: we see Helen, first weaving a story of the war fought on her behalf, and then sitting among the Trojan elders on the city ramparts, as we witness war from the point of view of those too old or too weak to defend the city themselves. But by the end of Book 3, Helen is back in bed with Alexander, and Menelaos has once again been abandoned as he was in Sparta, this time on the plains of Troy, prowling like a wild beast trying to find Alexander.

In one of the most startling scenes in the poem, Book 4 opens with a conference among the gods during which we learn that Zeus will allow Hera to destroy Troy and its people, most dear to Zeus ("Will nothing satisfy your malice before, penetrating the gates and long walls, you devour Priam raw, the children of Priam, and the other Trojans," 4.34–36), on the condition that she allow him, whenever he desires, to ravage a city dear to her. She quickly complies, offering by way of illustration Argos, Sparta, or Mycenae (cf. 4.51–53). We have examined the bargaining between Hera and Zeus before, but I return to it now because of its parallel with the proem of the poem. Achilles' divine wrath (*mēnis*), mentioned as the first word of the poem, was noteworthy because of its effect on the Achaean social order. A corollary of that wrath was the bestial devouring of the Achaean dead by dogs and birds. Now in the beginning of Book 4, Hera's (divine) anger (*kholos*) is directed against Troy, her own bestiality clear in her desire to eat Priam, the children of Priam, and the people of Priam. The wrath of the proem has expanded to take as its object not simply Agamemnon or his soldiers and not simply Trojan soldiers, but a civilized population including women and children embraced by emblematic walls. Only later in the poem, after Patroklos has died, will the wrath of Achilles against Agamemnon appear to merge with Hera's against Troy. In the final duel, Achilles scowls: "Would that my strength and spirit stirred me to eat you raw myself" (22.346–47; cf. 21.520–37, 22.352–54, 23.21).

The mēnis of Book 1, line 1, "formally" ends with the burning of the Greek ships in Book 16 when Zeus honors Achilles at the expense of his comrades (16.103–4 and 124–30). But that quarrel is clearly preliminary to a "second" wrath (cf. 21.520–25), or inhuman violence, evident in Achilles' desire to avenge his companion's death. Even if we mention Achilles' subsequent revenge for Patroklos and the heightened level of humanity, a kind of sophrosynē, that the hero gains in Book 24, we cannot consider Achilles the true subject of the poem. His wrath acquires its most far-reaching associations only when seen in the context of Hektor and its threat to Troy as evidenced by the funeral dirges that bemoan the ruin of Hektor and his city at the end of the poem. An analysis of the Iliad must, therefore, focus on both figures, and more properly on the relation between the two.

The stories of Hektor—whose "personality is already an example of the infiltration of the new ethics of the polis," as Werner Jaeger says[5]— and of Achilles in his elemental might are braided into the story of the city and of civilization. Each of the heroes represents the best of his side; as such, their personalities are to a significant degree "generic." Hektor's perspective on war and the heroic code is bound by his position as city-defender (cf. 6.441–46), whereas Achilles becomes the devastating image of consuming fire precisely at that moment when Troy's sacred river fears for its city. Inhuman might and city threat are inseparably linked in the river's words as it strives, leaping its own banks, to bury Achilles and extinguish his flame. First, addressing Achilles, the Skamandros says: "your strength is beyond that of men as are your inhuman [aisula] deeds; for the gods themselves always defend you" (21.214–15); then the river rebukes Apollo: "Shame! Is this how you obey your Father? Did he not tell you many times to stand by the Trojans and defend them until the evening dusk should cast its shadows over the fruitful fields?" (21.229–32); and finally he calls his brother, the river Simoeis, for help: "Let us both withstand the strength of this man since he will soon destroy the great city of lord Priam. . . . Defend [the Trojans] as quickly as possible. Fill your channels from the springs, replenish your mountain streams, raise a great surge, send it down . . . in order that we may stop this savage man" (21.308–14). The Iliad's true center of gravity is Troy, the point where the threads of events crisscross and the metaphysical place on which the sacred fiction of the poem turns.

The interplay between Achilles and Hektor over the question of Troy may perhaps best be demonstrated in Book 18, where the subject of revenge is also most prominent. As much as that book is pivotal in the story of Achilles' return to battle, it is equally crucial for Hektor and Troy. The two sections about Achilles which frame Book 18 (from the moment when he learns about Patroklos' death to his shout from the Achaean ditch, in the first section 18.1–242; and the making of the shield, in the second 18.314–617) are separated by a debate between Poulydamas and Hektor (18.243–313). The consequences of that debate reverberate through the next books up to the final meeting between the two main protagonists. Realizing that Achilles' reentry into the war poses a threat to Troy itself, Poulydamas suggests in the strongest terms that the Trojans move behind the city wall to face the danger from there. Hektor, encouraged by his previous success and hoping for the continued support of the gods, however, rebukes Poulydamas' cautious advice with equally strong sentiment: "Have you all not had your glut of being fenced in our ramparts [*purgos*]?" (18.287). This signals an error in judgment which the narrator himself criticizes and which Hektor will later criticize when alone outside the wall he speaks to his heart in soliloquy waiting for Achilles (18.250–52 and 310–13, and 22.99–110, respectively). Thus in this book of transition, Achilles at the beginning of his transcendent glory is balanced by Hektor in perhaps his moment of greatest delusion. The consequences of these events for Troy itself, implied throughout, are emphasized even in Book 18 by the similes that concern Achilles: the fire that burns from his head is compared to the fire with which a city under siege requests aid from its neighbors (18.206–14), and his shout from the trench comes as a "voice that is screamed out by a trumpet / by murderous attackers who beleaguer a city" (18.219–20).

Hektor's character, as urban defender, is far from simple. As so often in early literature, the "divided self" of the defender mentality is split into two figures, in the *Iliad* Poulydamas and Hektor, born on the same night. While Poulydamas, "who alone looked before and behind" and who was better in words," only recognizes the need to fight on the defensive from within the city, Hektor, better with the spear, is urged on by the spirit of war to fight in the open plain, free from the urban enclosure (cf. 18. 250–52). With a purely pragmatic view of defense, Poulydamas advises the Trojans to leave the plain and withdraw to the wall where the "towers, high gates, and the tall, well-polished doors

set therein, bolted fast, shall guard the city" (18.274–76). In the morning, he continues, when we fight again, "we shall gird ourselves in our
war gear / and make our stand on the towers. The worse for *him*, if he
desires, / coming from the ships, to fight us around the wall" (18.277–
79). The contrast between the plurality of Trojans ("we shall") and the
unspecified, solitary attacker accentuates the solace felt in being part of
a collective social order and in being secure behind city battlements.

Hektor, however, chooses with warrior courage to meet that single
enemy in the open field, face-to-face (*antēn,* 307). Not only does this
choice make for greater drama, it also underlines in a profound sense
the inherently paradoxical, or self-contradictory, nature of his position.
Although the advice of Poulydamas, like that of Andromache, is tactically sound, the urban enclosure thwarts the heroic spirit: again,
Hektor's telling line "Have you all not had your glut of being fenced in
our ramparts?" Even when Hektor later reprimands himself for trusting the defense of Troy to his own might (cf. 22.99–100), he sees his
city as a place of withdrawal and security, and not as a place from
which to fight. As in later Greek literature, Hektor places man, and
man without the protection of the walls, as the first and last defender of
the city.

As the themes of the poem broaden to include the fate of civilization,
so also the fate of Achilles acquires greater specificity as the poem
progresses. In Book 1, we learn that the greatest of warriors is doomed
to have a swift death (1.416–17), a fate bestowed on Achilles at birth,
without regard to the events at Troy or other individuals in the war. In
Book 9, Achilles claims that in fact he may choose between a short life
with glory at Troy or a long life without glory at home (9.410–16).
The choice is not difficult for him to make in Book 9, even if it seems
to contradict a fate marked out in Book 1. But after the death of
Patroklos, we learn for the first time, as perhaps does Achilles too, that
his death is intricately woven together with Hektor's.[6] Thetis informs
Achilles that he cannot die before Hektor, but that once the Trojan is
dead his own death will quickly follow. As the issues of war become
more dramatic, intense, and serious, so the meaning of Achilles' shortened life comes into sharper relief.

The increasing intertwining of Achilles' fate with Hektor's extends
to Troy's fate as well. Poulydamas understands this clearly enough:
"with [Achilles], the fight will be for the sake of our city and women"
(18.265). The rising fever of the poem may also be measured in the
similes that describe cities under siege (which must be a contemporary

and not a Dark Age Theme), all of which occur between Books 17 and 21.[7] The last of these is the most violent and suggests that the wrath of Achilles (mēnis) is transfigured after the fall of Patroklos into a burning force of city destruction:

> Meanwhile Achilles
> was destroying alike the Trojans and their horses
> as when smoke from a burning city reaches to the
> wide heavens, with the wrath of the gods [mēnis] let
>   loose upon it
> which inflicted pain for them all and sorrow on many,
> so Achilles inflicted pain and sorrow upon the Trojans.
>
> (21.520–25)[8]

It has been eloquently argued in recent years that Achilles as a character grows into himself during the course of the *Iliad*. This interpretation focuses our attention in the poem on Achilles himself and not on his balance with Hektor. As much as Achilles evolves into a hero who understands what it means to win honor (*timē*) from Zeus, he also grows into a figure who acquires the monumental, and inhuman, force required to overthrow the city of Troy. It is true that in the years of war before the poem opens, Achilles has already destroyed eleven poleis by land and twelve more by sea (9.328–29), but as we see him in Books 1–16 he is far from possessing that all-consuming fire, might, or view of mortality required to combat the imposing defense and sacred strength of Troy. A battle to the death with Hektor would be shallow at this point, compared with the resonances of that conflict which emerge as Achilles ripens into that ambrosia-fed and Hephaistean fire fury of Books 20 to 22.

If Achilles is unquestionably the best of the Achaeans, Hektor, as we have seen, is the fighting ideal of Troy. Alternately perceived as father and son, and as fighting at one time for the preservation of his *oikos* and at another for the polis at large, and for kleos as well, Hektor in his paradoxes personifies the very soul of city-holding defense. He boasts over Patroklos' corpse:

> Patroklos, you thought perhaps of devastating our city,
> of taking away the day of freedom from the Trojan women,
> and dragging them in ships to your dear fatherland.
> Fool! For in front of these women Hektor's swift horses
> strained with their feet to fight. And I with my spear

am conspicuous about the battle-loving Trojans, I who
  ward off for them
the day of necessity.

(16.830–36)

In paring down the respective sides to individual figures, Homer
expresses the clash over the city as a clash of warriors in single combat.
That ultimate conflict of the city, choreographed in the duel of Book 22
with both armies watching from the wings, has been anticipated twice
previously. In the first duel, and actually the first battle scene of the
poem, the fight between Alexander and Menelaos, the *Iliad* begins
with those who are personally and immediately responsible for the
war. But this duel introducing the conflict between Achaean and Trojan is designed to dismiss these figures from the center stage of the
poem. The gods break up the contest and refuse to let their single effort
end hostilities. The issue of the poem is not to be Helen, the major
figures of battle are not to be her lovers, and war between Achaean and
Trojan will not be settled by agreement.[9]

In the second and slightly more representative duel between the two
sides, Hektor and Telamonian Ajax emerge as the best of both camps.
In Seth Benardete's phrasing, "as the cause of the war has changed, so
too have the central characters."[10] When Hektor, as the undisputed best
of the Trojans, challenges any one among "the best of the Pan-
Achaeans" (7.73) to engage with him in a battle for undying glory
(*kleos,* 7.90–91), the Achaeans respond with silence. From a sense of
shame, Menelaos finally volunteers to meet the challenge, but now that
the cause of the conflict has been transformed from private to public,
Menelaos is no longer the appropriate Achaean representative. He is
pulled back by the other Achaean leaders who decide that the matter
will be settled by lot. Ajax's lot of course "leapt out," as it should have
(7.177–83). In the absence of Achilles he is in many ways the natural
choice. Like Achilles, Ajax is known for his stalwart defense (for
Achilles, see 1.284), exemplified nobly by his slow retreat at the burning ships in Book 15, but unlike Achilles, or even Diomedes, the fire of
the aggressor does not burn within him and he is the only Achaean
hero without an aristeia. Perhaps for these reasons, neither Hektor nor
Ajax is superior to the other, and their duel ends in a draw.

It is not until Book 22 that fighting again takes the intensified form
of single combat.[11] Although Benardete recognizes a shift in the
themes of war from the first to the second duel, he fails to recognize
the shift again in this third "man against man in bitter combat" (7.40).

By Book 22, the issue is no longer simply honor gained or lost but, as we have seen repeatedly, collective fate. Because this final duel is to be decisive, the arena has appropriately moved into focus from the plain to the perimeter of Troy. The Trojans will watch their captain from within the wall while their counterparts press against Troy in the plain. As the poem has progressively taught us, each of the contestants manifests in his being the essential nature of his side. It matters less that one is Trojan and the other Achaean, or any other such division, than that one is of the city and the other is not. In this confrontation we also witness the fate of Troy. The gods intervene as in the previous two combats, but now to ensure final resolution.

Now that we have established that the poem has increasingly focused on the consequences of war on Troy as the fate of Achilles becomes increasingly specific, and that the differences between Hektor and Achilles must be considered generic rather than specific, we can finally consider how their respective relations to the city determine the nature of their characters and their successes in war. The themes of the *Iliad,* like those of the *Odyssey,* are saturated in mortality: humankind is defined by the inevitability of death; the quality of the hero is measured by the degree to which he comes to terms with that definition. For both Achilles and Hektor, their perception of this fact, which shapes the nature of their being and therefore their strength on the battlefield, cannot be separated from their respective attitudes toward the polis.

Achilles' position toward mortality has long been discussed. In Book 9, he sees the question from a human point of view and chooses life and marriage over death and fame. But after the death of Patroklos he sees the question with an objective clarity and personal indifference that parallels the Olympian view. After his conversation with Thetis in Book 18, Achilles achieves a brilliant and prophetic vision of his own death that other heroes experience only in dying (see Patroklos, 16.854–55; Hektor, 22.355–61, cf. 22.296–306). The effect is a well-publicized, dehumanizing devastation that results in a slaughter of such proportion that war is reduced to an elemental, anthropomorphized struggle within nature itself. Achilles, in his association with fire and the fire-god, triumphs in that struggle. The most devastating quality of this violence, once Achilles decides to participate in war, is that he expects no life or action, either his own or others', to reach beyond the present. It is that unique capacity to sever himself from any thought of the future (or the past) that results in his glory (kleos) and which manifests the irrepressible force, invoked by the image of a star, that he bears against Troy:

> The aged Priam was the first to see him with his eyes,
> as a star in full-shining, sweeping across the plain,
> a star which comes in autumn whose brilliant rays
> outshine the many stars in the gloom of the night,
> the star they call Orion's Dog by name.
> It is the brightest of all but harbors an evil sign
> as it brings on great fever for wretched humankind.
>
> (22.25–31)[12]

Hektor, by contrast, cannot sustain this vision of time in the manner of Achilles. His motivation for fighting, as much as it aims toward kleos, is also bound by his relation to the past and future, as we have already seen in his relationship with his father and son. He cannot suffer long those rays of inhuman truth that Achilles is able to endure unflinchingly in Books 18 to 22. Hektor's position on the battlefield is forever the star in and out of a cloud:

> Hektor in the forefront bore his shield, a perfect circle,
> as out of the clouds a baleful star is conspicuous,
> full-shining, and enters again the darkening clouds,
> So Hektor would at one time be conspicuous among the first
> and then again among the hindmost, exhorting.
>
> (11.61–65)

When confronted by the stark reality of war, Hektor, like Achilles, can see his own mortality and the fall of Troy with heroic clarity—this vision most dramatically evident in his dispassionate answer to Andromache before the Skaian Gate (6.444–49). But, unlike Achilles, Hektor loses that focus the moment he turns to his son, and the star slips back behind the cloud. Although Hektor derives strength from the city, he is also its victim and its implement. With eyes focused on Skamandrios, he sees the city's continuity, if not for himself, at least for the collective. So he prays:

> Zeus and you other gods, grant that my son, just
> like me, be most conspicuous among the Trojans,
> as strong and brave as I, to rule mightily over Ilios.
> Some day let them say of him coming back from war: "That
> one is better by far than his father." Let him bring
>   home the blood-stained armor,
> having killed the enemy, and delight his mother's heart.
>
> (6.476–81)[13]

In his answer to Andromache, Hektor speaks with the masculine ethos of war clearly before him: men live in a world of confrontation and negation in what must ultimately be a futile effort against death. But when he turns to Astyanax, he peculiarly combines the combat ethic with a domestic one: though war is the perpetual state for the city, the city evades the natural consequences of war. Instead, in a vision that rings of a formulaic reality, Hektor sees war as glorious for son and father, in both present and future. War heightens an individual's sense of personal destiny, but the city of mortals lies outside the bonds of that destiny.

When Hektor turns his attention back to Andromache, his response to fate shows something of that Achillean indifference, or distance. He says to her: "Do not grieve excessively. No man will escape destiny, be he good or be he bad, once he is born."[14] But in light of his previous equivocation about his own future and the future of Troy, and in light of the various "delusions" that affect him,[15] this passage can also be seen as a kind of brushing aside of reality. Contrast Achilles' equivalent: "Then I will accept death at whatever time Zeus wishes to bring it about."[16] Despite Hektor's impulse to fight with the open freedom of the independent warrior, his response to the future can never afford to be unbiased or indifferent.

Their relationship with women helps set the two heroes apart. Before Patroklos' death, Achilles himself, like Hektor, seems to prefer love to war. Perhaps because he is a freer agent than Hektor, Achilles chooses to leave war altogether in order to enjoy something of that embrace, intimacy, and life which the glory of war foreshortens (9.394ff.). But it is in his relationship with Briseis that Achilles differs from Hektor. The circumstances of this affair echo in part those that prefigured Andromache's marriage to Hektor. The sister of three brothers who were killed while defending their city and the wife of a man whom Achilles had slain as he destroyed her city, Briseis looked to Achilles, as Andromache does to Hektor (6.414ff.), to supply that inner world taken from her. But in contrast to the shared emotion expressed between Hektor and Andromache on the wall of Troy, Briseis' experience of such intimacy consists only in melancholy reflection of what might have been. Achilles' complete severance from such embrace is marked by the fact that when Briseis reenters his camp, he does not address her. Possibilities of matrimony are only remembered in monologue as Briseis speaks to the body of Patroklos:

> You would never allow me, when swift Achilles slew
> my husband and plundered the city of godlike Mynes,

you would not let me weep but said you would make me the
   lawful, wedded bride
of godlike Achilles and that you would take me back
to Phthia and formalize my marriage among the Myrmidons.
Therefore I weep your death without ceasing, kind as you always
   were.

(19.295–300)

In his rejection of Briseis, Achilles rejects the world by which Hektor is bound. In the same scene, the implication of such rejection is
clearly brought forth. In a speech before his troops, Achilles acknowledges for the first time publicly the imminence of his death. In addition, he claims that he has already severed ties with his father, Peleus,
and imagines that, with the death of Patroklos, he has lost his last
protecting link with his own son, Neoptolemos (19.319–33).

But if Achilles and Hektor differ most in their relationships with
women, that difference acquires meaning only in the context of their
comprehension of time. As we have seen above and as his relationship
to Briseis testifies, Achilles now lives in a world that has no past or
future. Such godlike vision, emblematic of a heroic ideal, is fleeting for
most warriors, as it is for Hektor. Freed from his ties to father and son
and freed from the life-embracing affirmation of city and wife, Achilles
seeks neither stability in a world of mutability, permanence in a world
of impermanence, nor continuity in a world of death. An embrace of
the moment—what Alfred North Whitehead has defined in heroic
terms: "the complete sum of existence, backwards, and forwards, that
whole amplitude of life, which is eternity"[17]—is simultaneously an
embrace of death and a break in the chain of generational succession.
Paradoxically, to be open to a vision of eternity is to see oneself without future or past. To act without restraint in that moment, Achilles
demonstrates, provides access to the timeless (cf. 18.115ff., esp. 120–
21, and 21.64–113). And thus, in spite of, or because of, Hektor's
greatness in defending Troy, Achilles' moment in battle must be more
favored by Zeus.

The walled city, precisely because of its wall and the human order
held sacred within, protectively binds the range of heroic consciousness of those within. This is true as much for a Hektor as for a
Poulydamas. In his effort to sustain human life and hard-won civilization, a "holder of the city" is held back from perceiving the full application of the repeated claim about humankind in the Iliad: in the
words of one of the gods, "men, those wretched creatures who, like

the leaves, full of fire flourish for a little while on the bounty of the earth, but in a moment droop and fade away" (21.463–66; cf. 6.145–49). Not only must the gods not take the human being too seriously, but also from their perspective they can see his greatest and most sacred of achievements—the city—only in terms of its inevitable futility. The city's inability to secure its aggressive claims (i.e., to be arrēktos, or unbreakable), more than the crimes of Alexander and Laomedon, helps explain, I believe, the tragic weakness of Hektor and is the reason that Zeus and Athena, the city's most inspired creators and staunch defenders, in the *Iliad* help bring about Hektor's death and Troy's downfall.

So the city is at the end what everyone knew at the beginning, only an "illusion of immortality" and not the real thing. A realization of the city's limited scope becomes transparent when the city is cast within its cosmic setting. Perhaps this vision accounts for the unique phrasing of Zeus at the very moment he is about to grant Troy's destruction. Although acknowledging his love for Troy, Zeus speaks of the city from an Olympian perspective that seems to forecast Troy's doom:

> Of all the cities of men who live upon earth
> which dwell under the sun and starry heaven
> none has ever been more honored in my heart than sacred Ilios
> and Priam, and the people of Priam with the good ash spear.
>
> (4.44–47)

Reversing the direction from mountain homes to walled city in the plain as described in Aeneas' account of the founding of Troy, Zeus places the city back within the dispassioned framework of sun and stars. Although sacred and rich in sacrifices, Troy is also the place of people who live upon the earth as is recorded in the unique formula "the cities of human beings who live upon the earth" (*polées epichthoniōn anthrōpōn*). Outside the frame of human perspective, the walls are insubstantial divisions of natural space. The polis melts into the eternal. This chapter ends as it began. The generic truth that not only Troy but all cities are doomed is brought home when Hera a few lines later in reply coolly gives up for ruin the three cities most beloved by her:

> Of all cities there are three most dear to my heart:
> Argos and Sparta and Mycenae of the wide ways. All these
> whenever they become hateful to your heart, sack utterly.
>
> (4.51–53)

The other significant revelation of this "illusion" of a city's immortality comes on the Shield of Achilles. Often cited as portraying a fullness of life with its "distress and ardor, but above all with its joy"[18] that sharply contrasts with the self-doomed young hero, the shield also casts the city within an Olympian frame: "Upon it the earth he made, the sky and the sea's water / and the sun untiring and the moon at its full / and on it all the constellations that crown the heavens."[19] The two cities on the shield, labeled by their mortal inhabitants (*poleis meropōn anthrōpōn,* "cities of human beings"), as Zeus labeled Troy in Book 4, are only a part, though a significant part, of the formal unity of the world picture. Within the setting of the shield, cities are placed back into their mortal context; the walls of the polis no longer separate the human from the natural. What is true for a mortal (for Hektor)[20] is true for the human community. Like the leaves of the trees, the city of men, like man, experiences an end. F. Scott Fitzgerald has a glimpse of the city's illusion while standing on the top of the Empire State Building:

> From the ruins, lonely and inexplicable as the sphinx, rose the Empire State Building and just as it had been a tradition of mine to climb to the Plaza Roof to take leave of the beautiful city, extending as far as the eyes could reach, so now I went to the roof of the last and most magnificent of towers. Then I understood—everything was explained: I had discovered the crowning error of the city, its Pandora's box. Full of vaunting pride the New Yorker had climbed here and seen with dismay what he had never suspected, that the city was not the endless succession of canyons that he had supposed but that it had limits—from the tallest structure he saw for the first time that it faded out into country on all sides, into the expanse of green and blue that alone was limitless. And with the awful realization that New York was a city after all and not a universe, the whole shining edifice that he had reared in his imagination came crashing to the ground.[21]

As for those cities on Achilles' Shield, there is in Fitzgerald's vision a similar Olympian distancing which causes feelings of exuberant clarification and concomitant terror. It is a fatal vision, filled with awe and the dread suspicion that the ever-lasting man-made is no more than an imposing edifice after all. Does it explain why Hektor, in spite of his former heroic resolve to stand and wait for Achilles in front of the gates of Troy, when seeing the approach of the death star, turns in horror and runs?

Fitzgerald's and Homer's vision of the city may appear on the face of it to derive in some sense from a shared perspective, but much has intervened over time to separate the two views of urban life. Whereas the twentieth-century image of the megapolis is still under the spell of Romanticism's nostalgia for a preurban eden and is soberly aware of a postindustrial urban blight, the polis in Homer, as in later Greek philosophical writing, was exalted as the crowning achievement of humankind. But as Hektor encircles Troy's fate in his own as he runs around the wall of his city, Homer exposes, even more tragically than Fitzgerald, an order that is sacred but vulnerable to death and devastation, and one that is hardly arrēktos or stable in a world of mutability.

With the hero's death in Book 22, the *Iliad* reaches its climax. Although Achilles is gradually (and imperfectly) reintegrated with the social order through the funeral games of Patroklos, he himself still stands at a distance from that order: he gives away his own gifts and is psychically disengaged. While Achilles' shared meal with Priam restores, with fragility, the young warrior's long-absent humanity, it does so in the form of an elegy: as old and young man, father and son, each remembers that which he has lost. Although the last book balances and reverses the failures of supplication so fatal to the Achaeans in Book 1, this thematic closure masks a much deeper failure of closure.[22] The *Iliad* begins with Achilles, a mortal clothed in an immortal wrath, but it ends with the Trojans mourning for their favorite and only son, and with Troy itself, a mortal city clothed in a sacred veil. While Hektor's funeral prefigures both the death of Achilles and Troy's annihilation, it is the city's devastation which the poem recalls as Andromache very near the poem's end visualizes the day, soon to arrive, when an Achaean will hurl Astyanax from Troy's rampart.[23]

Nature and Technology
in Place Epithets

The number of epithets for places in the *Iliad* and the *Odyssey* is great. In the *Iliad,* there are eighty-one different epithets for *poleis* and other geographical sites (as best I can count), occurring a total of three hundred and six times; in the *Odyssey* fifty-two epithets are found, occurring one hundred and fifty-seven times.[1] If the seventy instances of epithetical usage in the Greek and Trojan Catalogues of Book 2 and the "Pylian" Catalogue of Book 9 are omitted from the Iliadic count, the discrepancy in numbers in the two poems would be considerably reduced: two hundred thirty-six in the *Iliad* to one hundred fifty-seven in the *Odyssey.* (All tabulations must be considered approximations.)

I shall list epithets here according to three categories: (1) those that describe natural features of the polis, (2) those that refer to man-made aspects of the polis, (3) those that fall in between these two poles and describe features of a city or domain that may be influenced by both man and nature. The numbers show that twice as many epithets in the *Iliad* as in the *Odyssey* describe man-made aspects of a city, whereas the opposite is true of the *Odyssey.* That is, while the natural features of a place in the main body of the *Iliad* are mentioned a total of thirty-five times, in the *Odyssey* they appear a total of seventy-one times. By contrast, seventy-four different occurrences in the *Iliad* describe man-made aspects of a city, but only thirty-eight instances exist in the *Odyssey.* In the third category, the ratio is ninety-five to sixty in favor of the *Iliad.* This statistical information needs to be put in context.

In general, the epithets of the first category describe the terrain, plant life, or special topographical features of the extended polis domain and are usually quite easy to identify. Of the thirty-five epithets in this group, a few are found quite frequently and seem to be generic in character: "wide" "fertile countryside," and "rocky" in four words of different metrical shape (*paipaloessa, petrēessa, trēkheia,* and *kranaa*); but most occur only once or twice even when they describe generic qualities of many places: "on the seashore," "by the sea," "sea-girt," and so on. The quantity of these epithets as well as their rarity is, then, noteworthy.

These epithets are much less common in the *Iliad* than in the *Odyssey*. It is true that twenty-eight of the thirty-five epithets in this group are found in the *Iliad,* but only fourteen of these occur in the main body of the poem. If found in the *Iliad,* they are most likely in the catalogues: fourteen from this group are exclusive to the catalogues of Books 2 and 9; four more are common to both the catalogues and to the poem proper. By contrast, of the nineteen epithets from this category in the *Odyssey,* many are used frequently, and only in this poem, i.e. *eudeielos* (seven times), *amphialos* (five times), *amphirutes* (four times). Furthermore, when characters in the *Odyssey* describe places with predicate adjectives (not in the following list), they tend to fall into this category. Telemachos' description of rocky Ithaca, unsuitable for horses, etc., is an obvious example. When the two poems do share epithets from this group, it is frequently the case that they come from the *Iliad*'s catalogues and not from the main body of the poem: *einosiphullos* (Cat. twice; *Od.* twice); *anthemoessa* (Cat. once; *Od.* twice); *trēkheia* (Cat. twice; *Od.* four times); *poiēeis* (Cat. once, Cat. of Book 9 once; *Od.* once).

The list from this group is as follows. (Epithets are arranged according to frequency of occurrence. Two numbers are listed under the *Iliad;* the first refers to the number of uses in the main body of the poem *exclusively,* the second, in parentheses, refers to catalogues usage.):

Epithet	Frequency		
	Total	*Iliad*	*Odyssey*
eureia (wide)	24	13	11
ēmathoeis (sandy)	12	3 (1)	8
piona dēmon (fertile territory)	10	5	5
paipaloessa (rocky)	10	2	8
eudeielos (bright? far-seen?)	7	0	7
petrēessa (rocky)	6	1 (3)	2
trēkheia (rough, rocky)	6	0 (2)	4
kranaa (rugged, rocky)	5	1	4
amphialos (sea-girt)	5	0	5

Epithet	Frequency		
	Total	Iliad	Odyssey
polubenthēs (with many recesses)	4	1	3
amphirutos (flowed around)	4	0	4
einosiphullos (covered with trembling leafage)	4	0 (2)	2
poiēeis (grassy)	3	0 (2)	1
anthemoessa (flowery)	3	0 (1)	2
ephalos (on the seashore)	2	0 (2)	0
polutrērōn (haunted by pigeons)	2	0 (2)	0
agkhialos (by the sea)	2	0 (2)	0
arginoeis (white, with cliffs)	2	0 (2)	0
lekhepoiēs (with grassy banks)	2	1 (1)	0
duskheimepos (wretched winters)	2	1 (1)	0
apeirōn (boundless)	2	2	0
koilēn Lakedaimona kētōessan (hollow Lake-daimon, among rifted hills)	2	0 (1)	
klōmakoessa (rugged, hilly)	1	0 (1)	0
leuka karēna (white head)	1	0 (1)	0
polis leuke (white city)	1	0 (1)	0
poluknēmos (with many mountain-spurs)	1	0 (1)	0
bathuleimos (meadows with deep grass)	1	0 (1)	0
bathuskhoinos (banks thick with rushes)	1	1	0
poludipsios (very thirsty)	1	1	0
hupoplakia (lying under Mount Plakos)	1	1	0
outhar arourēs (udder of fields)	1	1	0
platus (wide, broad)	1	0	1
aktē prouxousa (breach projecting out = Hellespont)	1	0	1
huponēios (lying under Mount Neium)	1	0	1
pikrē Aiguptos (bitter Egypt)	1	0	1
TOTAL	132	35 (26)	71

The list is undoubtedly incomplete because places such as the mythical White Rock in *Odyssey,* Book 24 and the many epithets for unnamed beaches, mountaintops, rocky crags, etc. (e.g., *paraplēgai, proukhousa, problētes*) have not been included.

The second category of epithets describes man-made construction, urbanized space, or in other ways suggests human imprint on the natural world. There are thirty (including alternative spellings) in this group, most of which refer to the city proper (although *eurukhoros, Akhaiikos,* and *Ithakēsios* are certainly exceptions, as may be *klutos* and *erateinos* as well). They tend to fall into three main groupings: those that describe the architectural stature of the polis (often with the prefix *eu*, which celebrates human technology), those that see the city as the place of human stories (famous or ill-famed), and those that mark the city as a place of human habitation (well-inhabited, Achaean, and so on). It is not feasible to list here the many references to a city in terms of its ruler and the city's people ("the city of Priam," "the children of Priam," and "the people of Troy;" "the city of Echion," etc.), but to do so would greatly enlarge the number of epithets referring, like the popular *eu naiomenos*, to the people of a polis (e.g., there are thirty references to Troy alone in this manner).

The balance between Iliadic and Odyssean usage is almost exactly reversed from that of the first category. Many of those that occur with great frequency in the main body of the *Iliad* seldom are found in the *Odyssey:* for example, *eu naiomenos* (thirteen to one), *astu mega* (thirteen to one), and *erateinos* (six to two). Many more are used only in the *Iliad:* *euteikheos* (seven times, always of Troy); *hupsipulos* (three times of Troy and of Thebes in the Troad); *hekatompulos* (once, of Thebes in Egypt); *eustephanos* (once, of Thebes in Boiotia); *eupurgos* and *ophruoessa* (once each and of Troy).

A list of these epithets appears below (again following the same format as with those in the first group; the number in parentheses refers to those in the catalogues):

Epithet	Frequency		
	Total	Iliad	Odyssey
euktimenos (*euktinos*) (well-built, furnished with fair buildings)	21 & 1	9 (7)	6
astu mega (great city)	15	13 (1)	1
erateinos (*erannos*) (lovely, fair, delightful, pleasing)	12 & 3	6 (7)	2
eu naiomenos (well-inhabited)	14	13	1
euruaguia (with wide streets)	12	8	4
eurukhoros (with spacious dancing floors)	9	2 (1)	6
euteikheos (well-walled)	7	7	0
polukhrusos (rich in gold)	4	3	1
Akhaiikos (Achaean)	4	1 (2)	1
klutos (*kleitos*) (famous)	3 & 1	2	2
astu perikluton (very famous city)	3	0	3
Kakoilion ouk onomastēn (Evil Ilion, not to be named)	3	0	3
hupsipulos (with lofty gates)	3	3	0
teikhioessa (walled)	2	0 (2)	0
heptapulos (with seven gates)	2	1	1

Epithet	Frequency		
	Total	*Iliad*	*Odyssey*
polukhalkos (rich in bronze)	2	1	1
Ithakesios (Ithacian)	2	0	2
hekatompolis (with 100 *poleis*)	1	0 (1)	0
hekatompulos (hundred-gated)	1	1	0
eustephanos (well-crowned)	1	1	0
eupurgos (well-towered)	1	1	0
ophruoessa (frowning)	1	1	0
hiera krēdemna (with holy diadem)	1	1	0
lipara krēdemna (shining diadem)	1	0	1
polueratos (very lovely)	1	0	1
megalē polis (great city)	1	0	1
hēmeteron astu (our city)	1	0	1
TOTAL	133	74 (21)	38

To this list, we may add a few epithets that modify the noun *polis* but never the proper name of a polis: *meropōn anthrōpōn* ("city of a mortal people": *Il.* 2; *Od.* 2) and *eparatos* ("lovely") of a *ptoliethron* (*Il.* 18.512 and 22.121) and of a cave (*Od.* 13.103). The list would also be a little longer if the predicate adjectives *arrēktos* ("unbreakable"), and *eudmētos* ("well-built" or "well-constructed") were included. Each occurs only once, and for Troy.

The epithets *erateinos* and *erannē* "lovely") properly belong in this category because they infer a love expressed in human companionship and social bonds. *Erannē* in Homer is used only with places;[2] *erateinos* has a wider field, referring as much to social bonds (*philotēs* ["friendship"], *hetaroi* ["comrades"], *homēlikiē* ["one's contemporary"], and *ēnoreē* ["manliness," prowess"]) as to cities.[3] So C. M. Bowra: "It has an emotional connotation but is in no sense descriptive."[4] Paolo Vivante's comments are also worth recording: "The epithets with the -*er* root would seem to convey a particular sort of beauty: the appeal of cities in that they are inhabited, loved, admired. A city becomes a pole of attraction. This explains how it shares these epithets with such ideals as youth, manhood, love."[5] Such emotions make these epithets particularly suited to the Catalogue of Book 2 and its invocation of the Greek homeland (cf. 2.532, 571, 583, 591, 607).[6] And such emotions make it fitting that when not in the catalogues, these epithets are used almost solely by characters in the poem (six of the seven occurrences), as they mention *poleis* or describe cherished human relationships.

The four occurrences of *erateinos* in Book 3 of the *Iliad* suggest a memory of a lost peace and fatherland. On the Skaian Gate, Helen curses herself for having left her young daughter and the "lovely friends with whom she had grown up" (*erateinēn homēlikiēn,* 3.175) and later recalls her brothers Kastor and Pollux in "lovely Lakedaimon" (3.239). As is appropriate for someone so absorbed in meditation upon her past and her past sins, when Helen speaks of cities from her past she continues to do so in terms of their people and bonds of intimacy. Confronted by Aphrodite, Helen asks: "Mistress, why do you desire to lead me astray thus? Will you drive me further on to any of the well-inhabited cities, either Phrygia or lovely Meonie, if someone of mortal men even there happens to be dear to you?" (3.399–401) One wonders whether Alexander does not trivialize Helen's sentiments of a violated social order when forty lines later he says that he has never desired her as much since the time he snatched her away from "lovely Lakedaimon" (3.443). Can and does Homeric language have the power to record through epithet a coarse indifference to social order so clearly evident in action?

The third category of place epithets is more problematic. The twenty-six epithets (including alternate spellings) of this group—which refer to the rich flocks, fertile lands, and abundant grapes—nicely illustrate the interplay of human being and nature, at once a statement of the earth's wealth and man's industry.

Of the epithets from this category, Iliadic usage is much greater than Odyssean occurrences: ninety-five (in the *Iliad* proper) to sixty. The difference we saw between Iliadic and Odyssean tendencies in the use of epithets from the first two categories applies here as well. The epithet *ēnemoessa* ("windy"), for example, in the *Iliad* refers only to cities;[7] whereas in the *Odyssey,* it refers only to the windy peaks, ravines, or promontories of Mount Parnassus, Mount Mimas, the Kyklopes' island, and so on. The epithet *aipus* ("steep") also applies with much greater frequency to mountains in the *Odyssey* than in the *Iliad.* (Similarly, in the nonurban world of similes and of Odysseus' travels, epithets from the other categories, such as "lofty" and "rocky," shift from polis to mountains and beaches.)

The list from this group is as follows:

Epithets	Frequency		
	Total	Iliad	Odyssey
aipus (aipeia, etc.) (steep, sheer, and of mountains)	10 & 20	22 (2)	6
hieros (hirē) (holy)	13 & 23	18 (6)	12
eribōlax (eribōlos) (fertile)	16 & 5	18 (1)	2
hippobotos (suitable for grazing)	15	7 (1)	7
dios (divine, holy)	15	3 (2)	10
ēnemoessa (windy)	12	8	4
ēgatheos (holy, very sacred)	7	3 (4)	0
kalligunaix (with beautiful women)	5	4	1
eupolos (with good foals)	5	2	3
mētera melōn (mother of flocks)	4	2 (1)	1
hedos (seat of a territory)	4	2	2
polupuros (with much grain)	4	0	4
ampeloessa (rich in vines)	3	1 (2)	0
polustaphulos (rich in grapes)	2	0 (2)	0
Aiguptiōn perikalleai agroi (very beautiful fields of Egypt)	2	0	2
polumēlos (rich in sheep or goats)	1	0 (1)	0
poluarnos (rich in sheep)	1	0 (1)	0
aphneois (rich)	1	0 (1)	0
kalos (beautiful)	1	0 (1)	0
botianeira (feeding men)	1	1	0
TOTAL	181	95 (26)	60

This list would also be expanded by including the predicate adjectives used by Telemachos and Athena to describe Ithaca and by Eumaios to describe the island of Syrie.

Perhaps surprisingly, the land's fertility is also more commonly specified in the *Iliad* than in the *Odyssey*. This is largely due to the popular usage of *eribōlax* ("fertile") in the *Iliad* (nineteen times), frequently but by no means exclusively applied to the Trojan plain (eight times). Otherwise, phrases such as *mētera melōn* ("mother of flocks"; three to one in favor of the *Iliad*) and *hippobotos* ("suitable for grazing"; eight to seven) are found in both poems rather equally. In the *Iliad* eight of these epithets referring to fertile land are found in the catalogues (five of the eight only in the catalogues; e.g., *polustaphulos*, "rich in grapes," *poluarnos*, "rich in sheep," and so on), and are similar in nature to Eumaios' description of Syrie in the *Odyssey*: that is, a land that it not populous, but good (*agathē*) nonetheless, good for cows (*eubotos*), good for sheep and goats (*eumēlos*), bearing wine in abundance (*oinoplēthēs*), and rich in wheat (*polupuros* (15.405–6).

When considering these three categories, the Greek Catalogue of Book 2 offers an interesting blend of Iliadic and Odyssean tendencies. In each territory, one or two well-founded (*euktimenos*) or walled (*teikhioeis*) poleis stand amid many which are described by epithets drawn from categories one or three. On the Greek mainland, the catalogue describes the following as *euktimenos:* Iolkos in Thessaly, Thebes in Boiotia, Medeon in Boiotia, Athens in Attika, Mycenae in Argos, Kleonai in Agamemnon's domain, and Aipu in Pylos (the epithet in this case has a unique spelling: *euktinos*).[8] In addition to these seven, Tiryns in Argos and Gortyna in Crete are said in the Catalogue of Book 2 to be walled (*teikhioeis*), an epithet unique to these references. Around these "well-founded" centers, the catalogue lists a myriad of "smaller" poleis which are epithetically described by their natural characteristics as if they were architecturally and politically less imposing. Historically, there can be no question that this configuration in mainland Greece of well-structured strongholds surrounded by satellite communities can only describe Mycenaean, or Late Helladic IIIC, patterns of acropolis center and outlying settlements. Neither the Greek Dark Age, nor the eighth-century, where the poleis in Greece proper were still in the process of coalescing or centralizing into a coherent teikhioeis form, suggests communities similarly organized.

As the three categories have amply shown, the epithets of the *Iliad* proper concentrate on the mighty, well-fortified, and centralizing polis. The smaller settlements of the catalogues, and their epithets, are for the most part ignored. In the *Odyssey,* the situation is reversed. Despite a claim made in the proem that the hero saw the cities (*astea*) of many men, descriptions of them almost never intrude on the narrative and with the exception of Scheria, there are few architectural statements about them. Rather, epithets tend to place poleis within their natural and geographical settings. Of all the epithets peculiar to that poem, not one describes man-made forms of the city.

In the *Odyssey,* sense of place is both broader and more specific than in the *Iliad:* broader in that the territory, not the polis, is the object of description, more specific in that the oikos, not the polis, is the object of desire. As mentioned in the introduction, the *Odyssey*'s gravitational pull toward the oikos corresponds to a non-Iliadic use of the epithets *euktimenos* and *eudmētos.*

Sacred Places

The lists that follow give all places in the *Iliad* and the *Odyssey* described by the epithets *hieros, zatheos, ēgatheos,* and *dios.* The most common of the four is *hieros,* used with the following places:

Place	Location	Frequency		Other modifiers
		Iliad	*Odyssey*	
POLEIS				
Ilios	Troad	23	2	*Il.*: well-inhabited, well-founded, steep polis, great astu of Priam, etc. *Od.*: Priam's ptoliethron, etc.
Troy		0	1	(see above)
Pergamon (Troy)		1	0	topmost, with a temple of Apollo (*nēos*)
Thebes	Troad	1	0	well-inhabited, under Plakos, polis of Eetion, lofty-gated
Zeleia	Troad	2	0	astu, below Mount Ida
Pylos	Messenia	0	1	*Il.*: well-founded ptoliethron, well-inhabited, etc. *Od.*: steep ptoliethron, mother of sheep, sandy, etc.

	Frequency			
Place	Location	*Iliad*	*Odyssey*	Other modifiers
Ismaros	Thrace	0	1	ptoliethron of the Kikones
ISLANDS				
Euboia	East of Boiotia	1	0	none (Cat. Bk. 2)
Echinai	Near Ithaca	1	0	none (Cat. Bk. 2)
SANCTUARIES				
Onchestos	Boiotia	1	0	shining grove of Poseidon (*Il.* Bk.2)
Sunion	Attica	0	1	promontory of Athens
OTHER				
cave of nymphs	Ithaca	0	1	lovely, misty
	TOTAL	30	7	

In addition, the walls of Boiotian Thebes are called *hieros,* as is the "veil" or diadem of towers metaphorically describing the walls of Troy. Furthermore, the circle of the agora in the city at peace on the Shield of Achilles is sacred. *Hieros,* thus, applies to seven poleis, two islands, two sanctuaries, one cave, one agora, and two city walls in the two poems.

Zatheos appears only in the *Iliad.* Its occurrences are as follows:

Place	Location	Frequency in *Iliad*	Other modifiers
POLEIS			
Killa	Troad	2	(protected by Apollo)
Pherai	Messenia	2	well-founded (Cat. Bk. 9)
Krisa	Phokis	1	none (Cat. Bk. 2)
Nisa	on Mount Helikon	1	none
ISLANDS			
Kythera	off southern tip of Lakedaimon	1	(where Aphrodite comes to mainland Greece)
SANCTUARIES			
none			

Place	Location	Frequency in *Iliad*	Other modifiers
OTHER			
hill (*oros*)	Boiotia	0	green (called holy at *Hymn to Apollo* 223)
	TOTAL	$\overline{7}$	

Except for Hesiod's *Theogony* (253), where *zatheos* modifies the winds (usually emended), this epithet in archaic hexamter appears only in conjunction with places. In Homer, it applies to four poleis and one island.

The similar epithet *ēgatheos* describes only one polis. Its references to places are as follows:

		Frequency		
Place	Location	*Iliad*	*Odyssey*	Other modifiers
POLEIS				
Pylos	Messenia	1	5	(see list for *hieros*)
ISLANDS				
Lemnos	off the Troad	3	0	*Il.*: well-founded, polis of godlike (*theios*) Thoas (also holy in Cat. Bk 2) *Od.*: well-founded ptoliethron
Lesbos	off the Troad	0	0	*Il.* well-founded, seat *Od.*: well-founded (called holy at *Hymn to Apollo* 37 and at Hesiod, *Theogony* 499)
SANCTUARIES				
Mount Nysa	Asia Minor	1	0	(part of Dionysus cult)
Pytho	Delphi	0	1	*Il.*: rocky, shining threshold
	TOTAL	$\overline{5}$	$\overline{6}$	

By analogy with Lesbos (*ēgatheos* in Hesiod), Lemnos is listed here as an island, but its description as polis and ptoliethron suggests that it should be identified in Homer under polis rather than island. Nevertheless, in this count, I shall tabulate it as above: thus *ēgatheos,* in Homer, applies to one city, one island, and two sanctuaries.

The fourth epithet in this grouping, *dios,* like *hieros,* has a wide range of usages; it modifies the following place names in Homer:

Place	Location	Frequency		Other modifiers
		Iliad	*Odyssey*	
POLIS				
Arisbe	Troad	2	0	well-founded (also holy in Tro. Cat. Bk. 2)
TERRITORIES				
Lakedaimon	Lakonia	0	6	*Il.*: hollow, lovely full of ravines *Od.*: hollow, with wide dancing floors
Elis	Elis	3	3	*Il.*: well-founded (also holy in Cat. Bk. 2) *Od.*: horse-nourishing, with wide dancing floors
SANCTUARIES				
none				
	TOTAL	5	9	

In sum, one polis and two territories are *dios* in Homer.

Sacred Cities
of the East

Capital Cities of Extended Kingdoms

In the Near East, as elsewhere in the Old and New World, capital cities of extended kingdoms were thought to possess a unique form of sanctity. So Babylon, Jerusalem, and Mecca for the Babylonians, Jews, Moslems, respectively, were thought to be holier than other cities. Like Nineveh, a capital of the Assyrian Empire, "whose ground plan" King Sennacherib said, "has been drawn since the beginning of time in the stars of the sky" (from Ursa Major),[1] such cities are earthly models of celestial archetypes, pure earth in profane space, founded at the moment of cosmogonic creation.[2]

The founding and building of Babylon exemplifies each of these points. When the Babylonian chief deity Marduk splits open the body of Tiamat, thereby bringing the universe into being, he surveys the heavens, defines the space where his temple, the Esharra, will be built, and then makes of that space the first firmament:

> Then the lord [Marduk] paused to view her [Tiamat's] dead body,
> That he might divide the monster and do artful works.
> He split her like a shellfish into two parts:
> Half of her he set up and sealed it as sky,
> Pulled down the bar and posted guards.
> He bade them to allow not her waters to escape.
> He crossed the heavens and surveyed the regions.
> He squared Apsu's quarter, the abode of Nudimmud,
> As the lord measured the dimensions of Apsu,
> The Great Abode, its likeness, he fixed as Esharra,

The Great Abode, Esharra, which he made as the firmament.
Anu, Enlil, and Ea he made occupy their places.

(*Enuma Elish* IV.135–46)[3]

Resting on top of the ziggurat or mountain at the center of the city of Babylon, the temple will lie midpoint between the primordial subterranean depths, or Apsu (I.71), and heaven:

Above the Apsu where you have resided,
The counterpart of Esharra which I have built over you,
Below I have hardened the ground for a building site,
I will build a house, it will be my luxurious abode.
I will found therein its temple,
I will appoint cellas, I will establish my sovereignty.
When you come up from the Apsu for assembly,
You will spend the night therein, (it is there) to receive all of you.
When you des[cend] from heaven [for assem]bly,
You will spend the night there[in], (it is there) to receive all of you.
I will call [its] name ["Babylon"] (which means) "the house of the
    great gods,"
I shall build it (with) the skill of craftsman.

(V.119–30)

Marduk's cosmic home and seat of his sovereignty, Esharra, is the *omphalos,* or embryonic center, of the cosmos as well as *axis mundi* ("the house of foundation of heaven and earth," VI.113) which links the upper and lower realms.[4] As "a likeness on earth of what he has wrought in heaven" (VI.113), the temple is equally an *imago mundi,* or earthly model of a celestial archetype.

Considerably before the creation of humankind, the gods themselves will build Marduk's temple and ziggurat, and then around that center erect their own shrines and the city of Babylon (cf. VI.67–72). The ziggurat and temple, and by extension the city itself, were of divine origin, sacred space in a profane world, at the center of the universe. Margaret Green, further, postulates that Babylon as the leading city of Babylonia attempted to imitate in its city planning the geography of the Mesopotamian plain, symbolizing in architecture and urban design the fact of its cosmic centrality.[5]

Babylon's special sanctity may be defined as follows: built in imitation of a celestial archetype, it is a sacred enclave at the center of the universe, where earth and sky, human and divine, nature and social order are in harmony. As one approaches Babylon, and more particularly the temple at the center of the city, one "transcends," in Mircea Eliade's phrase, "profane, heterogenous space and enters 'pure earth,'"[6] that is, one moves toward pure city and primordial universe. By reenacting that moment of city foundation through annual ritual and ceremony at the New Year Festival, historical humans break through profane space and time to share in the sacred act of cosmogonic creation.

Such exalted claims for capital cities are not the exclusive property of Sumerian and Babylonian propagandists. Once the Hebrews acquired a kingdom of their own, views of Jerusalem were often reminiscent of those prevalent for Near Eastern cities though, as Othmar Keel comments, "no attempt was made to trace the foundation of the Jerusalem sanctuary back to the time of the primal beginnings."[7] Yet much like Babylon, the city was founded and built by Yahweh upon the Holy Rock at the world's center.[8] Earthly Jerusalem and its temple translate into stone and brick during historical time a model conceived in heaven.[9] *Revelations* suggests the process will happen again at the time of the Second Coming: "The Holy City, New Jerusalem, coming down from God out of Heaven, prepared as a bride adorned for her husband" (21.2).

Whereas purity at Babylon was expressed primarily according to a vertical axis as one ascended the sacred mountain to the temple that crowned the ziggurat, in Jewish thought where the temple was less of a mountain, purity of the city and the temple at its center was perceived more in horizontal and geographical terms.[10] The city was set, as the Lord says, "in the center of nations";[11] within that center lay Mount Zion, "the center of the navel [*omphalos*] of the earth."[12] Jewish purification laws also expressed this purity according to a horizontal axis as the state of Israel itself was defined by a succession of symbolic boundaries, walls, and gates, the passing of each of which brings the visitor nearer to Jerusalem and its temple, the *omphalos* of Judea, the world, and the universe:

6. There are ten degrees of holiness. The land of Israel is holier than any other land. Where in lies its holiness? In that from it they may bring the omer, the first fruits, and the two loaves, which they may not bring from any other land.
7. The walled cities (of the Land of Israel) are still more holy, in that they must send forth lepers from their midst . . .
8. Within the wall (of Jerusalem) is still more holy, for there (only) they may eat the lesser holy things and the second tithe. The Temple Mount

is still more holy, for no man or woman that has a flux, no menstruant, and no woman after childbirth may enter therein. The Rampart is still more holy, for no gentiles and none that have contracted uncleanness from a corpse may enter therein. The Court of the Women is still more holy (restrictions cited). . . . The Court of the Israelites is still more holy (further restrictions cited). . . . The Court of Priests is still more holy . . .

9. Between the Porch and the Altar is still more holy . . . ; the Sanctuary is still more holy . . . ; the Holy of Holies still more holy, for none may enter therein save only the High Priest on the Day of Atonement at the time of the (Temple) service. (from Mishnah Kelim, 1.6–9)[13]

In identifying Jerusalem's unique status within the Hebrew kingdom, Gustave von Grunebaum has distinguished five interlocking criteria by which its hierarchical supremacy may be marked: (1) it was exalted above the territories surrounding it; (2) it was the origin of the earth; (3) it was the center of the earth; (4) it was the place of communication with the upper and lower worlds; (5) it was the medium through which food was distributed over the earth, a point not discussed here but consistent with the preceding themes.[14]

When the Moslems move the capital of their religion to Mecca, the city of Mohammed's birth, old Babylonian and Hebrew beliefs find new form. Consider the writings of the Moslem historian Azraqī who died circa A.D. 858: "Forty years before Allah created the heavens and the earth, the Ka'ba [the central Sanctuary in the center of Mecca] was a dry spot floating on the water and from it the world had been spread out."[15] In Grunebaum's account, city replaces sanctuary: "Before the creation of heaven and earth, the throne of god was on the water. When it ascended to the heavens, earth was created where the throne had stood. There the city was built."[16]

Contrary to Moslem views about holy Mecca, cities of commercial or military importance, either within the Moslem kingdom or connected to it through trade, were regarded as exclusively secular. For other cities in various states of impurity, the degree of sacredness depended on the extent to which their founding rituals imitated those of Mecca and whether prophets or saints were buried within or near the cities.[17]

But capital cities of extended kingdoms in the ancient Near East have a holiness unlike any other. Their unique sacredness derives from the fact that they were seen as occupying the first firmament of a nascent universe, that the chief deity of the kingdom selected this site as his cosmic home or as that point on earth where his presence could be felt in all its purity. In this sacred space human order could mirror divine order, and from this point the earth's fecundity could be generated.

Walled Cities of Mesopotamia

Although most cities of the ancient Near East could not be considered to imitate the cosmic centrality of a city like Babylon, in many other regards cities were considered holy and for many of the same reasons associated with Babylon's special purity. Analysis should begin with the Sumerians, whose ideas about religion and cities helped shape Mesopotamian thought for more than two thousand years.

Unlike the extended kingdom of the Babylonians, the earlier Sumerians lived in independent city-states, each region, with its outreaching agrarian economy and nuclei of suburban villages and hamlets, centered around one of the twelve to fourteen urban settlements.[18] The city proper, the Sumerian *uru*, defined by the city wall, consisted of palace, official residences, citizens' houses, and temples. But like Babylon, these urban centers were hierocentric and theocentric, that is, temple oriented (even if the temple itself may have been frequently located in one corner of the urban enclosure): the uru's ziggurat was always in the words of Samuel Kramer, "the largest, highest, and most important building in the city, in accordance with the theory current among the Sumerian religious leaders that the entire city belonged to its main god, to whom it had been assigned on the day the world was created."[19]

The prominence of the central temple complex is evident in the ancient literature, both sacred and secular. From the Sumerians to the Neo-Babylonians (circa 600 B.C.), the peoples of Mesopotamia make a strong distinction between the temple and outer city. Consider tablet one of the *Epic of Gilgamesh* (an Akkadian tablet):

> Of ramparted Uruk, the wall he [Gilgamesh] built,
> Of hallowed Eanna, the pure sanctuary.
> Behold its outer wall, whose cornice is like copper,
> Peer at the inner wall, which none can equal!
> Seize upon the threshold, which is from of old!
> Draw near to Eanna, the dwelling of Ishtar,
> Which no future king, no man, can equal.
> (*ANET* 73, lines 9–15)

City (Uruk) and temple (Eanna) are separately named and separately walled. Uruk is the *uru* where people live and work, with its outer wall ("whose cornice is like copper"); Eanna is the house (*é*) or hallowed sanctuary (in these texts called a *temenos*) where the tutelary dieties Anu and Ishtar live and where the administrative center of Uruk is located. This complex has its own walls ("which none can equal"). The description of the inner walls "from of old" suggests an archetypal model from the mythic past.

A Neo-Babylonian cosmogonic text fifteen hundred years later (sixth-century B.C.) shows how conservative is this tradition in the Near East of perceiving the city as made up of two parts: one of human beings, the other of its tutelary god. The inscription reads:

> A holy house, a house of the gods in a holy place had not yet been made;
> A reed had not yet come forth, a tree had not yet been created,
> A brick had not been laid, a brick mold had not been built;
> A house had not been made, a city had not been built;
> A city had not been made, a living creature had not been placed (therein);
> Nippur had not been made, Ekur had not been built;
> Uruk had not been made, Eanna had not been built;
> The *Apsu* had not been made, Eridu had not been built.
> A holy house, a house of gods, its dwelling, had not been made;
> All the lands were sea;
> The spring which is in the sea was a water pipe;
> Then Eridu was made, Esagila was built—
> Esagila whose foundations Lugaldukuga [= Lugal(king)-du(?)-ku(holy)] laid within the *Apsu*—
> Babylon was made, Esagila was completed;
> The gods the Anunnaki, he [Heidel: Lugaldukuga; King: Marduk] created equal.
> The holy city, the dwelling of their hearts' delight, they called it solemnly.[20]

At this late date, it has been forgotten that the Sumerian Enlil built Nippur, and that the Sumerian Inanna (the Akkadian Ishtar) built Uruk, and that the Sumerian Enki built Eridu, but the essential image of the city as a twofold creation persists. The formulaic language itself in this text underlines the essential dual image of the city: Nippur was made, its temple Ekur was built; Uruk was made, its temple Eanna built; Eridu made, Esagila built; Babylon made, its Esagila completed.

At this time in Babylon's history, the imperial king (*lugal*) had gained considerable power, exemplified by his palace The Hanging Gardens of Babylon, enclosed like the temple complex within its own walls and rival to it in splendor.[21] But in the hymn it is still as if Babylon were only of two parts, god's house and outer city. In such texts as the two just cited it is equally evident that of the two orders, the inner house (*é*) is always called pure (Sumerian *kù*, Akkadian *ellu*), whereas the outer city is rarely so designated. In our second cosmogonic story, only Babylon is called *kù* (or *ellu*), so identified perhaps because it is the capital city of its kingdom.

If not cosmic omphaloi, the Sumerian ziggurats are both local omphaloi ("Temple, whose interior is the vital-center of the country," to quote Sumerian Kes Temple Hymn I),[22] and *axis mundi* ("Temple, whose platform is suspended from heaven's midst / whose foundation fills the Abzu," Kes Temple Hymn II),[23] linking the three tiers of the cosmos.

As was true of Esharra in Babylon, the Sumerians believed that their gods founded and built the temple and attendant city, and as in the *Enuma Elish* account, all life emanates from the temple sanctuary. An incantation from the Kes temple reads: "Temple, which gives birth to countless peoples, seed which has sprouts, / Temple, which gives birth to kings [*lugal*], which determines the fate of the land."[24] In an inscription on the Gudea Cylinder, the tutelary deity of the Sumerian Girsu, Ningirsu, promises to his priestess, or *en* (circa 2100 B.C.): "With the founding of my house, overflow will come, / The large fields will grow high for you, / The canals will flood their banks for you, / . . . The North Wind, / From the mountain, the pure place, / Will blow the wind straight towards you . . . / (Because) I will have given the breath of life to the people."[25] The crucial transmission of divine power and blessings to the mortal city occurs at the lofty temple at the top of the ziggurat: at the beginning of every year, tutelary deity and city-priest or priestess (*en*), depending on the sex of the city god, unite at the ziggurat temple in a marriage that guarantees fecundity and prosperity for the entire city-state.[26]

As part of the daily routine, the major activities of the city-state were performed at the gates to the inner temple (and to a lesser extent at the city gates): "Temple, at whose gates is the ruler who decides cases," to quote from the Kes hymns again (Temple II, line 93). Here in the liminal space that separated the city of humankind from divinity, juridical control was exercised over business transactions, civic and legal orders of city life were administered, and the city food supply (barley, etc.), which was preserved in storehouses within the inner *temenos*, was regulated. The names over these gateways, as for example at Nippur, identify the kind of activities conducted there: Gate of Peace, Holy Judgment, Uncut Barley, The Lord Is Worldly Wise, and so on.

In Sumerian mythology, as in the Hebrew story of Eden, humans tended a world of divine making. Contrary to a tradition that stresses a pastoral paradise as the original setting of humankind, where Nature existed before the onset of civilization, in this world mortals come face to face with the god at the urban core ("sacred mound, where pure food is eaten," to quote the Kes Temple hymns again).[27] As one enters the city, and more especially the temple at the center of the city, one moves from a profane outer world toward, as the Sumerian Hymn to Enlil says, "the mountain, pure place, whose water is sweet . . . the center of the four corners;"[28] that is, as in the accounts about Babylon, humankind comes into the presence of pure divinity, pure earth, and pure city.

Both sacred and secular texts point in the same direction. If the power of the city god or goddess extends outward to city and country, the literature, in contrary fashion, trains its attention on the inner temple complex because therein lies the locus of power and the residence of the god. The textual and architectural evidence strongly suggest that the Sumerian phrase *uru-kù* ("sacred city") does not refer to the city at large but is, as Thorkild Jacobsen says, "a general term for the quarter of a city in which the main temples clustered."[29] The hymns, as we have seen, invariably exalt the temple enclosure as pure and holy ("the Holy of Holies" "uniting heaven and earth," "holy crown and pure place, scoured with soap"), but they are silent about the outer city in this context. Although the inner precinct is usually called the god's *é* ("house"), it is also possible that it be called metaphorically a *"uru"* ("permanent settlement"). For example, one text that I have found, again from the Kes hymns, proclaims jubilantly: "Indeed it is a city [*uru*], indeed it is a city [*uru*] / The Kes temple is indeed a city [*uru*]."[30] If the city of humankind partakes in the temple's purity, it does so as the first outer ring which embraces the place of godhead.

Perhaps this last formulation is stated too harshly. In a few instances, metaphors for the sacred complex expand to include the outer city, as if the larger city had absorbed the epithet of its inner temple. Witness the moment in one text when the phrase "mountain, pure place" applies to the city of Ninazu (*University Museum, Babylonian Section* XIII.41.20–

21). But there can be no dispute that if the whole city is sacred, the written testimony repeatedly makes clear it is so because its center is pure and of sacred origin. If Jacobsen is not right in fact, he certainly appears correct in spirit. The city's sacred identity derives directly from the god's presence and must be predominantly, if not exclusively, associated with his house, or inner city.

A carryover of this belief may explain the reactions of a Hittite king, Suppiluliuma I (1375–35 B.C.), when he conquered Carchemish in northern Syria on the upper Euphrates. Having utterly destroyed the lower city, he spared the "upper city," where he proceeded to worship the gods.[31]

Given the care with which Sumerians differentiated between the sacred and profane, we can easily understand the frequent metaphor of ziggurat temple as "head" and "crown" of the uru, a metaphor implied in the Sumerian name Esagila, "House with Lofty Head." Consider a temple hymn in praise of Eridu and its ziggurat Eunir:

> Eunir, which has grown high, (uniting) heaven and earth,
>
> . . .
>
> House, holy [kù] mound, where pure [kù] food is eaten,
>
> . . .
>
> Your great . . . wall is kept in good repair,
>
> . . .
>
> Mountain, pure place, scoured with soap,
>
> . . .
>
> Your prince, the great prince, a holy [kù] crown
> He has placed for you upon your head!
> O Eridu with a crown on your head![32]

Eunir dwarfs Eridu in this hymn as temple head dwarfs civic body. In such an image of the body politic, the city of humankind is the earthly body crowned, and absorbed, by the godhead into whose presence mortals (and civilization) have come.

Like the Babylonians, the Assyrians to the north divide their cities into two sharply differentiated parts. The city of mortals is protected by an outer wall and the inner citadel of god and king by "the great wall." As with the Sumerians and Babylonians, once again the inner citadel is the place of greater sanctity. But unlike the Akkadians and later Babylonians, the Assyrian king, as viceroy of Assur, placed his palace within the temple complex, a vivid testimony to the world that he and his supreme god acted as one.[33] In keeping with this exalted status, the Assyrian king called his royal palace, and not the temple on the ziggurat, the "head" of the city. So of the new palace at ancient Nineveh King Sennacherib boasts: "to the astonishment of all nations, I raised aloft its head. 'The Palace Without A Rival' I called its name."[34] Although the head of the body politic has shifted from god to king, the term continues to refer, as in Babylonian usage, to the place of greatest purity within the city enclosure.

Magical Defense

Whereas texts call only inner house or citadel pure, they commonly assert that outer wall and great wall are sacred, both under the aegis of the divinity and with supernatural force guarding mortals, city, and cosmic home. Here again, the inner wall, like the inner uru, more frequently commands attention in the literature. Consider a Sumerian text (circa 2100 B.C.) from Girsu that speaks of "sacred city" and inner wall. Ningirsuk, it says, employs a god (d)Lugal as guardian: in order "that the city be built, that (new) buildings be established, that the wall of the 'sacred city' be guarded, that its sergeant (of the guards) of the harem, 'Huge-Mace-head-of-White-Cedar-Wood,' go around (i.e. patrol) the temple, King Gudea let Lugal, the guardian of the 'sacred city' in person, go about his duties for the Lord Ningirsuk."[35]

Many forms of magic and ritual practice strengthen the well-hewed stones and the skilled craftsmanship of the two walls. An Assyrian text on the throne seat of King Shalmaneser III (858–24 B.C.) reveals that there as well inner and outer walls are holy, defended by god and magic rites (notice that "great wall" equals inner wall): "At that time the great wall of my city Assur, and its outer wall which the kings, my fathers, who lived before my time, had built aforetime,—those walls had become ruinous and old. . . . I completely (re)built them from their foundations to their top. The steles of the kings, my fathers, I returned to their places. / At that time I made a new (statue) of the god Kidudu, the guardian of the wall,—he had perished with that wall. . . . The name of the great wall is 'Whose Splendor Covers the Land.' The name of the outer wall is 'Oppressor of the Four Regions.' Ula is guardian of his city. Kidudu is guardian of his wall."[36] Like his fathers, Shalmaneser III placed a stele, or foundation inscription, in the wall as he rebuilt it ("Let some future prince return it to its place. [Then] Assur will hear his prayers."). These stele often faced inward and were clearly not intended for humans but were conceived as a personal note from the king to his overlord and protector. The unbroken chain of notes from earliest rulers to kings in the distant future offers a sign of immortality: although the material of the city wall may deteriorate over time, the god's presence, and protection, are continuous and ever present.[37]

Apotropaic magic in the form of human, animal, and plant talismans carved on walls and at gates manifests in more public view divinity and magical defense, visually warning all who entered city or inner home of the god that they were entering sanctified earth guarded by the city's tutelary deity. Sumerian literature frequently describes a "lion on its paws" at a gateway and "a great unblemished bull" at the bolt of a door (both quoted from the Kes Temple hymns; Gragg, Temple V. lines 92 and 95). Such figures incarnate the tutelary figure himself, "the great bull of the dwelling place" as one Sumerian text calls Enlil. A text from Assyria expresses much the same sentiment in prayer: "May the bull-colossi, guardian of life, the god who keeps (things) safe by day and night, not leave its side."[38] In a wonderful description of a Sumerian priest/king, not only does the *en,* or priest king, assume the animal power of the divine protector, but he also appropriates the architectural and engineering strength of the wall: "standing like a builder's wall, a wild ox of a man thou art."[39] Herodotus recounts that the Babylonian Queen Nitocris ordered that her body be entombed "in the upper part of one of the principal gateways of the city" (1.87).

Sculptures of lions, bulls, *sirrush* dragons, palms (or perhaps sacred trees) from Babylon, like the huge, winged bulls with human heads, attended by *genii* from the Assyrian capital Dur-Sharrukin (i.e., Khorsabad) and elsewhere, now in museums around the world, are the fossil remains of powerful city-defenders. Inscriptions written on outer and greater walls and over gateways had similar apotropaic power. The Assyrian Sennacherib called on divine aid in choosing names to be inscribed over the fifteen city gates in his rebuilding of Nineveh. Pausanias says that words were similarly inscribed over Thebes' seven gates in Greece.

Copper figurines at the corners of city walls, temple foundations, passageways, doorways, or stairwells provided further forms of cosmo-magical defense. Popular from the earliest Sumerian period until Neo-Babylonian and Assyrian times, these figures, often in the shape of a semi-kneeling god, were thrust vertically into soil or mud-brick or placed in boxes. Their precise function is uncertain, but it appears as if they were meant to nail the temple god to the temple foundation so that he or she might never depart.[40] Furthermore, fine layers of sand seemed to have been placed underneath temple foundations, as at Dur-Sharrukin, as well as large numbers of small objects of little value.

Sargon II, founder of that city, even boasts that he aligned the masonry (of the temple foundation?) on gold, silver, copper, precious stones, and cuttings (of fragrant resins) from Amanus, in order to "lay its foundation and make its brickwork firm."[41]

Walled Cities of Anatolia

Centered in Central Anatolia, the Indo-European Hittites came to occupy over time much of the territory between Mesopotamia and the eastern Aegean coastline, starting around 1600 B.C. when they, with the Hurrians, overran much of Hammurabi's Babylonian dynasty. A hundred and fifty years later, the first kings of the New Kingdom (1450–1206) expanded their territory westward as far as Old Smyrna and Miletus (Hittite Milawata?) on the Aegean shores. Adopting many of the gods of the Anatolian Hurrians, as well as their religious practices, and to a lesser extent incorporating the stories and gods of the Babylonians into their own, these remarkable peoples developed a rich and complex civilization characterized by its unique synthesis of Eastern and "Indo-European" elements.[42] Although the Hittite/Hurrian Empire came to a catastrophic end circa 1200 B.C., a segment of their culture continued in northern Syria for another five hundred years, a culture this time strongly marked by Assyrian influence.

The literary evidence indicates that two cities in the Anatolian Hittite culture were especially sanctified: Nirek and Arinna, both of ancient Hatti origin and both to date having escaped modern discovery. The supreme male deity of the Hittites, the Weather God of Hatti, himself much like the Hurrian weather god Teshub, built Nirek, and it was there that all Hittite gods annually convened to celebrate the *purulli* festival. In the manner of the Babylonian New Year Festival which celebrated the creation of the cosmos, in this city festival, as the texts state, "the beginning of the year, of heaven and earth, took place."[43] The other major holy city, Arinna, was the home of the chief Hittite goddess, their Sun Goddess, who has much in common with the Hurrian Hebat, or Hebit, consort of Teshub. If other Hittite cities were less holy, they were, nevertheless, like the walled, temple-oriented cities of Mesopotamia, of sacred origin and said to have been built by their gods ("It is not we who have (really) built it, all the gods built it."[44]).

In contrast to the clearly demarcated temple complex "at the center of" the Mesopotamian walled city, the location of holy places within a Hittite city appears highly decentralized. At Hattusas, the capital city of the Hittite Empire (near modern Bogazkale), we see at least three major religious and sacred areas: the great temple complex to the Weather God of Hatti and to the Sun Goddess of Arinna located on a small plateau in the walled lower city; a multitempled "sanctuary complex," for want of a better term, in the walled upper city; the royal residence in a separately walled citadel between the other two areas. Only slightly larger than the Great Temple Complex in the lower city and at a distance from the rest of the community, the citadel appears to have been the center for the major administrative and economic activities of state, where it is also conjectured that the city's tutelary deity resided.[45] It was not until the last phase of building activity during the Empire period that this complex of citadel, upper and lower cities, sprawling across four hundred fifteen acres, was enclosed within a single, massive circuit wall, accented by the magnificent artificial mound at the highest point of the city, called Yerkapi.[46]

Although Hattusas clearly appears to be a temple-oriented city, the architectural styles and the placement of the various temple complexes within the long sloping "urban" area do not suggest direct Mesopotamian influence. The asymmetrical and labyrinthine design of the Great Temple Complex rather suggests, to many, the palace arrangement at Knossos.[47] It is set off by an enclosing wall, but one that is not on the scale of the Mesopotamian inner walls; nor is there anything of the Babylonian ziggurat elevation or urban centrality. The multitemple sanctuaries in the upper city were conspicuously displayed so as to be seen easily from outside the city, but they do not follow a homogeneous plan and are not aligned according to a common axis. Like the buildings of Troy VI, contemporary with this construction, they appear to those within the city to be randomly arranged.[48] The royal administrative center, and possible home of the city's tutelary deity, however, does suggest possible Assyrian influence.

In spite of the fact that in the Assyrian manner a Hittite ruler served as the god's regent[49] and Hittite cities were said to have been built by the gods, demarcation between human and divine space is not sharply drawn at Hattusas. There is not the Babylonian contrast between city and ziggurat, each separately walled and named; temples are labyrinthine rather than mountain-like heights; the priest/king lives outside the major temple areas. That difference in urban design is also seen in the hymn literature. In contrast to a Babylonian poet who sings of city and temple (e.g., "Then Eridu was made, Esagila was built") or an Assyrian writer who records the building of the outer wall and the great wall, a Hittite storyteller appears to speak of the city as a single entity and its tutelary deity identified with the city at large: "The Sun-God (here male) dwells in Sippar, / The Moon-God dwells in Kuzina, / The Weather-God dwells in Kummiy, / Ishtar dwells in Kissina, / And in Babylon dwells Marduk."[50]

The sanctity of Hattusas cannot properly be understood without reference to the large open sanctuary two kilometers from the city fortifications at Yazilikaya (Turkish for "Inscribed rock") and connected by a sacred road.[51] Sixty-three gods in all are depicted in these rock outcroppings marching in procession, with the males generally on one side and the females on the other, toward a central panel. There the Weather God of Hatti and the Sun Goddess of Arinna meet with outstretched hands. Although without textual evidence for corroboration, the scene undoubtedly commemorates a sacred marriage. The most recent suggestion is that the sanctuary may be regarded as embodying the House of the New Year's Festival, which, like the sacred marriage at Babylon between tutelary deity and en, celebrated the renewal of life and the fertility of the earth.[52]

The Babylonian festival (later appropriated by the Assyrians), from which this seems to have derived, celebrated Marduk's defeat of the Dragon Lady Tiamat in a twelve-day festival. On all but the tenth day of the festival, ceremonies were conducted at Esagila within the city. On the tenth day, when the actual battle took place, Marduk went outside Babylon to the akitu temple, joined to Babylon by sacred road, where presumably he defeated Tiamat. On the eleventh day, the en, god, and procession returned to Esagila where victory was celebrated, as the organization of state, the building of city, the cosmogonic creation of the cosmos, and the election of Marduk were ritually reenacted.[53] The Hittite festival, by contrast, took thirty-eight days in order to accommodate the many gods and goddesses and, more important, was primarily an extraurban celebration in the open, unsettled country of Yazilikaya.

Whereas the urban design of Hattusas does not suggest Mesopotamian influences, Hittite religious and magical beliefs owe much to Babylonian/Assyrian beliefs of cosmomagical defense. Much like the Assyrian bull, giant Hittite lions, here sculpted in the round, guard city gates (cf. their presence also at the Neo-Hittite Carchemish and Zinjirli in northern Syria and at Malatya in Taurus). These figures most likely represent the Sun Goddess of Arinna, who must, as a result, be considered the major protecting deity of Hittite cities. On the city side of the long vaulted tunnel at Hattusas, two sphinxes facing toward the city flank the entrance way (see also sphinx gate watchers at Alaca Huyuk, slightly north of Hattusas). Again on the city side at a third gate, in high relief carved out of the stone pillar, stands an image of the War God, undoubtedly the male protecting deity of the city.[54] While these figures are inspired from the East, they may themselves have influenced those westward. "The possibility of Hittite influence on the development of Mycenaean religion in later times," as Bogdan Rutkowski says with great circumspection, "cannot be ruled out."[55] The two animals (heads now missing) on the "Lion Gate" at Mycenae were most likely regarded as animal representations of a protecting citadel goddess, similar in nature to two sphinxes painted over a doorway depicted on a Mycenaean fresco now in the Pylos Museum.

As far as we can tell, Hittite kings did not place foundation steles in city walls and temple foundations. Although physical remains of foundation deposits have not been found, ritual texts do reveal that the Hittites, like the Mesopotamians, made foundation offerings of silver, gold, lapis-lazuli, jasper, copper, iron oxen with silver yokes, etc., at the four corners of a temple. The tablets explain their efficacy as follows: "See! Beneath the foundations they have deposited gold for (firm) founding. Just as the gold is firm, (as) moreover it is clean (and) strong, (as) the mind of the gods be set on this temple (and) let it be dear (to them)!."[56] At the *center* of the temple a copper *mina* was secured "on all sides" by four bronze pegs "with a small iron hammer" and a prayer: "Just as this copper is secured, (as) moreover it is firm, even so let this temple be secure! Let it be firm upon the dark earth!"[57] Yet, contrary to Mesopotamian practice, there is no indication that such pegs were personified in the image of divinities.

Although the architectural structures of Trojan defenses, contemporary with those of Hattusas, show little use of Hittite techniques,[58] magical forms of defense are evident there as well. Several monolithic stone pillars of cultic function were placed along the front of the flanking tower near the South Gate and in front of the Northwest Gate. As Carl Blegen says, these massive aniconic pillars were visual symbols of a city protected and kept pure by it deities and are clearly "analogous to the monumental gateways characteristics of Hittite sites where sculptured lions display a more portentous spirit."[59] As mentioned above, the pillar flanked by two animals on the "Lion Gate" at Mycenae appears to be of similar kind. Blegen et al. (p. 253) suggest that the "Anta House" to the right of the South Gate at Troy may have had a shrine on "sacred ground" guarding the city entrance, like the shrine inside a nearby flanking tower. Servius claims that the body of

Laomedon was buried over the Skaian Gate.[60] The potency of such burial may be inferred in Plautus when he comments that the fate of Troy was secure only so long as the image (the *signum* or Palladium) was not removed from the citadel, Troilus did not die, and the "upper lintel of the Phrygian Gate" (presumably Servius' Skaian Gate) was not torn away. (From this perspective, the Greeks would have made the Trojan Horse larger than the gate so that, when breaking the wall to maneuver the horse into the city, the Trojans would undo that magic.)[61]

After the Hittite and Trojan (Luvian?) civilizations were utterly destroyed c. 1200 B.C., urban settlements vanished in Anatolia for close to five hundred years. Ekrem Akurgal writes: "It is striking that up to date not only no Phrygian, but no cultural remains of any sort have been found which might belong to the period between 1200 and 800 B.C. This could indicate that Central Anatolia at that period was either very thinly populated or occupied by nomad tribes who left no material remains in the dwelling mounds. The results of Thracian invasion must have been altogether catastrophic if no urban settlements could be formed until the emergence of the Phrygian state about 750 B.C."[62]

Neo-Hittites, however, continued to flourish for another five hundred years in northern Syria, where they rebuilt the devastated cities of Charchemish, Malatya, etc., and built "new cities" like Zinjirli. The Assyrian influence on Neo-Hittites in urban design, as in art, is unmistakable. Once again, there is an inner and outer city, each massively walled, the former home of king and god. As in the older Hittite cities, however, lions rather than bulls flank gateways for both greater and outer walls. The particularly striking, perfectly circular walls at the new city of Zingirli suggest sacred circles and must undoubtedly be of magical significance.[63] Deioces' capital city of the Medes, Ecbatana, was built, as Herodotus describes it (I.101), with seven concentric circles painted white, black, red, blue, orange, silver, and gold progressively as one moves toward the royal palace and treasury in the innermost ring. The people had to build their houses outside the circuit of the seven walls. As with Mesopotamian cities, the whole city was magically protected and built in imitation of the heavens (Ecbatana presumably modeled on the circuits of the planets), and as in Mesopotamia, all attention is centered on the inner citadel where human and god meet.

To summarize: despite regional and national divergences, there appears to be considerable uniformity throughout the Near East across almost two millennia and in a variety of cultures, concerning the sacredness of walled, temple-oriented cities of sacred origin. Built by the gods, protected by a holy acropolis, secured at their outer boundaries by sacred walls and by invisible fields of magical force, the temple cities of the Near East seem to be of a common type. An annual sacred marriage between priestess or priest/king and the tutelary deity of the city, or the *purulli* festival between king and Hittite Weather God, magically ensured the earth's fertility and the city's plenty. Both literary sources and urban design testify to the theocratic and theocentric nature of these cultures and their view of sacred cities. As mortals approached the center of the city, they underwent a process of cleansing, moving increasingly toward the center of the cosmos, godhead, and sacred earth. In contrast to Eden, such pure earth was not lost to humankind in an irretrievable mythical past, but was experienced throughout the year in ritual and in the activities of civilization.

It seems equally clear that as one moves westward, the beliefs that originated among the Sumerians many hundreds of years earlier shift their focus. Although the Hittite king was considered the god's regent, the strong theocentric focus on inner house (with or without royal palace) of the Mesopotamian cities seems to become diffused as major temple centers at Hattusas are spread throughout the upper and lower city and are even located outside the city, linked by a sacred umbilical road. There also seems a Mesopotamian borrowing in Hittite magic connected with temple foundations, but the Hittite use of straight pegs rather than nails in the form of a deity abstracts and makes symbolic what was previously (frequently) representational. Similarly, the aniconic pillars at Troy are more referential than figurative, and the seven concentric walls of Ecbatana suggest a rhetorically expansive and highly schematized expression of the original Sumerian distinction between godhead and human being. But in spite of such changes, the overriding similarities of walled, temple-oriented cities and of holy, magically defended walls remains relatively constant. Throughout the Near East, the city's patron deity lends magic and purificatory powers to the walled enclosure of urban achievement.

Abbreviations

AA	*Archaölogischer Anzeiger*
AAnthung	*Acta Antiqua Academiae Scientiarum Hungaricae*
AJA	*American Journal of Archaeology*
AJP	*American Journal of Philology*
AIPhO	*Annuaire de l'Institut de Philologie et d'Histoire Orientales et Slaves de l'Université Libre de Bruxelles*
BCH	*Bulletin de Correspondance Hellénique*
BSA	*The British School at Athens, Annual*
CA	*Classical Antiquity*
CAH	*Cambridge Ancient History*
CJ	*Classical Journal*
CP	*Classical Philology*
CQ	*Classical Quarterly*
CR	*Classical Review*
CW	*Classical World*
DA	*Dissertation Abstracts*
GRBS	*Greek, Roman, and Byzantine Studies*
HSCP	*Harvard Studies in Classical Philology*
JFA	*Journal of Field Archaeology*
JHS	*Journal of Hellenic Studies*
JPh	*Journal of Philosophy*
LEC	*Les Études Classiques*
LSJ	H. G. Liddell, R. Scott, H. S. Jones, *A Greek-English Lexicon* 9th ed. (Oxford, 1968)
MH	*Museum Helveticum*
OJA	*Oxford Journal of Archaeology*
PMG	D. L. Page, *Poetae Melici Graeci* (Oxford, 1962)
PP	*Parola del Passato*
PRIA	*Proceedings of the Royal Irish Academy*

QUCC	Quaderni Urbinati di Cultura Classica
RE	Paulys Realencyclopädie der classischen Alterumswissenschaft
REG	Revue des Études Grecques
RFIC	Rivista di filologia e di istruzione classica
RhM	Rheinisches Museum für Philologie
RHR	Revue de l'Histoire des Religions
SMEA	Studi Micenei ed Ageo-Anatolici
SO	Symbolae Osloenses
TAPA	Transactions of the American Philological Association
VKNA	Verhandelingen der Koninklijke Nederlandse Akademie van Wetenschappen
WS	Weiner Studien
YCS	Yale Classical Studies

Notes

Introduction

1. W. G. Runciman, "Origins of States: The Case of Archaic Greece," *Comparative Studies in Society and History* 24 (1982), 351–77. All translations of Homer and other classical authors are mine, unless otherwise attributed.

2. Cf. A. A. Snodgrass, *Archaic Greece: The Age of Experiment* (London, 1980), 61. See below, Chapter 6.

1. Toward a Definition of the Polis in Homer

1. C. Blegen, *Troy and the Trojans* (New York, 1963), 13.

2. Priam's palace (*dōmos* and *megaron*) included fifty separate sleeping quarters, their walls made of smoothly worked stone. Many of Priam's sons, including presumably Hektor and his family, slept within the complex. Opposite the fifty chambers and through a court were twelve more chambers, also of polished stone, in which Priam's sons-in-law slept with his daughters.

3. See 7.344–46. Perhaps it was at this assembly (7.344ff.) or another like it (cf. 11.138–42) that Antimakhos, taking bribes from Alexander, spoke up in defense of Alexander (cf. 11.123–25).

4. In addition to Priam's palace and Alexander's residence, Deiphobus, another of Priam's sons, and later husband of Helen, is also said to have had a house (*dōmata*) of his own with several rooms. No other domestic dwellings at Troy are described.

5. For Athena's freestanding temple, a *nēos*, with its seated cult image of the "city-protecting deity," see 6.297–304. For Apollo's freestanding temple, also a nēos, with inner shrine (*aduton*), see 5.446–48 and 7.83. It is also "down from the highest part of the city" (*kat' akrotatēs polios*) that Ares yells encouragement to the Trojans (20.52).

6. *Kata* is often associated with downward motion and could imply here "down through."

7. Blegen, *Troy and the Trojans*, 16.

8. See C. Watkins, "The Language of the Trojans," in *Troy and the Trojan War* (proceedings of a symposium held at Bryn Mawr College, October 1984), ed. M. Mellink (Bryn Mawr, Pa., 1986), 58–59.

9. The term "village" is recorded on the Mycenaean tablets in the word *da-mo,* usually in the dative singular *paro damoi,* interpreted as meaning "from the village." There are also the terms *da-mo-de-mi* and *da-mo-ko-ro,* translated as "but the village says" and as a title for a village functionary; see M. Ventris and J. Chadwick, *Documents in Mycenaean Greek* 2d ed. (Cambridge, 1973), 254. In Homer, however, *dēmos* does not mean "village" but a well-defined "territory" and all the free "people" who inhabit it; see W. Donlan, "The Social Groups of Dark Age Greece," *CP* 80 (1985), 288–89. The word *kome* first appears in Greek literature, including the Linear B tablets, in "Hesiod's" *Shield* 18. See di G. Maddoli, *"Damos e Basilēes,* contributo allo studio delle origini della *polis,"* *SMEA* 12 (1970), 17–40, esp. 17–19 and 37–38. Also W. Hoffmann, "Die *Polis* bei Homer," in *Festschrift Bruno Snell,* ed. H. Erbse (Munich, 1956), 153. Finally, see W. Donlan, "Changes and Shifts in the Meaning of *dēmos* in the Literature of the Archaic Period," *PP* 25 (1970), 381–95.

10. Cf. J. V. Luce, "The *Polis* in Homer and Hesiod," *PRIA* 78 (1978), 8, who states that "the *polis* in Homer can cover different types of settlements from village to town to city. . . . Thucydides (1.8) is probably reflecting epic usage when he describes early Greece as consisting of 'unfortified *communities* dwelling in *villages*', a phrase which combines *polis* and *kome*" (emphasis his).

11. P. Chantraine, *Dictionnaire étymologique de la langue grecque, histoire des mots,* vol. 1 (Paris, 1968), 129–30, translates *astu* as "ville, agglomérat urbain"; for Chantraine's comments on *polis,* see vol. 3 (Paris, 1974), 926.

12. See D. R. Cole, "Astu and Polis: 'City' in Early Greek" (Ph.D. diss., Stanford University, 1976), *DA* 37 ([10 April] 1977), 6460A. See G. Glotz, *The Greek City and Its Institutions,* trans. N. Mallinson (New York, 1930), 10–12. J. Myres in *The Political Ideas of the Greeks* (New York, 1927), 67–72, esp. 72 n. 25, draws interesting distinctions between compounds with *polis* and *astu,* between "fortress" and "lord of a people in its homes."

13. E. Lévy, "*Astu et polis* dans l'*Iliade*," *Ktema* 8 (1983), 55–73.

14. J. Hurwit, *The Art and Culture of Early Greece, 1100–480 B.C.* (Ithaca, N.Y., 1985), 74.

15. In the *Iliad, polis* (and *ptolis*) appear one hundred thirty-two times, *astu* eighty-seven times, and *ptoliethron* only twenty-two; in the *Odyssey, polis* (and *ptolis*) appear one hundred and four times, *astu* forty-nine times, and *ptoliethron* only eight.

16. See P. Vidal-Naquet, "Land and Sacrifice in the *Odyssey:* A Study of Religious and Mythical Meanings," in *The Black Hunter,* trans. A. Szegedy-Maszak (Baltimore, 1986; originally *Le chasseur noir* [Paris, 1981]), 15–38, esp. 20–25). For the tendency to ignore the countryside in the arts and literature of the classical

period, see R. Osborne, *Classical Landscape with Figures: The Ancient Greek City and Its Countryside* (London, 1987), 16–21.

17. Vidal-Naquet, "Land and Sacrifice," 26.

18. Nausikaa deviates from this general tendency when she describes to Odysseus how to get from the outfields and farm plots (*agroi, erga*; 6.259) to the city of Scheria. In this transition she refers to her father's *temenos* and blooming orchard, "as far from the city as a person's voice will carry" (6.294). This *temenos* is part of a meadow that surrounds a grove of poplars sacred to Athena and a spring (just off the road to Scheria) (6.291–94). See W. Donlan, "Homeric *temenos* and the Land Economy of the Dark Age," *MH* 46 (1989), 130–31.

19. See S. Schein, *The Mortal Hero* (Berkeley, 1984), 73–76. William Sale, in private correspondence, has particularly stressed that most of the Trojans, perhaps with the exception of Hektor, had peacetime occupations prior to the war, and it is to him that I owe the reference to Lykaon in this context.

20. For an account of the thickly vegetated, uncultivated meadowlands along river banks in Homeric descriptions of horse and cattle grazing and of plains, see Donlan, "Homeric *temenos*," 136. See also, W. Richter, *Die Landwirtschaft im homerischen Zeitalter* (Göttingen, 1968), 41–43; cf. 107 (also cited by Donlan).

21. For the language of gods and men in Homer, see J. Clay, "Human and Divine Names in Homer," *Hermes* 100 (1972), 127–31 (and bibliography cited therein).

22. This is assuming that *thrōsmos pedioio* ("rising of the plain") corresponds with Kallikolone; see 10.159–61, 11.56–57, 21.1–3.

23. See *Il.* 8.489–90 and 560–63; 10.414–15; 11.369–72 and 497–99; 24.349–51. For B. Quiller, "The Dynamics of the Heroic Society," *SO* 56 (1981), 143, the tomb of Ilos, who was the son of Tros and mythical founder of Troy (20.216), "symbolizes Trojan sovereignty over the territory" (see 10.414–15), and it "shows the rise of hero-cult and the formation of polis society" because it is the place where Trojan leaders come together. For the action of the war shifting to the seashore "alternating between the defence of a besieged settlement and a contest at sea," see M. Lynn-George, *Epos: Word, Narrative, and the "Iliad"* (Atlantic Highlands, N.J., 1988), 262. From an archaeological perspective, the geological camp of the Troad suggests that the Achaean camp, if one ever existed, was located on the Aegean coastline at Besik Bay, not "on the Hellespont"; see G. Rapp, Jr., and J. A. Gifford, *Troy: The Archaeological Geology*, Suppl. Mono. No. 4 (Princeton, 1982), 3–5. See also M. Korfmann, "Troy: Topography and Navigation," and "Beşik Tepe: New Evidence for the Period of the Trojan Sixth and Seventh Settlements," in *Troy and the Trojan War* (note 8, above), 1–16 and 17–28, respectively.

24. On the other hand, many references to agricultural lands occur in the similes describing men in battle. See *Il.* 11.67–70; 11.555–64; 12.417–26; 13.701–8.

25. V. Ehrenberg, *The Greek State*, 2d ed. (New York, 1964), 94. For the difficulties of translating *polis* as "city-state," see R. Osborne, *Demos: The Discovery of Classical Attika* (Cambridge, 1985), 6–10, and M. I. Finley, *The Ancient Greeks* (New York, 1963), 37. See below, Chapter 4, note 1.

26. C. Thomas, "The Greek Polis," in *The City-State in Five Cultures*, ed. R.

Griffeth and C. Thomas (Santa Barbara, Calif., 1981), 43; see also her comments on Ehrenberg, 31. For Aristotle on the essential components of citizen body and territory, see *Pol.* 1325b40; also 1276a19ff. In considering the rise of the polis, Ian Morris makes an important distinction between "the rise of the city" and "the rise of the state." He defines the former "by its political, economic and social relationships to the surrounding countryside," while he describes the state (at least with a preliminary definition) as "a complex, permanently hierarchical social and political organisation, with formal offices of government"; see I. M. Morris, "The Early *Polis* as City and State," in *City and Country in the Ancient World*, ed. J. Rich and A. Wallace-Hadrill (London, forthcoming).

27. G. M. Calhoun, "Polity and Society: The Homeric Picture," in *A Companion to Homer*, ed. A. J. B. Wace and F. H. Stubbings (London, 1962), 432. Most scholars agree that the Homeric polis, if Ithaca is chosen as the model, is not yet a *state;* see, most recently, J. Halverson, "The Succession Issue in the *Odyssey,*" *Greece and Rome* 33 (1986), 119–28, and W. G. Runciman, "Origins of States: The Case of Archaic Greece," *Comparative Studies in Society and History* 24 (1982), 351–77. See also below, Chapter 4, note 7; Chapter 6, note 24; Chapter 7, notes 4–6 and 19. But some scholars, taking a broader perspective, observe correctly that in Homer and Hesiod the polis as an urban complex already exists in all essential aspects; see E. Lévy, "Lien personnel et titre royal: *ANAX* et *BASILEUS* dans l'*Iliade,*" in *Le système palatial en Orient, en Grèce et à Rome*, ed. E. Lévy (Strasbourg, 1987), 291–314; I. M. Morris, "The Use and Abuse of Homer," *CA* 5 (1986), 94–104; B. Quiller, "The Dynamics of Homeric Society," *SO* 56 (1981), 109–55; O. Murray, *Early Greece* (Sussex, 1980), 64–66; G. Nagy, *The Best of the Achaeans* (Baltimore, 1979), 116; see also below, Chapter 6, 239 notes 42–46.

28. For a similar definition of the polis in the fifth and fourth centuries expressed in much of the same language, see S. Benardete, "Leo Strauss, *The City and Man,*" *Political Science Reviewer* 5 (1978), 1–20.

2. The Sacred Polis

1. Homeric reference to the hestia (found only in the Ionic form, *histie*) is restricted to the *Odyssey* and to this formula (see 14.159 = 17.156 = 19.304 = 20.231). Attic forms, however, are evident in the compounds *ephestios* and *anestios*. Except for this formula, in Homer the word for hearth is *eskharē*. For the hearth, in addition to the altar and sacrificial pit, as a place of sacrifice, see W. Burkert, *Homo Necans: The Anthropology of Ancient Greek Sacrificial Ritual and Myth*, trans. P. Bing (Berkeley, 1983), 5 n. 20. On the double role of Hestia as both the virginal figure at the center of the house and as a mother-like source of life giving nourishment to the house, see J.-P. Vernant, *Myth and Thought among the Greeks* (name of translator not given) (London, 1983), 127–75. In *Greek Mythology and Poetics* (Ithaca, N.Y., 1990), 148 n. 21, G. Nagy points out *eskharē*, unlike *hestia*, is potentially movable.

2. Kirke's glens (*bēssae*) are sacred, we may imagine, because they are in the immediate vicinity of her dwelling (*Od.* 10.275). For the temple developing out of the "hearth-house," see H. Drerup, *Griechische Baukunst in geometrischer Zeit. Ar-*

chaeologica Homerica Kap. O (Göttingen, 1969), 123–28; see also Burkert, *Homo Necans,* 10 n. 43 and bibliography. A temple is called a god's oikos as well as domos; see Burkert, *Homo Necans,* 122 n. 33 and 215 n. 9.

3. J. T. Hooker, *Hieros in Early Greek,* Innsbrucker Beiträge zur Sprachwissenschaft 22 (Innsbruck, 1980), 7.

4. Ibid., 27.

5. *The Athenian Agora* (1983), 16. On the agora's religious significance, see G. E. M. de Ste. Croix, *The Origins of the Peloponnesian War* (Ithaca, N.Y., 1972), 267–84, esp. 271–72, and Appendix 43, 397–98. See, as well, R. Martin, *Recherches sur l'agora grecque* (Paris, 1951), 164–201, and R. Parker, *Miasma: Pollution and Purification in Early Greek Religion* (Oxford, 1983), 19 and 125. For the law barring those with unclean hands from entering the agora, see Demosthenes, *Against Timokrates* xxiv.60.

6. E. Benveniste, *Indo-European Language and Society,* trans. E. Palmer (Coral Gables, Fla., 1973), 461. For a full study of this question in regard to Rome, see my "Cities in Italy's Golden Age," *Numen* 35 (1988), 69–78.

7. W. Burkert, *Greek Religion,* trans. J. Raffan (Cambridge, Mass., 1985), 269; see also 17–18. Cf. Hooker, *Hieros in Early Greek;* A. Pagliaro, *Saggi di critica semantica,* 2d ed. (Florence, 1961), 93–124; U. von Wilamowitz-Moellendorff, *Der Glaube der Hellenen,* 2 vols. (Berlin, 1931), 1:21–22. All of these authors avoid the temptation, followed by many scholars, to find a double etymology for the word ("strong," following Vedic parallels, and later "sacred" or "pertaining to the god"). For the movement in the word between the civilized and the natural realms, but always with the presence of a god, see the excellent observations by J. Rudhardt, *Notions fondamentales de la pensée religieuse et actes constitutifs du culte dans la Grèce classique* (Geneva, 1958), 29–31. For further discussion of *hieros,* with bibliography, see M. Schmidt, "H(I)EROS," in *Thesaurus Linguae Graecae: Lexicon des frühgriechischen Epos,* ed. B. Snell (Göttingen, 1989), no. 13, 1138–45. For the difference between *hieros* and *hagnos* (both referring to realms of the sacred in archaic usage), see E. Williger, *Hagios: Untersuchungen zur Terminologie des Heiligen in den hellenisch-hellenistischen Religionem* (Giessen, 1922), and B. Gentili, *Poetry and Its Public in Ancient Greece,* trans. T. Cole (Baltimore, 1988), 217–20. Gentili summarizes well: *hagnos,* which inspires deep reverence and religious awe, "designates everything in the sacred which is disturbing and forbidden or taboo to man" (218). On the evolution of *hieros* from Mycenaean *ijero,* see note 13 below.

8. Benveniste, *Indo-European,* 461 (and generally 456–61).

9. Burkert, *Greek Religion,* 269.

10. Ibid., 272.

11. Benveniste, *Indo-European,* 460–61. This insistence on strict divisions of categories is even more surprising since it comes after an analysis of *hieros* and *theios* in Homer. The terminology for cities is further complicated by Pindar's *daimonion ptoliethron* describing Athens; see B. Snell, ed., *Pindari Carmina* (Leipzig, 1964), Frag. 76.

12. P. Wülfing–von Martitz, "*Hieros* bei Homer und in derältern griechischen Literatur," *Glotta* 38 (1960), 272–76. A scholiast does specify, at *Il.* 4.103, that Apollo was especially worshiped at Zeleia. Wülfing–von Martitz's work, it ap-

pears, influenced Burkert when he wrote that hieros "may be predicated of a city like Troy" (*Greek Religion*, 269), as if some, but not all, cities were sacred.

13. For the etymology of *hieros* from Mycenaen *i-je-ro*, see O. Szemerényi, "ETYMA GRAECA IV (22–29): Homerica et Mycenaica," *SMEA* fasc. XX (1979), 207–11. M. Doria argues, unconvincingly I believe, that Mycenaean Greek also attests the contracted form *hiros;* see "Testimonianze di *hiros* (= *hieros*) in Miceneo," *Kadmos* 19 (1980), 29–37. In *Les traits éoliens dans la langue de l'épopée grecque* (Rome, 1970), 356–57, P. Wathelet argues for the Aeolic origins of the contracted *hiros.* M. L. West in "The Rise of the Greek Epic," *JHS* 108 (1988), 163 (cf. 165) believes that *hiros* is proto-Aeolic, attested in Lesbian at a time "early enough to overlap with the last few decades of Troy VIIb2" (164), before becoming the Ionic *hieros* and *hiros.* Proto-Aeolic origins of this form are extremely unlikely since *hiros* is largely localized to Asia Minor. In "PROTI ILION HIRĒN," *Mnemosyne* 26 (1973), 387–90, R. S. P. Beekes says that the contracted form, found almost exclusively with Ilios in Homer, is an archaism from Old Lesbian, and "handed over to the Ionians," although he recognizes that "it cannot be wholly excluded that it [*hirē* with Ilios] was made at a late date" (both quotes from 389). Contrary to Beekes, D. G. Miller regards *proti* as Old Ionic, rather than Aeolic, in which case *proti Ilios hirēn* would not be the pure archaism Beekes claims it to be; see Miller, *Homer and the Ionian Epic Tradition* (Innsbruck, 1982), 139. R. Janko makes the interesting observation in *Homer, Hesiod, and the Hymns: Diachronic Development in Epic Diction* (Cambridge, 1982), x, that while *hiros* compared with *hieros* is used 36.1 percent of the time in the *Iliad* and 22.1 percent of the time in the *Odyssey*, it is not found in the rest of the epic corpus.

14. For small temple complexes near the perimeter wall of walled Mycenaean citadels, see C. Renfrew, *The Archaeology of Cult: The Sanctuary of Phylakopi*, British School of Archaeology at Athens Suppl. 18 (London, 1985), 398–413; B. Rutkowski, *The Cult Places of the Aegean* (New Haven, Conn., 1986), 169–99, 209, 232–33; G. Mylonas, *Mycenaean Religion: Temples, Altars, and Temenea*, Pragmateiai tes Akademias Athenon 39 (Athens, 1977), 92–94 and 124–27. The distinction between *polis* and *astu* is blurred somewhat in the last phase of Mycenaean Tiryns when citadel and lower town were both walled. Cult objects have been found in the walls surrounding the lower town. See Chapter 6, note 3.

15. For the Ionic form *neos*, see Miller, *Homer and the Ionian Epic Tradition*, 130; cf. F. Bechtel, *Die griechischen Dialekte* (Berlin, 1963), 3:47–48. For similar conclusions about Homeric Troy, see W. M. Sale, "The Formularity of Place-Phrases in the *Iliad*," *TAPA* 117 (1987), 38: "Such a city belongs to the eighth century or later."

16. See C. Bowra, "Homeric Epithets for Troy," *JHS* 80 (1960), 17. Archaeologists have unearthed temple precincts within "the city" of Hissarlik (Troy VIIa strata, commonly identified as the Troy of the Homeric poems), but a number of Mycenaean sites, such as Pylos, which are called sacred in Homer (both *ēgatheos* and *hieros*) show no evidence of special temple areas within the polis. From the Linear B tablets, it is clear, however, that Poseidon and a goddess (or goddesses), under the name Potnia, were of special importance at Pylos. Blegen, for example, identified a small room (3.10 by 3.40m) in the northeast *insula* of Nestor's palace as

a shrine with an altar where a tablet was discovered with the name Potnia Hippeia on it. Cf. C. W. Blegen and M. Rawson, *The Palace of Nestor at Pylos in Western Messenia* (Cincinnati, 1966), 305, and L. R. Palmer, *The Interpretation of Mycenaean Greek Texts* (Oxford, 1963), 226. There is no reason, however, to assume that the Homeric reference to the sanctity of these sites derives *necessarily* from Mycenaean origins. For further discussion and bibliography, see note 38 below.

17. T. E. Shaw, trans., *The "Odyssey" of Homer* (New York, 1932); cf. Hooker, *Hieros in Early Greek*, 7, and S. Schein, *The Mortal Hero: An Introduction to Homer's "Iliad"* (Berkeley, Calif., 1984), 170.

18. This appears to be W. B. Stanford's favored view, although he also acknowledges that city sanctity may derive from the city's temples: "*hieron:* here simply 'holy' with reference, perhaps, to its foundation by Poseidon and Apollo or else to its many temples." See his *"Odyssey" of Homer,* 2d ed. (London, 1959), at 1.2. Stanford here seems to imply that some cities are more sacred than others, or sacred for different reasons. Following a similar line of reasoning, Jan Kamerbeek offers this explanation for Sophocles' calling Athens hierai: "Often gods have built the walls and the town is under divine protection" (at *Ajax* 1221) (Leiden, 1953).

19. Cf. Burkert, *Homo Necans,* 3: "Sacrificial killing is the basic experience of the 'sacred'. *Homo religiosus* acts and attains self-awareness as *homo necans.*" Later in the same work, Burkert discusses the relation between sacrifice and community (37–38). For the association of *hieros* in the neuter plural (*hiera*) with sacrifice, see J. P. Locher, *Untersuchungen zu hieros hauptsachlich bei Homer* (Bern, 1963), 16–30, 33–36, and 64; cf. J. Casabona, *Recherches sur le vocabulaire des sacrifices en Grèc* (Aix-en-Provence, 1966), 5–7.

20. The relation between this story in Homer and that of Anchises and Aeneas in the Homeric *Hymn to Aphrodite* is hotly debated; see Burkert, *Greek Religion,* 154 (and 409 n. 26 for related bibliography). For the oriental associations of the myth, see Burkert's *Die orientalisierende Epoche in der griechischen Religion und Literatur* (Heidelberg, 1984), 93–94.

21. For general comments on this achievement, see O. Spengler, *The Decline of the West,* trans. C. F. Atkinson (New York, 1928), 91–94, and N. O. Brown, *Life against Death* (Middletown, Conn., 1970), 281–82. But see also C. Starr, "The Early Greek City-State," *PP* 12 (1957), 97–108.

22. L. Mumford, *The City in History* (New York, 1961), 37.

23. Cf. Callimachus' *Hymn to Zeus* (92–111), in which the god is particularly identified with the protection of cities. Zeus favored rulers of cities over sea captains, soldiers, or poets: "And so you chose them to sponsor, / gave them cities to guard, and took your position / in the high citadels, a monitor of judgments / straight and crooked, to see how they govern" (*Callimachos: Hymns, Epigrams, Select Fragments,* trans. S. Lombardo and D. Rayor [Baltimore, 1988]). Here Zeus is concerned more with preserving order within a city than with protecting the city from outside danger, but surely the principle is the same. Cf. Heraclitus, frag. 44: "the demos should fight for its laws as it does for its walls."

24. Comparative analysis of any kind must be handled with great care, but the importance of the Near East in understanding Greek religion as well as Homeric and Hesiodic epic has certainly not been lost on the profession. Such comparison is

part of a long and continuing tradition of Homeric scholarship that goes back to figures such as Jackson Knight, T. B. L. Webster, P. Walcot, and M. L. West among others. See, most recently, Burkert, *Die orientalisierende Epoche*, and Miller, *Homer and the Ionian Epic Tradition*, 16–21.

25. Translation is by E. A. Speiser in J. B. Pritchard, ed., *Ancient Near Eastern Texts (ANET)*, 3d ed. (Princeton, 1969), 73. Tablet I.9–15.

26. The first quote is from S. N. Kramer, trans., "Hymn to Enlil, the All-Beneficient," in *ANET*, 57, line 65, describing the Duranki or Eduranki, central temple at Nippur, city of the chief Sumerian god Enlil. The second is in G. Gragg, *The Kes Temple Hymn*, printed with A. Sjoberg and E. Bergmann, *The Collection of the Sumerian Temple Hymns* (Locust Valley, N.Y., 1969) (catalogued under Sjoberg).

27. Gragg, *Kes Temple Hymn*, Temple I, line 29.

28. Ibid., Temple II, lines 35–36.

29. M. Eliade, *Patterns in Comparative Religion*, trans. R. Sheed (New York, 1974), 376. See the useful summaries in T. Gaster, "Myth and Story," *Numen* 1 (1954), 184–212, esp. 191, as well as in P. Wheatley, *City as Symbol*, Inaugural Lecture, University College London, 20 November 1967 (London, 1969), 9.

30. Cf. L. L. Orlin, "Ancient Near Eastern Cities: Form, Function, and Idea," in Orlin, ed., *Janus: Essays in Ancient and Modern Studies* (Ann Arbor, 1975), 51.

31. Gragg, *Kes Temple Hymn*, Temple III, lines 58–59.

32. Cf. T. Jacobsen, *Toward the Image of Tammuz and Other Essays on Mesopotamian History and Culture*, ed. W. Moran (Cambridge, Mass., 1970), 379 n. 49, where different evidence is cited. In *The Harps That Once . . . : Sumerian Poetry in Translation* (New Haven, Conn., 1987), 436 n. 43, Jacobsen with little discussion rescinds this reading of *uru-kù*, feeling instead that all references to *uru-kù* are to the city Uru-kù in the Lagash region, called Sacred-City of Al Hibba (of Lagash?).

33. The Greek division of space between city and nature corresponds with Aristotle's division of the soul between an irrational lower part, motivated by corporeal appetites, common to animals and all living things, and a rational upper part, possessed with reason, shared by humankind and divinity alone. The upper portion of the soul can be awakened, or exercised, only when the person is *within* the *polis*, as it is only there that humanity can aspire toward the divine within (see *Nicomachean Ethics*, chap. 1. 1102a26ff. and chap. 10, passim).

34. Sjoberg and Bergmann, *Sumerian Temple Hymns*, Hymn 1, lines 11–13; cf. Gragg, Hymn 1, lines 6–9.

35. Even in small, quotidian rituals garlands have been seen in the larger sense of city sanctity; cf. Parker, *Miasma*, 153: "The garland marked with a certain sanctity many areas of Greek life outside the strictly religious sphere; the participants at dinner parties put one on, but certain public offices too were 'garland-wearing'. This last detail shows, as do the lustral stoups around the agora and the preliminary purification of the assembly, that the community itself was in a sense a sacred entity." For the association of garlands with sacrifice, see Burkert, *Greek Religion*, 56, 99, and 368 n. 5. For a modification of this initial interpretation of polis and veil, see above, page 33. Also see Chapter 5, note 5.

36. L. Muellner, *The Meaning of Homeric eukhomai through Its Formulas*, Innsbrucker Beiträge zur Sprachwissenschaft 13 (Innsbruck, 1976), 70, where he also

credits Nagy, lecture, 1969. Muellner dates this phenomenon to the Late Bronze Age, but the archaeological record more reasonably suggests a date ca. 700 B.C. for Athens and other cities in mainland Greece.

37. Mumford, *City in History*, 37.

38. Potnia is a title of honor used in the historical period chiefly when addressing females, whether goddesses or mortal women. As a substantive, it is frequently translated "lady," "mistress," or "queen"; as an adjective, it equals *timia*, "revered, august." (There is no masculine equivalent.) The word is of Mycenaean origins. Some scholars believe that the term on the Linear B tablets is generic and honorific for the five venerated Olympian goddesses: Hera, Athena, Demeter or Leto, Artemis, and Aphrodite. See J. C. van Leuven, "Mycenaean Goddesses Called Potnia," *Kadmos* 18 (1979), 112–29. Others think that there was one great nature goddess, derived from the mother goddess figure of Minoan religion, celebrated in several different capacities. Fur further discussion, see S. Hiller, "Mykenische Heiligtümer: Das Zeugnis der Linear B-Texte," in R. Hägg and N. Marinatos, eds., *Sanctuaries and Cults in the Aegean Bronze Age* (Stockholm, 1981), 95–125, esp. 109–25, and the general discussion of the participants at the conference, 210–11 and 215. See also O. Tsagarakis, *Nature and Background of Major Concepts of Divine Power in Homer* (Amsterdam, 1977), 93 n. 16.

39. In the classical period, Athena alone with her father shares the title *Polieus* (of the polis) as Athena Polias. See L. R. Farnell, *The Cults of the Greek States*, 5 vols. (Oxford, 1896), 1:293–94; see 52–64, 299, and 319, where the especially important cult of Athena Polias at Ilios is mentioned. Cf. M. P. Nilsson, *Geschichte der griechischen Religion*, 2d ed., 2 vols. (Munich, 1961), 2:433–37.

40. N. Loraux, *The Invention of Athens: The Funeral Oration in the Classical City*, trans. A. Sheridan (Cambridge, Mass., 1986), 128.

41. In other stories about Troy from the Greek archaic period, the city's invulnerability depends on the image of the small Pallas, or Palladion, remaining within her temple. See Apollodorus 3.143 and Dionysius of Halicarnassus *Ant. Rom.* 2.66; L. Ziehen, "Palladion," *RE*, 18, part 3, 171–89, and Burkert, *Greek Religion*, 140 and 404 n. 10.

42. Cf. Burkert, *Greek Religion*, 140: "As goddess of citadel and city she manifests herself in the evocative image of the armed maiden, valiant and untouchable; to conquer a city is to loosen her veils (see *Il.* 16.100)." The epithet "well-crowned" used both for the polis and for the heroine Mykene shows how the figure of a local tutelary goddess merges easily with the portrait of the polis itself. For the virginal nature of this goddess, see the Homeric *Hymn to Aphrodite* 5.7–15; M. Detienne, "Le Navire d'Athena," *RHR* 178 (1970), 137–38, comments that even in the agricultural realm, Athena's actions are more associated with technology than with fecundity.

43. M. Nagler, "Towards a Generative View of Oral Formula," *TAPA* 98 (1967), 279–80 and 298–311; see also his *Spontaneity and Tradition* (Berkeley, Calif., 1974), 44–55 and 64–111. See also Odysseus' statement that the Achaeans "loosed the shiny veil of Troy," *Od.* 13.388.

44. Nagler, "Towards a Generative View."

45. The role of male protector of the female veiled head can also be performed

by mortals; see *Hymn to Demeter* 151–52, "the men of Eleusis guard the krēdemna of the city." It is thought from both archaeological evidence and literary reference (see ibid., 270–72) that the Late Mycenaean acropolis at Eleusis was enclosed by a fortification wall. See J. N. Travlos, "The Topography of Eleusis," *Hesperia* 18 (1949), 138, and G. E. Mylonas, *Eleusis and the Eleusinian Mysteries* (Princeton, 1961), 33–34.

46. See, for example, such modest temple precincts at Ayria Irini on Keos (from the Middle Helladic period), at Mycenae itself (from Late Helladic IIIB), at Phylakopi on Melos (from the same period), and at Tiryns (from LH IIIC). According to one scholar: "It is highly likely that temples appeared fairly early in Greece, parallel with the development of the settlements." He continues that "on the Greek mainland the cult places in the citadels, villages and towns played a minor role in the lives of the inhabitants" (Rutkowski, *Cult Places of the Aegean*, 197 and 209, respectively; see 169–99 with bibliography). Also see Renfrew, *Archaeology of Cult*, 405–13.

47. Mylonas, *Mycenaean Religion*, 115, and his *Cult Center of Mycenae*, Pragmateiai tes Akademias Athenon 33 (Athens, 1972), 39–40. But see Renfrew, *Archaeology of Cult*, 432–33.

48. Cf. M. P. Nilsson, *Minoan-Mycenaean Religion*, 2d ed. (Lund, 1968), 406–12 and 491–501; cf. Burkert, *Greek Religion*, 140 and 362 n. 46. In addition to the comments of Renfrew and Mylonas (see notes 46 and 47), for criticism of Nilsson's "household goddess" theory, see J. C. van Leuvan, "Problems and Methods of Pre-Hellenic *naology*," in Hägg and Marinatos, eds., *Sanctuaries and Cults in the Aegean Bronze Age*, 11–25.

49. For Ishtar, see M. T. Barrelet, "Les déesses armées et ailées: Inanna/Ishtar," *Syria* 32 (1955), 222–60; for Anat/Athena, see R. du Mesnil du Buisson, *Nouvelles études sur les dieux et les mythes du Canaan* (Paris, 1973), 48–55.

50. See Farnell on Kybele: " The Phrygian goddess who rides on the lion has her counterpart in the Babylonian-Assyrian religion; the armed Cappadocian Ma—the mother goddess, a divinity of like nature with Cybele, is a type that recalls the armed Astarte of Ascalon; . . . as the Semitic goddess was the tutelary genius of cities, so Cybele came to wear the turreted crown" (*Cults of the Greek States*, 2:644; see 3:288–302, for a connection between this figure and Rhea). Also see the testimonia of Kybele as tutelary goddess in C. Cadoux, *Ancient Smyrna* (Oxford, 1938), 24–25 and 214–21.

51. These include Miletos, Kolophon, Ephesus, Priene, Erythrai, Klazomenai, Phokaia, and Old Smyrna. See E. Akurgal, *Ancient Civilizations and the Ruins of Turkey* (Istanbul, 1983).

52. Farnell, *Cults of the Greek States*, 4:161. For more about Apollo and city walls, see Chapter 3.

53. See Burkert, *Greek Religion*, 144–46 (with relevant bibliography).

54. The first is to a cult at Sminthe, a polis in the Troad where Apollo was especially worshiped, the second to a cult of Zeus (and not Apollo) among the Carians. In addition to Apollo's presence at Troy itself, sacred Killa in the Troad, according to Khryses, is under Apollo's protection, as is Khryses' own cult center,

Khryse. Apollo's epithet *Lykegenes,* wolf-born, may equally derive from a regional affiliation of the god with the Trojan Lycia under Mount Ida.

55. For Aphrodite's affiliations with cities and with Ishtar/Astarte, see Farnell, *Cults of the Greek States,* vol. 2; Nilsson, *Geschichte der griechischen Religion,* 2:520f; Burkert, *Greek Religion,* 152–56; F. Laumonier, *Les cultes indigènes de Carie* (Paris, 1958), 482–500; P. Friedrich, *The Meaning of Aphrodite* (Chicago, 1978).

56. Cf. V. Scully, *The Earth, the Temple, and the Gods* (New Haven, 1962), 21–22; see also notes 23 and 49 above. Does Hera's regional affiliation with the Argolid (see Callimachus, *Hymn to Delos:* "but Leto avoided Sikyon and Argos since these lands were Hera's," 1.75–76) similarly contribute to her passionate defense of the Argives? Cf. Pindar, *Nemean* 10.2.

57. See Rotkowski, *Cult Places of the Aegean,* 220.

58. See F. G. Maier, "Torgötter," in *Eranion,* Festschrift für Hildebrecht Hommel, ed. J. Kroyman (Tubingen, 1961), 93–104, and C. A. Faraone, "Hephaestus the Magician and Near Eastern Parallels for Alcinbus' Watchdogs," *GRBS* 28 (1987), 266–75. Several Greek cities in the historical period claimed to possess the Trojan Palladion. The most notable of these were Argos and Athens, but to this list we must add the city of Heraclea in Lucania, not to mention Roman claims at Lavinium in Latium and at Luceria in Apulia. Cf. Sir James Frazer, ed., *Publii Ovidi Nasonis, Fastorum Libri Sex,* 5 vols. (London, 1962), 4:258–65. For comment on a wide variety of magical beliefs documented from Homer to the end of antiquity, see G. E. R. Lloyd, *Magic, Reason, and Experience* (Cambridge, 1979), 1–5, 29–32, including 29 n. 98.

59. W. F. Jackson Knight, *Vergil: Epic and Anthropology* (London, 1967), 109–10, 113–15, 210–11. Virgil may have been expressing similar views when he says, with some surrealism, that "the fatal [Trojan] horse went with a leap over steep Pergamon" (*super ardua . . . Pergama; A.*6.515–16). Knight further suggested that the wall's circular shape, as a perfect form, had magical powers; compare F. Robert, *Thymélè* (Paris, 1939), for holy circles in religious architecture in Greece, and E. Neumann, *The Origins and History of Consciousness,* trans. R. F. C. Hull (New York, 1954), chap. 1 on the Ouroboros.

60. Burkert, *Homo Necans,* 158–60.

61. For a different interpretation of the circling around Troy, see W. R. Platon, "The Dragging of Hector," *CR* 27 (1913), 45–47.

62. See Knight, *Vergil,* 124. The unique use of the participle in this description, *astu periplomenon,* meaning "going around the city," may support the interpretation that the music from the trumpet, like the enemy, encircles the town. For the discussion of music in the context of Greek wall construction, see Chapter 3. In the the historical period in Greece, we know that flute players accompanied the demolition of the "Long Walls" at Athens in 404 B.C. The use of music in this event may contain a reference to ritual practice in the desecration of walls or, as Xenophon explains, it may merely express the spirit of jubilation for the day of freedom in Greece (*Hellenica* 2.2.23).

63. For the elaborate Hittite rituals involved with this practice, see Goetze, "Evocatio," in *ANET,* 351–53. For Roman practice, thought to derive from

Etruscan ritual, see Livy 5.21 and R. M. Ogilvie, *A Commentary on Livy Books 1–5* (Oxford, 1965), 674–77.

64. See J. Cooper, *Curse of Agade* (Baltimore, 1983); S. Kramer, *Lamentation over the Destruction of Ur* (Chicago, 1940), lines 162–64; C. J. Gadd, *Ur Excavation Texts, Literary and Religious Texts* 6 (London, 1963), pt. 2, nos. 124–34. See also T. Jacobsen, *The Treasures of Darkness: A History of Mesopotamian Religion* (New Haven, 1976), 89–91, and his *Toward an Image of Tammuz*, 43–44, 168–69, and 331–32 n. 24. Cf. M. Green, "Eridu in Sumerian Literature" (Ph.D. diss., University of Chicago, 1975), 277–374, esp. 304–10.

65. To this list of magical events, we should add Erichthonios' mares that dance over ears of corn and the waves of the sea (20.226–29). Because of such evidence, one cannot simply say, as J. Griffin ("The Epic Cycle and the Uniqueness of Homer," *JHS* 97 [1977] 41) and others do, that all magical scenes are alien to Homeric narration.

66. Cf. Dionysius of Halicarnassus *Ant. Rom.* 2.69.3. See Griffin, "Epic Cycle," 40 and 46; cf. *Iliou Persis*, frag. 1.

67. Such violation of a wall is not limited to the Trojans in the *Iliad*. The weakness of the Achaean wall at Troy, otherwise arrēktos, can be ascribed among other reasons to the impiety of the Greeks when they, equally surprisingly, neglect to perform sacrifices to the gods when building that structure.

68. Cf. Schein, *Mortal Hero*, 21, who also notes that the Antenor scene in Book 7 effectively calls to mind the beginning of the war nine years prior to the present action.

69. For the defense of *atē* (instead of *archēs*), questioned in antiquity, see T. C. W. Stinton, *Euripides and the Judgement of Paris*, Society for the Promotion of Hellenic Studies Suppl. No. 11 (London, 1965), 72. For the meaning of *atē*, see W. S. Barrett, *Euripides: Hippolytos* (Oxford, 1964), at 241. Against those who claim that Homer was unaware of Paris' judgment, see K. Reinhardt, "Das Parisurteil," now in *Tradition und Geist* (Göttingen, 1960), 16–36. M. Davies, "The Judgement of Paris and *Iliad* XXIV," *JHS* 101 (1981–82), 56–62, argues that, unlike the mortals Achilles and Priam, the gods (Athena, Hera, Poseidon), seen in their "malicious and unforgiving aspects," cannot learn to forgive (60). The fate of Troy, however, has been sealed long before this moment; its annihilation, though deferred, is prefigured in Hektor's circling of Troy, his death, and the *threnos* that follows. See also Chapter 8, note 22.

70. Drawing a distinction between *philoi* and *alloi*, M. Nagler, "Towards a Semantics of Ancient Conflict: Eris in the *Iliad*," *CW* 82 (1988), 87, comments that Hera, like the other gods in the Olympian council, sees human cities as "other" "for the purposes of drawing off *neikos* from that of the gods."

3. The Walled Polis

1. The walls of Pheia are mentioned only once (by Nestor at 7.135); the walls of Kalydon are mentioned only in Book 9 (by Phoinix); the walls of Thebes in Egypt only once (by Achilles in Book 9); Tiryns and Gortyna are called walled

(*teikhioessa*) only in the Greek Catalogue of Book 2, the only place in the *Iliad* where that epithet appears.

2. If Homer does not mention the walls of Mycenae or Athens directly, perhaps they may be inferred from the formula *euktimenon ptoliethron* in the Greek Catalogue of Book 2.

3. P. Vivante, *The Epithets in Homer: A Study in Poetic Values* (New Haven, 1982).

4. M. Arthur, "The Divided World of *Iliad* VI," in *Reflections of Women in Antiquity,* ed. H. Foley (New York, 1981), 31. For further discussion of this article and of Book 6, see Chapter 4.

5. For weaving as a "worthy archetype of the poetic craft" in the words of the scholia, see most recently G. Kennedy, "Helen's Web Unraveled," *Arethusa* 19 (1986), 5–14; cf. A. Bergren, "Helen's Web: Time and Tableau in the *Iliad,*" *Helios* 7 (1979), 19–34; L. L. Clader, *Helen: The Evolution from Divine to Heroic in Greek Epic Tradition* (Leiden, 1976), 6–11; B. Peabody, *The Winged Word* (Albany, N.Y., 1975), 82–83.

6. Many have noticed that such a duel belongs more appropriately in the first year of the Trojan war, rather than in the ninth. But A. Bergren (see note 5, above) argues that this scene is neither an epic mistake nor a violation of chronology, since, like other scenes in the *Iliad,* it creates a sense of epic timelessness. Also see C. Whitman, *Homer and the Homeric Tradition* (Cambridge, Mass., 1958), 264–68. M. Lynn-George in *Epos: Word, Narrative, and the "Iliad"* (Atlantic Highlands, N.J., 1988), 27–37, commenting on all of Book 3, observes a deliberate narrative "indeterminacy" in which the shrouded, distant past is framed within events seen as if for the first time, in which the already experienced is entwined within the just now observed. For Lynn-George's views on the metaphor of language as weaving, what he calls the "braided word," see 103–4. On Helen and Priam, see M. Edwards, *Homer, the Poet of the "Iliad"* (Baltimore, 1987), 191–95.

7. For the political connotations of this scene, see K. Rauflaub, "Homer and the Beginning of Political Thought in Greece," in *Proceedings of the Boston Area Colloquium Series in Ancient Philosophy* 4 (1988), 1–25. That the Trojans recognize the illegitimacy of Alexander's claim over Helen, see K. J. Atchity, "The Message of Idaios: Formulaic Departure?" *CP* 68 (1973), 297. (See, in addition, Chapter 4, note 14.)

8. This tendency in Homeric depiction of siege warfare is not fully consonant with the many Mycenaean portraits of siege warfare seen on frescoes and the famous silver rhyton. As in the Homeric scenes at Troy, in Mycenaean art women (not children) take an active interest in the course of battle and seem to have a clear role in the story; their portrayal in art is perhaps the visual equivalent to the oft-repeated Homeric formula "fighting on behalf of the women and children." Unlike Homeric portrayal, however, Mycenaean art depicts ladies observing the war both from the walls *and* from the palace windows. For discussion and illustration of Mycenaean scenes of siege warfare, see T. B. L. Webster, *From Mycenae to Homer* (New York, 1964), 58–61, and Sir Arthur Evans, *Palace of Minos* (London, 1930), 3:81–106. S. Schein observes in *The Mortal Hero* (Berkeley, Calif., 1984), 189, that as Cassandra is the first traditionally to see the fall of Troy in her visions so here she

is the first to catch sight of the returning Hektor, whose death foretells the city's doom.

9. Cf. Hektor who, rebuking Alexander, says that the Trojans "are falling in action round the town and the steep walls" (6.327–28); cf. 9.352–55.

10. In Book 6, Andromache refers to an attack earlier in the war when the best of the Achaeans (Achilles not mentioned among them) tried to scale the wall at its weakest point (cf. 6.435–37). In the *Cypria* a *teikhomakhia* is mentioned shortly after the Greeks arrived.

11. For a discussion of Scheria as existing between "mythical" and "real" worlds, see C. Segal, "The Phaeacians and the Symbolism of Odysseus' Return," *Arion* 1 (1962), 17–63; cf. P. Vidal-Naquet, "Land and Sacrifice in the *Odyssey*," in his *The Black Hunter,* trans. A. Szegedy-Maszak (Baltimore, 1986), 26–30.

12. See W. B. Stanford, ed., *The "Odyssey" of Homer,* 2 vols. (New York, 1967), 1 at 6.9. Although the economy of the Homeric polis was primarily an agrarian one dependent on its adjoining farmlands, this is the only reference in Homer to a division of lands associated with the founding of a polis. M. I. Finley, "Homer and Mycenae: Property and Tenure," *Historia* 6 (1957), 136, believes that the practice is contemporary with Ionian colonization rather than a remembrance inherited through the oral tradition. For the agrarian economy of early Greek cities, see Finley, *Early Greece: The Bronze and Archaic Ages* (London, 1970), 91. For the unit of town and country in the classical period, see Aristotle, *Pol.* 1252b29.

13. E. Braun, "The Poet of the *Odyssey*," *The College* (St. John's College, Annapolis, Maryland) 26 (April 1974), 5. Also see S. Bassett, *The Poetry of Homer* (Berkeley, 1938), 91.

14. Aeneas' use of this verb in the perfect when describing the founding of Troy equally implies a city wall (*Il.* 20.217).

15. For a similar phrase about the Achaean wall, see *khthamalōtaton* ("nearest to the ground"), found in the narrative at 13.683–84. When referring to the attack on Thebes by the Epigonoi, Sthenelos similarly discusses architectural or engineering weak points in city defenses: "we even took the seat of Thebes, seven-gated, / although we were a smaller force under a stronger wall" (*hupo teikhos areion*), 4.406–7. The scholia consider the comparative *areion* as referring to a wall stronger than the one the Achaeans are now facing (cf. the same phrase at 15.736), but it is equally possible that the phrase here refers to a stronger wall than the one the fathers of the Epigoni found at Thebes. Others, improperly, understand the adjective as meaning "belonging to Ares." The comparative speaks directly to the relative strength and weakness of all human construction.

16. For the sanctity of city walls, see Chapter 2, above. The wall made of bronze enclosing King Aeolus' island is not "sacred" but it is "unbreakable" (*arrēktos, Od.* 10.2–3), as is the Achaean, otherwise unloved by the Olympians (*Il.* 14.53–54). Agamemnon suggests that this quality of the Greek wall derived less from human *tekhnē* than from divine providence: the Greeks had hoped that with their work "the wall would be an unbreakable defense for their ships and for them but it was to be dear to Zeus that the Achaeans were to be destroyed here far from Argos" (14.66–70; cf. 14.55–56). Gatekeepers of the Achaean wall are, again also generically, called "sacred" (*Il.* 24.681). (All applications of the epithet *arrēktos* in regard

to things of the human world, i.e., city, defensive wall, or bard's voice, are found in contrary-to-fact environments. The same is true of the reference to gatekeepers as sacred.)

17. M. Eliade, *Patterns in Comparative Religion*, trans. R. Sheed (New York, 1974), 371.

18. R. Wycherley, *The Stones of Athens* (Princeton, 1978), 18. P. Wülfing-v. Martitz, by contrast, identifies the sacredness of city walls with the shelter and invulnerability it offers to those within; see his "*Hieros* bei Homer und in derälteren griechischen Literatur," *Glotta* 38 (1960), 287.

19. As noted in the previous chapter, Poseidon's construction is usually ignored by the heroes in the *Iliad*. There is only one exception to this rule. Wanting to camp in the plain for the night, Hektor advises his heralds: "Summon the young lads and the grey-haired old men to bivouac through the city on the walls built by the gods. Let the women build a great fire in every home, and post a guard lest the enemy steal into the city while the host is way" (8.517–22). *Theodmēton*, "built by the gods" (compare the more common *eudmēton*, "well-built"), occurs only here in Homer and may convey a confidence that the gods with the aid of young lads, old men, and household fires will keep the city of Troy, although unmanned, secure for the night. For the epithet *theodmētoi* describing Athens, see Soph. *El.* 707 and Eur. *Hipp.* 974.

20. L. R. Farnell, *The Cults of the Greek States*, 5 vols. (Oxford, 1907), 4:11; cf. p. 14. Also see his *Critical Commentary to the Works of Pindar* (1932; reprint Amsterdam, 1965), at *Olympian* 8.30–51.

21. For the many parallels in the divine origins of these two cities, see W. R. Halliday, "The Cults of Hector at Thebes and Achilles at Tanagra," *Annals of Archaeology and Anthropology at Liverpool* 11 (1924), 3–24, esp. 3–6; cf. W. F. J. Knight, *Vergil: Epic and Anthropology* (London, 1967), 219, 221, 292–93, 301; and G. R. Levy, *The Gate of Horn: A Study of the Religious Conceptions of the Stone Age, and Their Influences upon European Thought* (London, 1948), 249–54.

22. The Kyklopes, descended from Ouranos and Ge in Hesiod, exhibit a similar duality. If Polyphemos, fathered by Poseidon, is the paradigm of precivilization in the *Odyssey*, the Kyklopes in the later tradition were assistants in Hephaistos' smithery and considered the builders of the ancient Mycenaean walls.

23. Cf. a third-century B.C. inscription, *Inscriptions de Delos*, ed. F. Durrbach (Paris, 1926), 290.116. At Sparta, Poseidon was worshiped as *domatites*, "builder of the house" (in the late Roman period; cf. *C16* 1446), a title Apollo enjoyed at Aegina (cf. Paus. 3.14.7). In the *Theogony* (1.733), he builds the bronze gates for the wall that holds the Titans in Tartarus.

24. Cf. Plutarch, *Thes.* 6. The worship of Poseidon in Trozen was undoubtedly connected with the stories of his fathering Trozenian hero Theseus. Poseidon was also Father at Eleusis, and the descendants of Hellen sacrificed to him as *patrigeneios*. For references, see L. R. Farnell, *Cults of the Greek States*, 4:9–12. Also see his role in Plato's account of Atlantis, *Critias* 113Cff., especially in regard to making it well-defended.

25. See Knight, *Vergil*, 114. M. Detienne finds similar distinctions between the civilizing tendencies of Athena and the cruder *tekhnē* of Poseidon in regard to their

jurisdiction over the horse; see "Athena and the Mastery of the Horse," *History of Religions* 11 (1971), 161–84.

26. Farnell, *Cults of the Greek States*, 4:161.

27. *Hymn to Apollo* 55–57. For a chorus of Thebans represented as if they were rebuilding the walls of Thebes, see G. Nagy, *Pindar's Homer* (Baltimore, 1990), 145 and n. 45. The making of songs and hymns is also commonly associated with weaving (cf. Bacchylides 5.9). The connection between song and foundation on the one hand and song and weaving on the other may show how weaving became associated with the city foundation as well as demonstrate how song could be regarded as the magic that binds the stones of the city's circumvallation. For a survey of the weave metaphor, see R. Schmitt, *Dichtung und Dichtersprache in indogermanischer Zeit* (Wiesbaden, 1967), 300–301. For more on this much-discussed relation between song and weaving, see (in addition to the works cited in note 5, above): I. D. Jenkins, "The Ambiguity of Greek Textiles," *Arethusa* 18 (1985), 109–32; P. de Man, *Blindness and Insight: Essays in the Rhetoric of Contemporary Criticism*, 2d ed. (Minneapolis, 1983), 17; J. M. Snyder, "The Web of Song: Weaving Imagery in Homer and the Lyric Poets," *CJ* 76 (1981), 193–96.

28. The Achaean wall, though never called sacred, equals the Trojan wall at least in its epithet *arrēktos*. (See note 16, above.) Apollo, of course, only intends to prevent Troy from falling before its time; his divine intervention delays a destruction that is already divinely determined and repeatedly anticipated in the epic. About such narrative indeterminacy, in Lynn-George's words (see note 6 above): "The *Iliad* suggests that that which is not narrated as a present event, the immediate destruction of a city, is nevertheless already indefinitely present" (224).

4. The People of the Polis

1. In commenting on the abstract nature of the Greek polis, E. Benveniste notes that politēs (citizen) is subordinated to polis, whereas in Latin, to the contrary, it is the *civis* (citizen) who gives definition to the *civitas* (state); cf. "Deux modèles linguistiques de la cité," originally in *Echanges et communications: Mélanges offerts à Claude Lévi-Strauss* (The Hague, 1970), 589–96, now reprinted in *Problèmes de linguistique générale*, 2 vols. (Paris, 1974), 2:272–80, esp. 278–80. For the tendency in fifth-century literature to see the polis in abstract terms, see D. Lanza and M. Vegetti, "L'ideologia della città," *Quaderni di Storia* 2 (1975), 1–37, esp. 20 and 27; J. Stambaugh, "The Idea of the City: Three Views of Athens," *CJ* 69 (1974), 309–19; B. M. W. Knox, *Oedipus at Thebes* (New Haven, 1957), 160–61.

2. N. Loraux, *The Invention of Athens: The Funeral Oration in the Classical City*, trans. A. Sheridan (Cambridge, Mass., 1986), passim, esp. 78–79, 264–87, and 328–38. See also A. Parry, "Thucydides' Use of Abstract Language," *Yale French Review* 54 (1970), 3–20, esp. 14, and H. R. Immerwahr, "Ergon: History as a Monument in Herodotus and Thucydides," *AJP* 81 (1960), 261–90, esp. 285–90.

3. See *Il.* 4.234–39.

4. *Il.* 21.583–89; translation by E. V. Rieu, *The Iliad* (New York, 1950).

5. G. Vlachos, *Les sociétés politiques homériques* (Paris, 1974), 66; cf. G. Nagy, *The Best of the Achaeans* (Baltimore, 1979), 116.

6. M. Austin and P. Vidal-Naquet, *Les èconomies et sociétés en Grèce ancienne* (Paris, 1972), 54 = *Economic and Social History of Ancient Greece: An Introduction*, trans. and rev. M. Austin (Berkeley, Calif., 1977).

7. See W. G. Runciman, "Origins of States: The Case of Archaic Greece," *Comparative Studies in Society and History* 24 (1982), 351–77, esp. 335–73; J. Halverson, "Social Order in the *Odyssey*," *Hermes* 113 (1985), 129–45. Also see Austin and Vidal-Naquet, ibid., 53, and G. M. Calhoun, "Polity and Society: The Homeric Picture," in *A Companion to Homer*, ed. A. J. B. Wace and F. H. Stubbings (London, 1962), 434. (See below, Chapter 7.)

8. See A. Andrewes, "Phratries in Homer," *Hermes* 89 (1961), 134–37, who discusses it together with *hetairos*. See also W. Donlan, "The Social Groups of Dark Age Greece," *CP* 80 (1985), 300–301; cf. H. Gates, *The Kinship Terminology of Homeric Greek* (Baltimore, 1971), 28–31.

9. Cf. E. Benveniste, note 1, above.

10. Sir John Myres, *The Political Ideas of the Greeks* (New York, 1927), 70. For *laos* evolving into a synonym for *dēmos*, see Donlan, "The Social Groups of Dark Age Greece," 299.

11. See G. Redard, *Les noms grecs en -tes, -tis* (Paris, 1949), 20–33; P. Chantraine, *La formation des noms en grec ancien* (Paris, 1933), 311; C. D. Buck, *The Comparative Grammar of Greek and Latin* (Chicago, 1933), 336.

12. A survey of various lexica indicates the following: *LSJ*, "citizen"; Cunliffe, "the dwellers in a town or city, citizens"; Ebeling, "*incolas urbis*, the *Landsleute*" (with less of a political connotation than Cunliffe or *LSJ);* cf. Calhoun, "Polity and Society," 433.

13. See 22.515 = 24.746. The same phrase at 24.746 describes women who mourn after men began a dirge; compare 23.1 where we hear that "they (gender unspecified) mourned through the city." The same formula as 22.515 describes women mourning Patroklos (19.301); a similar formula describes Achaean chieftains: *epi de stenakhonto gerontes* (19.338).

14. The political order of Troy, mostly ignored by Homer, is certainly dynastic. As Priam's claim to the throne goes back to Dardanos, founder of Dardania, so he is in the position to pass it on to Hektor, and Hektor to Astyanax. But this dynastic rule does not also mean that Priam rules Troy alone. On one occasion the narrator describes how the young and old, all assembled together, gathered for a conference (*agoras agoreuon*) at Priam's door (2.788–89), and on another he describes a gathering of Trojans (*Trōōn agora*) who meet on the acropolis in front of Priam's palace to discuss the possible return of Helen (7.345–46). Unlike Agamemnon in Book 1, Priam proves to be an exemplary leader in this debate. Mediating between Antenor speaking for the people and Alexander expressing narrow self-interest, he convinces the two parties, and the Trojans, to follow his advice. "Well-minded toward them both" (7.367), as Nestor was when mediating between Achilles and Agamemnon (1.253), Priam succeeds because of his power of persuasion more than because of an expressed regal authority, as is seen in the public reception of Priam's

speech: "Priam's advice was very well received, and they [the people] were per-suaded" (*hoi d'ara tou mala men kluon, ēde pithonto,* 7.379). (For the persuasive powers of a king's words, see Hesiod, *Theogony,* 89–93.) For some of the political connotations of this scene, see K. Rauflaub, "Homer and the Beginning of Political Thought in Greece," in *Proceedings of the Boston Area Colloquium Series in Ancient Philosophy* 4 (1988), 1–25. About Trojans who sided with Alexander in this debate (cf. *Il.* 11.123–25) and about Priam's political authority, W. M. Sale writes: "Troy is a *polis,* governed not by Priam alone but by the elders, *dēmogerontes,* the bribery of one of whom, Antimachus, made it possible for Paris to keep Helen and neces-sary for Troy to go to war (*Iliad* 11.125)," in "The Formularity of the Place-Phrases in the *Iliad,*" *TAPA* 117 (1987), 38. (See Chapter 3, note 7, above.)

15. References to "the city of Trojans" are less frequent and are found at fewer places within the line:

Position	Phrase	Number of occurrences
Middle of the second foot	*Trōōn te polis*	1
	Trōōn te polin	2
	Trōōn de polis . . . pasa	1
After first short of second foot	*polin (perthai) Trōōn agerōkhon*	1
Middle of the third foot	*Trōōn polin*	3
	Trōōn polin euruaguian	1
	Trōōn eis astu alenton	1
	TOTAL	10

Juxtaposed with the single example of *Priamou polis euruaguia* (*Od.* 22.230) is *Trōōn polin euruaguian* (*Il.* 14.88), each appearing only once. Denys Page (*History and the Homeric "Iliad"* [Berkeley, Calif., 1959], 294) labels the former "antitraditional," and he well may be right, but precedent for substitution of Priam for Troy is certainly not uncommon and the form *Priamou* is hardly uncommon itself. Also see Chapter 5, note 5.

16. For a late sixth-century reference to the polis itself in the first-person plural (i.e., "we, the polis"), see H. Van Effenterre, "Le contrat de travail de scribe Spensithios," *BCH* 97 (1973), 31–46; cf. Loraux, *The Invention of Athens,* 282–84. This unusual expression, both authors argue, suggests an unusual equivalence between the polis and the community of inhabitants. In Homer, one might com-pare the phrase "the whole polis of the Trojans, filled with courage, went out [against us]" (*Trōōn polis . . . pasa . . . tharsunos, Il.* 16.69–70). Hektor also speaks of "my city" (*polin amēn*): "Patroklos, you thought to destroy my city and to take away the Trojan women" (*Il.* 16.830), phrasing which suggests again the strong equivalence between polis and polis inhabitant.

17. The narrator attempts to equate warriors outside Priam's family with those within the house when he says that Deikoon was honored by the Trojans as though equal with the sons of Priam, 5.535. Also see the reference to the leaving of Helen behind as a boast to Priam and the Trojans (2.160, 176 and 4.175). Here an *oikos*-related problem is cast in a polis setting.

18. For the last quote, see E. Lobel and D. Page, eds., *Poetarum Lesbiorum Fragmenta* (Oxford, 1955), Z 103; for the Alcaeus quote above, see *Poetarum Lesbiorum Fragmenta*, E 1.10. Compare Xenophon when in the *Memorabilia* (3.5.27) Socrates asks Pericles whether he does not think that the young Athenians, lightly armed, living in the mountains, would be a harm to the enemy and a great bulwark (*megalēn probolēn*) to our citizens; compare Sophocles, *Oedipus Tyrannos* 56–57. For the notion that a city is where "you settle yourselves" (*kathezesthe*), see Nicias' statement to the Athenian troops in Sicily (Thuc. 7.77.4), itself reminiscent of Pericles' famous statement that Athens is not a city of houses but a city of men (Thuc. 1.143.5).

19. Occasionally texts discuss human valor and walled defense working in conjunction with each other. Euripides in the *Hekabe* (1208–10), for example, remembers the time when Troy was well off, its rampart (purgos) ran around the city, Priam was alive, and Hektor was flourishing with spear. We hear that without great men, the weak (*smikroi*) are a perilous defense of the rampart (purgos), i.e., of the polis (Sophocles, *Ajax* 158–59). The opposite sentiment may equally be expressed: Themistokles argues that a guard of a few men, even those who are most weak, is sufficient if they can fight behind a wall (Thuc. 1.93.6).

20. Plato, *Laws* 778e–79a, trans. R. G. Bury (Cambridge, Mass., 1926); cf. Aristotle, *Pol.* 1330b.32ff.

21. *Il.* 7.207. Except for *panta*, this phrase is like those at 3.328, 13.241, and 17.210. The shield is so large that Ajax does not wear the typical thorax. Two telamons guard his skin from chafing; cf. 14.402–6 and the scholia at 14.402. For a general description, see W. Whallon, "The Shield of Ajax," *YCS* 19 (1966), 25.

22. *Il.* 3.229, 6.5, 7.211, as is Achilles once (1.284) and as are the Achaeans once (4.299). In the *Odyssey*, Ajax himself and not his shield is called a "tower" (11.551).

23. Hektor's role in defense is often greater than that of the actual wall, the men of Troy, or the city's allies. For the importance of the allies, see Agamemnon's comments at 2.119ff. Sarpedon rebukes Hektor by saying the allies more than the Trojans are saving the city (5.472–92). Hektor addresses the multitude of allies at 17.220–24.

24. Cf. A. Fick and F. Bechtel, *Die griechischen Personennamen* (Göttingen, 1894), 389. G. Macurdy ("Homeric Names in *-tor*," *CQ* 23 [1929], 24–25 and 27) argues that "Hektor" should be considered a shortened form of Hechelaos; but for "Hektor" as "holder" of the city, see Nagy, *Best of the Achaeans*, 146–47, and for Astyanax as named after one of his father's primary heroic characteristics, see ibid., 146 n. 9. Hektor as coming from Hechepolis is also closer to the ancient Greek view of him: in the fifth century B.C., Hektor is called *poliokhon kratos* and associated with the "city-holding rule" of Troy, *poliokhou turannidos*, *Rhesus* 821 and 166. See also Plato, *Cra.* 394b–c.

25. The epithet is applied to Athena or Pallas by Pindar, *Olympian* 5.10; by Herodotus 1.160; by Aristophanes, *Knights* 581, *Clouds* 602, *Birds* 827. It is applied to Zeus in Plato's *Laws* 921c; to Artemis by Apollonius Rhodius 1.312; and to the gods and daimons in Aeschylus' *Seven against Thebes* 312 and 822, respectively. For Poseidon, see page 52, above.

26. In a unique usage of *eukhomai* and in what proves to be an isolated instance in

the poem, Hektor boasts that he is honored by the Trojan women as if he were a god (*Il.* 8.538–41); cf. L. Muellner, *The Meaning of Homeric eukhomai through Its Formulas* (Innsbruck, 1976), 50, and Nagy, *Best of the Achaeans,* 142–50. Against this interpretation of 8.538ff., see F. M. Combellack, "The Wish without Desire," *AJP* 102 (1981), 115–19, and Nagy's rebuttal, "On the Range of an Idiom in Homeric Dialogue," in *Studies Presented to Sterling Dow: GRBS* 25 (1984), 233–38; rewritten in Nagy, *Greek Mythology and Poetics* (Ithaca, N.Y., 1990), 294–301.

27. Cf. note 16, above.

28. Cf. J. M. Redfield, *Nature and Culture in the "Iliad"* (Chicago, 1975), 124–25; cf. G. Nagy, note 24, above.

29. Erichthonios, father of the Trojans, was the namesake of the Erichthonidai (cf. *Inscriptiones Graecae* 3, 771). That the reference to Erichthonios in the *Iliad* predates that hero's entry into Attika and for the genuineness of this passage, see E. Heitsch, *"Aphroditehymnus", Aeneas und Homer. Hypomnemata* 15 (Göttingen, 1965), 124–35. But the question is much debated; see K. Reinhardt, *Die "Ilias" und ihr Dichter* (Göttingen, 1961), 507–21. (Cf. note 37, below.)

30. Aeneas does not specify the exact founder of Ilios, but by implication it appears to lead back to Erichthonios.

31. According to legend, Tithonos left Troy when he married the goddess of dawn, who gave him a son Memnon as well as immortality, but without a concomitant gift of eternal youth. For the story of Tithonos, see most recently H. King, "Tithonos and the Tettix," *Arethusa* 19 (1986), 15–36; cf. C. Segal, "Tithonos and the Homeric *Hymn to Aphrodite*: A Comment," *Arethusa* 19 (1986), 37–47; J. Clay, *The Wrath of Athena: Gods and Men in the "Odyssey"* (Princeton, 1983), 141–48; P. Smith, *Nursling of Mortality: A Study of the Homeric "Hymn to Aphrodite"* (Frankfurt, 1981), 77–86. (Cf. note 38, below.)

32. No children of the brothers of Priam are mentioned; but they are contemporaries and therefore perhaps of a different category. Reference to Priam's brothers may suggest the health of the royal line at the time of Aeneas' telling. For a sensitive analysis of the father-son succession in Anchises' line, see P. Smith, "Aineiadai as Patrons of *Iliad* XX," *HSCP* 85 (1981), 46–51 and 57–58. On Ganymedes in Homer, see K. Reinhardt, *Die "Ilias" und ihr Dichter,* 509–10; on Ganymedes' abduction, see Smith, *Nursling of Mortality,* 71–77. (Cf. note 38, below.) For the meaning of *polis meropōn anthrōpōn,* see P. Chantraine, "Homerique *meropōn anthrōpōn,*" *AlPhO* 4 (1936), 121–28, and H. Keller, *"Polis meropōn anthrōpōn,"* Glotta 46 (1968), 18–26.

33. A hero whose father is divine, dead, or senile, as in the cases of Herakles, Achilles, or Odysseus, finds it easier to grow into full manhood. The stature of Diomedes' father still hangs over his head; Antilochus, son of Nestor, never became a prominent figure at Troy, and, according to mythological testimony, not one of Nestor's sons at Pylos ever became a major figure because, one must imagine, of the Zeus-like longevity of their robust father. On the divine level, Apollo suffers in related ways. For a conflict between fathers and sons in Homer, see especially Sthenelos' boast at *Il.* 4.405ff. For the importance of individual fame and honor at the expense of public welfare in classical Greek culture (i.e., "the dysfunctions of the contest system"), see A. W. Gouldner, *Enter Plato: Classical*

Greece and the Origins of Social Theory (New York, 1965), 41–77, esp. 52–55 and 66–70.

34. Redfield, *Nature and Culture in the "Iliad,"* 110; cf. 109–13 (and see note 33, above).

35. With Tithonos' absence, Priam is the eldest son and legitimate heir. In spite of what we hear at *Il.* 13.460 (cf. 20.179–83), the family line of succession appears to be secure at Ilios, because Priam seems to be in control of the geras, the dignities or honors of a king; cf. Odysseus, who asks his mother in Hades whether his father and son "still hold my geras, or already some other man has it" (*Od.* 11.176), and whose prayer for the Phaiakians is that the gods grant them prosperity during their own lifetime and that each be able to pass to their sons the possessions in their halls and "the geras which the dēmos have granted" (*Od.* 7.150). Cf. Redfield, *Nature and Culture in the "Iliad,"* 111–12. (Cf. note 14, above.)

36. H. Arendt, *The Human Condition* (Chicago, 1958), 21. Cf. Redfield on Homer: whereas nature is eternal and the things of culture transient, "it is also true that the creatures of nature are ephemeral, while institutions of culture—its families, cities, traditions—are in principle immortal. . . . But culture does not thereby redeem man from death" (*Nature and Culture in the "Iliad,"* 126).

37. Cf. H. Frisk, *Griechisches etymologisches Wörterbuch* (Heidelberg, 1960), 561. The agricultural aspects of the Attic hero Erichthonios are discussed in L. R. Farnell, *The Cults of the Greek States*, 5 vols. (1896; reprint New York, 1977), 4:47–55. Is there a coincidence between the name and the epithet of men when associated with cities in Zeus' phrase *polées epikhthoniōn anthrōpōn* (*Il.* 4.45)?

38. For the polis-man as a figure suspended between the animal and divine worlds, see Aristotle's description of man (*Pol.* 1253a27–29): "The man who is unable to join in partnerships or does not need to because of his self-sufficiency is not part of a city; he is either a beast or a god" (after Wardman); see also 1253a.1ff. For the sterile union of Ganymedes and Zeus on Olympos, see C. Segal, "The Homeric *Hymn to Aphrodite*: A Structuralist Approach," *CW* 67 (1973/74), 205–12. (Cf. notes 31 and 32, above.)

39. For the representation of the city as a woman in the Classical (goddesses) and Hellenistic periods (personified abstractions), see C. Picard, *Manuel d'archéologie grecque. La sculpture*, vol. 2 (Paris, 1939), 838 (fifth century); vol. 3 (Paris, 1948), 98 and 104 (fourth century); and vol. 4 (Paris, 1963), 1258–59. See also N. Loraux, *The Invention of Athens*, 282–84, with bibliography cited esp. at 450 n. 111 and 466 n. 4. Cf. Redfield on the family: "It is as if the father were the social or cultural parent, the mother the natural parent. . . . The son's social task is to replace his father," *Nature and Culture in the "Iliad"*, 119.

40. Cf. H. Monsacre, *Les larmes d'Achille* (Paris, 1984), 78–93, and M. B. Arthur, "The Divided World of *Iliad* VI," in *Reflections of Women in Antiquity*, ed. H. Foley (New York, 1981), 19–44. Cf. C. Segal, "Andromache's Anagnorisis, Formulaic Artistry in *Iliad* 22.437–76," *HSCP* 75 (1971), 33–57. (Cf. note 46, below.)

41. J. T. Kakridis, *Homeric Researches* (Lund, 1949), 19–27 and 152–64, comparing Kleopatra's plea to that of Andromache, observes that the order of the suppliant list in Book 9 has been changed to fit the context. Although fine works in general, both Kakridis and Arthur ("The Divided World of *Iliad* VI"), who builds off of his

work, fail to notice the central importance of the polis in each of these supplications. M. Edwards in *Homer: The Poet of the "Iliad"* (Baltimore, 1987), 208–9, sees the Hektor/Andromache scene anticipated in a more conventional farewell scene described a few hundred lines earlier when the narrator recalls Sarpedon having taken leave of his wife and infant son (5.478–80).

42. Arthur, "The Divided World of *Iliad* VI," argues oddly that Andromache does not "ask Hector to refrain from going out to battle" (32); she wants simply that he not seek kleos. Such a reading ignores Andromache's anxiety that the city wall will be overrun (6.433–39). Aristarchus athetized these lines on the grounds that it was not fitting for Hektor's wife to act like a rival commander (*antistrategein*). Cf. both Ameis-Hentze and Leaf, at 6.433–9; also see G. M. Bolling, *The Athetized Lines of the "Iliad"* (Baltimore, 1944), 99–101. In light of the other references to women and city walls, it is perfectly within her feminine character, and part of a larger undercurrent running throughout Book 6, to ask that the city protector fight from within the city wall.

43. The verb for loosening used here, *aniemenē*, somewhat rare with this meaning in the *Iliad*, is used approximately one hundred and fifty lines earlier when the Trojans "loosened" (*anesan*) their gates to offer safety for the warriors retreating from the monstrous Achilles: "So Priam spoke. The Trojans loosened the gates and thrust back the bars. With the gates swung open, there was some hope of salvation" (*Il.* 21.537–38).

44. Cf. J. T. Kakridis, "The Role of the Women in the *Iliad*," *Eranos* 54 (1956), 24 and 26. A. W. Gouldner, in modern dress, sees Hektor's "sexual surrender to the aggressive competitor" as a homosexual response (*Enter Plato*, 60). M. Lynn-George sees Hektor's memory of "whispered intimacies" as a world set apart from "a landscape in which language is abandoned or annulled," in *Epos: Word, Narrative, and the "Iliad"* (Atlantic Highlands, N.J., 1988), 130.

45. Compare the narrator's description of an Achaean bowman who, running behind Ajax's tower shield, is called a "child [running] to the arms of his mother" (*Il.* 8.271). A similar dichotomy between heroic action and mothering city may be suggested two and a half centuries later by Plato in the *Euthyphro*, the prologue as it were to the philosopher/hero's struggle against an imperfect state. Socrates charges that Miletus ran to the state "as a boy to his mother" (2c.7–8). There is the same implication that the city, as nurturing female, here using law, constricts adulthood, truth, and fullness of being.

46. Cf. A. Schmidt, "La polarité des contraires dans la rencontre d'Hector et Andromaque," *LEC* 31 (1963), 129–58, esp. 133–48.

47. By contrast, Arthur, "The Divided World of *Iliad* VI," sees overtones of sexual excitement in Helen's invitation.

48. See the sensitive comments of Schmidt on this question, in "La polarité des contraires," 152–53. Arthur, "The Divided World of *Iliad* VI," sees "resolution of competing interests" (35), but Andromache's effort to influence Hektor's heroism, it needs to be recognized, fails when she, like Hekabe and Helen, tries, unsuccessfully, to lure Hektor away from the danger of the open field of war. Although husband and wife meet at the city gate where each partially enters the other's world, the best the couple can achieve is a smile through their tears as Andromache

departs to weave (a floral design, cf. *Il.* 22.441, and not Helen's *Iliad*) and Hektor goes to almost certain death. Momentary mediation here underscores deeper division. (For a study of Hektor's prayer in this scene, see Chapter 8.) For other recent studies of the female in this book and in epic generally, see Monsacre, *Les larmes d'Achille,* 97–132; H. Foley, "'Reverse Similes and Sex Roles in the *Odyssey,*'" *Arethusa* 11 (1978), 7–26; C. Beye, "Male and Female in the Homeric Poems," *Ramus* 3 (1974), 87–101.

5. City Epithets and Homeric Poetics

1. Of these five examples, one is in the narrative, four in speeches. They are as follows: the narrator says that Achilles never expected Patroklos to sack the citadel without him (*ekpersein ptoliethron* begins the line, 17.407); Achilles says that he had told Patroklos' father that he would bring his son home, having sacked Troy (*Ilion ekpersanta* begins the line, 18.327); Nestor says at 2.367–68 that the Greeks will learn whether divine will or their cowardice will prevent them from destroying the city; Priam says bitterly to his surviving sons that he would sooner go to Hades than look upon the city destroyed and plundered (*prin alapazomenēn te polin keraizomenēn te,* 24.245). Diomedes tells Agamemnon that the rest of the Achaeans will remain behind "until we destroy Troy: (*eis ho ke per Troiēn diapersomen* at the beginning of the hexameter, 9.46).

2. The three instances in the narrative are as follows: twice when the gods are said to hate Troy (8.551–52 and 24.27–8) and once when the narrator foretells that Troy will fall in the tenth year (12.15).

3. One also finds the phrase "the city of the proud Trojans" twice in the *Iliad,* both times in speeches. The formulaic usage in the two instances is almost identical, and the context similar to other formulas for Troy with *perthō.* Apollo tells Patroklos to withdraw, in one: it is not fated for you "with your spear to sack the city of the proud Trojans" (. . . *polin perthai Trōōn agerōkhōn,* 16.708). Agenor, inspired by Apollo, tells Achilles, in the other: it may be your hope "on this day to sack the city of the proud Trojans" (21.584). G. Nagy, in *Greek Mythology and Poetics* (Ithaca, N.Y., 1990), 74–75, points out that the direct objects of *perthō* in the Homeric tradition are confined to *polis* and related words.

4. "The city of Priam" is subject in the following phrase: *pertheto de Priamoio polis dekatōi eniautōi* (12.15).

5. The two formulaic phrases are: "*the polis of lord Priam* would have nodded or tottered to its fall [*ēmuseie*] / having been seized and sacked [*halousa te perthomenē te*] under our hands" (2.373–74 = 4.290–91) and "*your well-inhabited polis* will very likely [*phthaiē*] / be seized and sacked [*halousa te perthomenē te*] under our hands" (13.815–16). The close overlap of these phrases suggests the "polis of Priam" and the "well-inhabited polis" express closely related ideas about the polis. That is, in the first phrase, Priam symbolizes in his person the life of the city, shorthand for the women, children, and old men, implied in the second. The verb *ēmuo* in the first phrase literally means "to droop or nod," as the heads of wheat do late in the

season, and refers metaphorically to the "head" (*karēna;* cf. 2.16–18) of a city, a metaphor continued in the image of the walls as "well-crowned" and a "holy veil."

6. In its one non-Troy usage, the formulaic phrase differs but the context is similar: with *perthō* and in speech. Achilles says at *Il.* 16.57: "I won her with my spear, having stormed the well-walled city" (*douri d'emōi kteatissa, polin euteikhea persas*).

7. P. Vivante, *The Epithets in Homer: A Study in Poetic Values* (New Haven, 1982), 174–75.

8. Ibid., 13.

9. Ibid., 13 (both quotes).

10. A. A. Parry, *Blameless Aegistus: A Study of "amumon" and Other Homeric Epithets,* Mnemosyne Suppl. 26 (Leiden, 1973), 4. Also see S. Scully, "The Language of Achilles: The *ochthēsas* Formulas," *TAPA* 114 (1984), 11–27; M. Nagler, *Spontaneity and Tradition: A Study in the Oral Art of Homer* (Berkeley, Calif., 1974); C. Segal, *The Theme of Mutilation of the Corpse in the "Iliad,"* Mnemosyne Suppl. 17 (Leiden, 1971); J. Russo, "Homer against His Tradition," *Arion* 7 (1968), 275–95; W. Whallon, "The Homeric Epithets," *YCS* 17 (1961), 47–412, where he concludes that the formulaic language shows variety and accuracy, that "neither the metrical nor the literary function of epithets is an impediment to the other" (142). J. B. Hainsworth, "Phrase-clusters in Homer," in *Studies in Greek, Italic, and Indo-European Linguistics* offered to L. R. Palmer, ed. A. M. Davies and W. Meid (Innsbruck, 1976), 83–86, interprets, too readily I believe, formula-clustering as stock formulas temporarily remembered, then forgotten. Here again, more attention should be paid to context. Five of the eight usages of the epithet *euruaguia* ("of wide ways") in the *Iliad,* for example, occur in Book 2, all in speeches, for Troy and usually after a verb of plunder (see 2.12, 28, 66, 141, 329). Compare 14.88 where the epithet is again used of Troy, in speech, and in similar context. At 9.28 it is used with the future indicative, again with Troy (cf. 2.141, 329).

11. In all these examples (six times), the epithet declines like a first- and second-declension adjective. All examples are within the first nine books. In a seventh example, as if a third-declension adjective, the epithet is used by Achilles in describing his destruction of Lyrnessos, "the well-walled polis" (16.57).

12. Six of the fifteen occurrences are found in the Greek Catalogue (discussed above in Chapter 3). It occurs another four times in the narrative after the preposition *en, ek,* or the verb *peraō* ("to sell into slavery"). In speech, it appears twice in catalogue listings. None of the above examples describes Troy.

13. Other than these examples, the formula *euktimenon ptoliethron* appears only in the Greek Catalogue. In *Epic Verse before Homer: Three Studies* (New York, 1981), A. Hoekstra says that the form *euktimenon* is pre-Ionic, derived from the earliest traceable usage of epic composition (see 46); and that the epithet *euteikheos,* by contrast, is of very late origin (see 82 nn. 7 and 8).

14. In another variation, without mention of divine support, men defend Troy: "Sooner we must kill the Argives," Hektor shouts to his troops, "or else utterly / sheer Ilios will be stormed and her citizens killed" (15.557–58).

15. Cf. H. Koch, "*aipus olethros* and the Etymology of *ollumi,*" *Glotta* 54 (1976), 216–22. For a similar play between noun and verb, see *tēid' atēid aasas, Il.* 8.237. For

examples of *schema etymologica* in the *Odyssey,* see W. B. Stanford, *The "Odyssey" of Homer* (New York, 1967), xxii. For an analysis of inner balance and syncopation of an orally composed couplet by the Yugoslavian *guslar* Ugljanin, see Albert Lord, *The Singer of Tales* (Cambridge, Mass., 1960), 56–57.

16. The use of *aipus* with Troy in the *Odyssey* parallels its usage in the *Iliad* with minor variations. Always in speeches and in the context of destruction (3.130, 8.516, 11.533, 13.316), the verb is in the past tense rather than the *Iliad's* future indicative or optative mood.

17. See M. Finkelberg, "Formulaic and Nonformulaic Elements in Homer," *CP* 84 (1989), 179–97. For a study of the systematic extension of formulas, see J. B. Hainsworth, *The Flexibility of the Homeric Formula* (Oxford, 1968), 9, passim; for this and the study of epithets in speech and narrative, see N. Austin, *Archery at the Dark of the Moon: Poetic Problems in Homer's "Odyssey"* (Berkeley, Calif., 1975), chap. 1. For the study of formulaic modifications, see A. Hoekstra, "Homeric Modifications of Formulaic Prototypes: Studies in the Development of Greek Epic Diction," *VKNA* 71 (1965), 1–172; for "adapted" formulas, see G. S. Kirk, *Homer and the Oral Tradition* (Cambridge, 1976), 37–38, 73–78, and 186–90.

18. Vivante, *Epithets in Homer,* 27.

19. Ibid., 33.

20. For the epithet after *proti* in the *Iliad,* see 7.413, 7.429, 13.657, 17.193. All Iliadic occurrences with *es* involve Iris coming down from Mount Ida to Ilios (11.196, 15.169, 24.143). *Hieros,* rather than *hirē,* occurs twice, both at the beginning of the line contrary to *Ilios hirē's* place at the end. One example is with the preposition *eis* (7.20), the other with *ein* (5.446). The remaining four examples from the narrative do not occur within propositional phrases. In one, Apollo is said to have entered sacred Ilios (21.515) (similar to the prepositional phrases); in two other passages, the narrator says that the Olympians "hate sacred Ilios" (8.551 and 24.27); in the fourth, from the proem of the *Odyssey,* Odysseus is said to have destroyed the sacred city of Troy (1.2).

21. In the *Iliad,* the epithet with Ilios is found once after *proti,* see 7.82; in the *Odyssey,* it appears after *eis,* see 11.86 and 17.293. All the examples of sacred Ilios in speech occur in the *Iliad:* 4.46, 4.164–65, 4.416, 6.96, 6.277, 6.448–49, 20.216, 21.128, 24.383, and 16.100 where the epithet describes Troy's diadem of towers; cf. *theios* of Troy's towers (21.526).

22. D. G. Miller, *Homer and the Ionian Epic Tradition* (Innsbruck, 1982), 44.

23. Austin, *Archery at the Dark of the Moon,* 29.

24. Ibid., 39.

25. Ibid., 53.

6. History and Composition

1. A. A. Snodgrass, *Archaic Greece: The Age of Experiment* (London, 1980), 18.

2. The central position of the wanax in Mycenaean society is summarized well by K. Kilian, "The Emergence of Wanax Ideology in the Mycenaean Palaces," *OJA* 7 (1988), 291–302. One should also see: L. Godart, "Le rôle du palais dans

l'organisation militaire mycénienne," in *Le système palatial en Orient, en Grèce et à Rome*, ed. E. Lévy (Strasbourg, 1987), 237–53; S. Deger Jalkotzy, "'Near Eastern Economies' versus 'Feudal Society': zum mykenischen Palaststaat," *Minos* 20–22 (1987), 137–50; O. Panagl, "Politische und soziale Struktur," in *Die frühgriechischen Texte aus mykenischer*, ed. S. Hiller and O. Panagl (Darmstadt, 1986), 278–88; J. T. Killen, "The Linear B Tablets and the Mycenaean Economy," in *Linear B, a 1984 Survey*, ed. A. Morpurgo Davies and Y. Duhoux (Louvain la Neuve, 1985), 241–98.

3. At Mycenae in the thirteenth century, a number of town houses were also built within the acropolis wall, but the most striking new evidence comes from Tiryns, where, in addition to the walled upper citadel, a "lower citadel," also walled, includes many dwellings for habitation, commerce, and cult worship. Cf. K. Kilian's excavation reports of Tiryns lower citadel in *AA* (1978), 449–70; (1979), 379–411; (1981), 149–94.

4. Population studies reveal many small settlements within any one Mycenaean kingdom and one, or perhaps two, large centers. Of 129 sites in Mycenaean Messinia examined in one report, 107 were under 2.4 hectares and widely dispersed; cf. J. Carothers and W. A. McDonald, "Size and Distribution of the Population in Late Bronze Age Messinia: Some Statistical Approaches," *JFA* 6 (1979), 433–54; cf. W. A. McDonald and G. R. Rapp, Jr. (eds), *The Minnesota Messenia Expedition: Reconstructing a Bronze Age Regional Environment* (*MME*) (Minneapolis, 1972). For a study of the natural environment and human settlement patterns in Boiotia during the Mycenaean Age, see J. L. Bintliff and A. M. Snodgrass, "The Cambridge/Bradford Boeotian Expedition: The First Four Years," *JFA* 12 (1985), 137–39; and for surface studies in the Argolid, see T. H. van Andel and C. Runnels, *Beyond the Acropolis: A Rural Greek Past* (Stanford, Calif., 1987), 94–98. See also Panagl, "Politische und soziale Struktur," 280–82. For a study of place names on the Linear B tablets and the Homeric Catologue of Ships, see note 50, below.

5. Cf. K. Kilian, "Zur Funktion der mykenischen Residenzen," in *The Function of the Minoan Palaces*, ed. R. Hägg and N. Marinatos (Stockholm, 1987), 21–38 and his "L'architecture des résidences mycéniennes," in *Le système palatial*, 203–17.

6. Cf. T. B. L. Webster, *From Mycenae to Homer* (New York, 1964), 58–61; Sir Arthur Evans, *The Palace of Minos*, 4 vols. (London, 1930), 3:81–106. See W. S. Smith, *Interconnections in the Ancient Near East: A Study of the Relationship between the Arts of Egypt, the Aegean, and Western Asia* (New Haven, Conn., 1965), chap. 5 (63–95) on the Mycenaean character of the Silver Siege Rhyton. Also see S. Marinatos, *Excavations at Thera VI* (Athens, 1974), plates 108, 110a, 112; see also its compendium *Thera Color Plates and Plans* (Athens, 1974), plates 7 and 9; cf. E. Vermeule, *Greece in the Bronze Age* (Chicago, 1964), 100–105. For the important links between Mycenaeans and Minoans suggested by these frescoes, see S. A. Immervahr, "Mycenaeans at Thera: Some Reflections on the Paintings from the West House," in *Greece and the Eastern Mediterranean in Ancient History and Prehistory: Studies Presented to Fritz Schachermeyr*, ed. K. H. Finzl (Berlin, 1977), 173–91. Also see P. Warren, "The Miniature Fresco from the West House at Akrotiri, Thera, and Its Aegean Setting," *JHS* 99 (1979), 115–29, and A. Sakellariou, "Scene de bataille sur

un vase mycenien en pierre?" *Revue archéologique* (1971), 1–14. And for the Cretan elements of the Thera frescoes, see G. Saflund, "Cretan and Theban Questions," in *Sanctuaries and Cults in the Aegean Bronze Age,* ed. R. Hägg and N. Marinatos (Stockholm, 1981), 196–202, with related bibliography there.

7. For the pertinent bibliography, see notes 24–34, below.

8. M. I. Finley, "Homer and Mycenae: Property and Tenure," *Historia* 6 (1957), 159.

9. For an argument that the Submycenaean period lasted for only a quarter of a century (1075–1050 B.C.), see S. Iakovidis, "The Chronology of LHIIIC," *AJA* 83 (1979), 454–62. For a discussion of this and other problems in dating and length of Submycenaean, see I. M. Morris, *Burial and Ancient Society: The Rise of the Greek City-State* (Cambridge, 1987), 11–18.

10. The depopulation of Greece was not uniform. Major losses occurred in a line that cut across Greece from Boiotia, through Corinth to Laconia and Messinia. Eastern Attika was left untouched and its population may even have increased, as is also true of the mountainous regions in Achaia and of the Ionian islands. Cf. N. K. Sandars, *The Sea Peoples: Warriors of the Ancient Mediterranean, 1250–1150 B.C.* (London, 1978), 182–83. For evidence of depopulation in Messinia, see W. A. McDonald and R. H. Simpson, "Archaeological Exploration," 142–43 (and Pocket Maps 8–15), and H. E. Wright Jr., "Vegetation History," 188–99, both in *MME* (see note 4, above). For migration movements, see V. Desborough, *The Greek Dark Ages* (London, 1972), 106–7, 262–63, and 332–41; J. Sarkady, "Outlines of the Development of Greek Society in the Period between the 12th and 8th Centuries B.C.," *AAntHung,* 23 (1975), 113–14; E. Kirsten, *Die griechische Polis als historisch-geographisches Problem des Mittelmeerraumes* (Bonn, 1956), 78–81. See also R. J. Hopper, *The Early Greeks* (New York, 1976), 68–82; G. L. Huxley, *The Early Ionians* (London, 1966), 23–39, 160–68; and the seminal work by M. B. Sakellariou, *La migration grecque en Ionie* (Athens, 1958), 21–357.

11. The collapse was accompanied by the disappearance of the ruling and bureaucratic classes, and the number of skilled craftsmen probably dwindled dramatically. The archaeological testimony from this period is summarized well by J. Hurwit, *The Art and Culture of Early Greece, 1100–480 B.C.* (Ithaca, N.Y., 1985), 34–44; cf. J. N. Coldstream, *Geometric Greece* (New York, 1977), 41. In addition to the many theories that the Mycenaeans were overthrown by returning Heraklids, invading Sea Peoples, hit-and-run raiders, civil wars, or subjects in revolt, Nancy Sanders in *The Sea Peoples* attributes the weakening, and then collapse, of the Mycenaean kingdoms to five causes: (1) overspecialized economy, (2) too great a dependency on central administration, (3) overpopulation, (4) difficulty of safe trade routes for tin, (5) exhaustion of marginal land (72–79 and 183–84). But see J. Carothers and W. A. McDonald, *JFA* (1979), 450, who argue that there is little evidence to support claims of overpopulation or of land exploitation. (See further bibliography in note 4 above.)

12. Cf. Desborough, *Greek Dark Ages,* 18–19 and chap. 24, and his *The Last Mycenaeans and Their Successors: An Archaeological Survey, c. 1200–c.1000 B.C.* (Oxford, 1964), 241–44 and 258–63; A. A. Snodgrass, *The Dark Age of Greece: An Archaeological Survey of the Eleventh to the Eighth Centuries B.C.* (Edinburgh, 1971),

192, 377, 380–88; J. N. Coldstream, *Greek Geometric Pottery* (London, 1968), 332–90, and his *Geometric Greece,* 25–54, on the isolation of the Greeks even into the early ninth century B.C. See also P. Betancourt, "The End of the Greek Bronze Age," *Antiquity* 50 (1976), 40–45. For the discovery of Eastern objects at Lefkandi in the tenth century, see M. R. Popham, E. Touloupa, and L. H. Sackett, "Further Excavations of the Toumba Cemetery at Lefkandi, 1981," *BSA* 77 (1982), 213–48. By 1050 B.C., the Iron Age is well-developed in Greece, although there are examples of iron use as early as c. 1200, especially but not exclusively on Cyprus; cf. A. A. Snodgrass, "Iron and Early Metallurgy in the Mediterranean," in *The Coming of the Iron Age,* ed. T. A. Wertime and J. D. Muhly (New Haven, Conn., 1980), 335–74. (Also see note 18, below.)

13. C. G. Thomas, *The Earliest Civilizations: Ancient Greece and the Near East, 3000–200 B.C.* (Washington, D.C., 1982), 59, and 74–77. The count was first published in 1971 by A. A. Snodgrass, *Dark Age of Greece.*

14. Morris, *Burial and Ancient Society,* 146. Concerning two hard-of-access Early Iron Age sites in Crete, see B. Hayden, "New Plans of the Early Iron Age Settlement of Vrokrastro," *Hesperia* 52 (1983), 367–87, and J. D. S. Pendlebury, *The Archaeology of Crete* (London, 1939) on Karphi. Cf. K. Nowicki, "The History and Setting of the Town at Karphi," *SMEA* 85, fasc. 26 (1987), 235–56.

15. Cf. Morris, *Burial and Ancient Society,* 146.

16. Hurwit, *Art and Culture of Early Greece,* 42. Even more pessimistic was F. Tritsch fifty years ago ("Die Stadtbildungen des Altertums und die griechische Polis," *Klio* 22 [1929], 61–62): "the impulse towards state organization, to the creation of the *Polis,* was wholly lacking."

17. See J. M. Wagstaff, "A Note on Settlement Numbers in Ancient Greece," *JHS* 95 (1975), 163–83; Snodgrass, *Archaic Greece,* 18–35, and his "Two Demographic Notes" in *The Greek Renaissance of the Eighth Century B.C.,* ed. R. Hägg (Stockholm, 1983), 167–69. Small village clusters sprang up at Lefkandi, Athens, and Argos in Submycenaean times and continued into the Protogeometric period, but again population density was greatly diminished when compared to Mycenaean standards.

18. For several eleventh-century houses at Asine in the Argolid, see B. Wells, *Asine II.4.2.3: The Protogeometric Period* (Stockholm, 1983); for one freestanding oval-shaped house from Old Smyrna in Asia Minor, see H. Drerup, *Griechische Baukunst in geometrischer Zeit, Archaeologia Homerica,* Kap. O. (Göttingen, 1969), 25–31, 79–87. One piece of well-cut stone (at Iolkos in Thessaly) is known. "Elsewhere we are lucky to find the flimsiest foundations," as A. Johnston says in *The Emergence of Greece* (Oxford, 1976), 52. Against this evidence is the remarkable apsidal structure dating to 1000 B.C. at Lefkandi. It measures fifty by ten meters and may well have been a peristyle, laced with columns. The two graves beneath its floor, one of a man and the other of a women jeweled in gold, suggested to some that this large and architecturally advanced building served as a place to honor and house the worship of the community's founding hero. If so, it anticipates, in size and function, the great *hekatompedon* temples of the eighth century by two hundred years. Cf. *Lefkandi, The Iron Age,* ed. M. R. Popham and L. H. Sackett (London, 1980), and Popham et al., "The Hero of Lefkandi," *Antiquity* 56 (1982), 169–74.

The interpretation of this building as a *heroon* has been questioned by A. Mazarakis-Ainian, "Contributions à l'étude de l'architecture religieuse grecque des Ages Obscurs," *Antiquité Classique* 54 (1985), 5–48.

19. Morris, *Burial and Ancient Society*, 195.

20. O. Murray, *Early Greece* (Sussex, 1980), 65–66. Cf. Snodgrass, *Archaic Greece*, 22–24. See Snodgrass, "Population in Late Eighth-Century Attica" (169–71), and D. Schilardi, "The Decline of the Geometric Settlement of Koukounaries at Paros" (173), as well as the general discussion on this question (210–12), all in *The Greek Renaissance*.

21. The earliest of these was Cyzicus along the Sea of Marmara, the first of over ninety colonies founded by Miletos (756 B.C.), Naxos in the Aegean (735 B.C.), and in Sicily Syracuse (734 B.C.), Leontini, and Catania (729 B.C.) founded, respectively, by the Chalcidians under Thycles, by the Corinthians, and by the Sicilian Naxians. Cf. Snodgrass, *Archaic Greece*, 18–19 and 40–42. For the colonization in the east, see J. M. Cook, *The Greeks in Ionia and the East* (London, 1962), "The Expansion of Ionia," 46–60. For the expansion in the west, see Coldstream, *Geometric Greece*, 221–45.

22. Snodgrass, *Archaic Greece*, 31.

23. For Argos, see R. Hägg, "Zur Stadtwerdung des dorischen Argos," in *Palast und Hutte. Beiträge zum Bauen und Wohnen im Altertum von Archaologen, Vor -und Fruhgeschichtlern* (Mainz, 1968), 297–307. For Athens and Corinth, see Snodgrass, *Archaic Greece*, 154–59. For Eretria, see A. Mazarakis-Ainian, "Geometric Eretria," *Antike Kunst* 30 (1987). In *Burial and Ancient Society,* Morris also sees a population expansion in the eighth century but "not at the same astronomical rate at which numbers of burials grows" (156; cf. 156–67).

24. N. G. L. Hammond, "The Physical Geography of Greece and the Aegean," in *A Companion to Homer,* ed. A. J. B. Wace and F. H. Stubbings (London, 1962), 98. That the Ionians were forerunners in the creation of the Greek city-state is argued by many and for many reasons. See the early work of V. Ehrenberg, "When Did the Polis Rise?" *JHS* 57 (1937), 147–59. C. Starr, "The Early Greek City-State," *PP* 12 (1957), 97–108, like Ehrenberg, sees the emergence of polis-life in Ionia, but he considers what he calls a sudden crystallization of the political attitudes underlying the city-state to have occurred about a century later than does Ehrenberg and after the time of Homer. "The Greek city-state is, I suggest then, a fairly sudden development toward the end of the eighth century B.C., a reflection in essence of the desire of men in certain areas to live in closer spiritual bonds," he says (108). See further J. M. Cook, "Greek Settlement in the Eastern Aegean and Asia Minor," *CAH,* 2d edition (Cambridge, 1961), 2 (chap. 38):773–804; E. Akurgal, "The Early Period and the Golden Age of Ionia," *AJA* 66 (1962), 372–73. Against the view that the city-state first emerged in Ionia, see G. M. A. Hanfmann, "Ionia, Leader or Follower?" *HSCP* 61 (1953), 1–37. D. A. Roebuck in "Some Aspects of Urbanization in Corinth," *Hesperia* 41 (1972), 96–127, sees early signs of the polis in Corinth circa 750–700 B.C. The archaeological evidence supports, I believe, Ionia over the mainland as the forerunner in this development and Ehrenberg's dating over Starr's.

25. See A. Wokalek, *Griechische Stadtbefestigungen* (Bonn, 1973): Old Smyrna,

48–50; Larissa on the Hermos River, 36–37; Emporio, 31–32; Phaistos, 39–44; Zagora, 55. See also Coldstream, *Geometric Greece*, 257–62, 267–68, 303–16; Drerup, *Griechische Baukunst*, 41–57, 87–105, esp. 100–103. For the detailed study of the three stages of city wall construction before the seventh century at Old Smyrna, see R. V. Nicholls, "Old Smyrna: The Iron Age Fortifications and Associated Remains of the City Perimeter," *BSA* 53–54 (1958–59), 115–19.

26. Coldstream, *Geometric Greece*, 304. For similarities between construction at Troy VIa and Smyrna's walls, see Nicholls, "Old Smyrna," 117; Drerup, *Griechische Baukunst*, 79–87 and Nicholls' review of Drerup in *Gnomon* 44 (1972), 698–704, esp. 702–4. For walled communities in northwestern Anatolia, see F. G. Maier, "Ausgrabungen in Alt-Paphos: Stadtmauer und Belagerungswerke," *AA* (1967), 303–29.

27. Coldstream, *Geometric Greece*, 303.

28. Snodgrass, *Archaic Greece*, 61; second quote from A. A. Snodgrass's Inaugural Lecture, *Archaeology and the Rise of the Greek State* (Cambridge, 1977), 24. More recently, F. de Polignac, *La naissance de la cité grecque* (Paris, 1984), expanding on Snodgrass' claims that temples should be regarded as evidence for the emerging polis, intriguingly observes that, in addition to urban sanctuaries, many poleis at this time established major rural sanctuaries in the hinterlands at the liminal point between tilled land and the mountain wilds, magnifying thereby the differences between humanity and nature (cf. esp. chap. 2, 41–92). Also see Morris, *Burial and Ancient Society*, 192.

29. See note 18, above.

30. In the Dark Ages, worship generally appears to have occurred in the open air; even in the Geometric period most sanctuaries have no temple buildings. Cf. Desborough, *Greek Dark Ages*, 280–87, esp. 281, and Snodgrass, *Dark Age of Greece*, 394–401. There are, however, a few noteworthy exceptions. See, for example, a sanctuary at Kommos on Crete dating back to the Early Proto-Geometric period (perhaps the latter half of the tenth century), reported by J. W. Shaw, et al., *Hesperia* 47 (1978), 129–54, and later by Shaw alone: *Hesperia* 48 (1979), 162–73; 49 (1980), 218–37; 50 (1981), 224–51. At Eretria, two sanctuaries are dated from the Geometric period (circa 750 B.C.), one to Apollo Daphnephoros and the other perhaps to Astarte/Aphrodite; cf. A. Mazarakis-Ainian, "Geometric Eretria," *Antike Kunst* 30 (1987), 10–14.

31. In addition to the temples mentioned in the text, there were apsidal temple structures at Solyceia (modern Galataki) in Corinth (to Hera), and Mycenae (to Athena). A narrow, megaron-shaped temple may also have been built at Tiryns (to Hera) and at Asine (to Apollo).

32. See Coldstream, *Geometric Greece*, 317–32; Drerup, *Griechische Baukunst*, 5–21 and 70, and Hurwit, *Art and Culture of Early Greece*, 74–78.

33. Nicholls, "Old Smyrna," 77. For the modeling of the capitals of this temple on Near Eastern prototypes, see P. Betancourt, *The Aeolic Style in Architecture: A Survey of Its Development in Palestine, the Halikarnassos Peninsula, and Greece, 1000–500 B.C.* (Princeton, 1977), 58–63.

34. See Nicholls, "Old Smyrna," 77 n.189; Snodgrass, *Archaic Greece*, 21–22, tends to date the temple to 750.

35. D. Schilardi, "The Decline of the Geometric Settlement of Koukounaries," 180–82.

36. S. Iakovidis, *Vormykenische und Mykenische Wehrbauten. Archaeologia Homerica* Kap. E (116–221) (Göttingen, 1977), 219.

37. See Drerup, *Griechische Baukunst*, 101.

38. J. M. Cook, "Old Smyrna, 1948–51," *BSA* 53–54 (1958–59), 12; cf. Nicholls in the same volume, 108. Nicholls also comments that placement of stakes in a ditch some distance from the face of the wall as the Achaeans did at Troy parallels contemporary Ionian defensive techniques (118). Building with timber and stone (*dourata, phitroi, laes*), but not mud-brick, resembles seventh-century methods; see F. Winter, *Greek Fortifications* (Toronto, 1971), 126–28, and Nicholls, "Old Smyrna," 119.

39. Cf. J. M. Cook, "Old Smyrna," 22–23.

40. For the ancient testimonials concerning this question, see C. J. Cadoux, *Ancient Smyrna: A History of the City from the Earliest Times to 324 A.D.* (Oxford, 1938), 10–12 and 70–77.

41. Cf. Finley, "Homer and Mycenae," 138; S. Humphreys, *Anthropology and the Greeks* (London, 1978), 200–201.

42. W. Jaeger, *Paedeia*, trans. G. Highet (New York, 1943), 3 vols., 1:17–18. For the polis ideology of the poems, also see G. Nagy, *The Best of the Achaeans* (Baltimore, 1979), 115–16. For those of a contrary persuasion, see Chapter 7, notes 1–4.

43. Cf. Hurwit, *Art and Culture of Early Greece*, 78.

44. Cook, "Old Smyrna," 37.

45. Sarkady, "Outlines of the Development of Greek Society," 123.

46. Murray, *Early Greece*, 64; cf. I. M. Morris, "The Use and Abuse of Homer," *CA* 5 (1986), 81–138, esp. 94–104.

47. In addition, the main body of the poem mentions the rivers Skamandros (Xanthos), Simoeis (4.473–77), Satnioeis (6.34; 14.443), Rhodios, Karesos, Heptaporos, and Grenikos, the last four listed in two lines (12.20–21).

48. Twenty-seven leaders, in sixteen continents grouped in five geographical areas, are mentioned by name. Of these twenty-seven leaders, eight never appear again and seventeen die within the *Iliad*, although the names of some contingent leaders do not agree with those in the main body of the poem. Many of these deaths are forecast within the catalogue itself as if it were designed with the poem in mind, but the inconsistencies mentioned above suggest just as well that the list of Trojan allies predates this particular poem and has been adapted to fit its present location. The contingents are grouped in five geographical areas, the first including Troy and its allies in the Troad, the rest in groups radiating outward from Troy. To the north and west, there are the European allies: Thrakians, Kikonians, and Paionians. On the southern shore of the Black Sea, Troy is helped by the Paphlagonians and Halizonians. Continuing in a counterclockwise direction, in the north-central area of Asia Minor, the Mysians and Phrygians come to Troy's defense. Finally, from the western shores of Asia Minor come numerous contingents: under Mount Tmolus and near Lake Gygaian are the Maionians; around the city of Miletos and near the River Maiandros as well as under Mount Mykale are the

Karians; and continuing south along the coast, by the River Xanthos, we find the Lykians. Strikingly, the area around Old Smyrna and Ephesus, perhaps under Lelegian rule at the time of the catalogues' formulation, is not part of the Trojan allied forces; cf. Cadoux, *Ancient Smyrna*, 49–52. The islands of Chios and Samos are also absent from this list. Of most note perhaps, Miletos is said to be in the hands of barbarian-speaking Trojan allies, when historically we know that this city was a Mycenaean settlement, probably walled, until shortly after the Trojan war and soon thereafter was occupied, if not ruled, by emigrating Greeks. Either the Trojan catalogue displays great restraint on the part of an Ionian poet to avoid anachronisms (there is no mention of the Ionian migrations), or, as is often said, the making of the catalogue occurred at a time after the Trojan war but before the Greek migrations when western Anatolia was under native Anatolian rule.

For further discussion of this catalogue, see G. S. Kirk, *The "Iliad": A Commentary*, vol. 1 (Cambridge, 1985), 248–63; R. H. Simpson and J. F. Lazenby, *The Catalogue of Ships in Homer's "Iliad"* (Oxford, 1970), 176–83; D. Page, *History and the Homeric "Iliad"* (Berkeley, Calif., 1959), 137–45. See also H. G. Huxley, *Achaeans and Hittites* (Oxford, 1966), 31–36, and T. W. Allen, *The Homeric Catalogue of Ships* (Oxford, 1921), 147–67.

49. In twenty-nine contingents, forty-four men led one thousand eighty-six ships against Troy, or, in the words of Simpson and Lazenby, "a sledge hammer to crush a comparatively small nut" (*Catalogue of Ships*, 161). The account was clearly not created for its present purpose of mustering Greeks into battle in the ninth year of a war, although it has been adapted in a number of places for its new design (cf. R. H. Simpson, "The Homeric Catalogue of Ships and Its Dramatic Context in the *Iliad*," *SMEA* 6 (1968), 39–44; H. T. Wade-Grey, *The Poet of the "Iliad"* (Cambridge, 1952), 49–57. Although the hasty assemblage of Trojan allies which follows claims to be a response to this Greek gathering as it is perceived to "advance across the plain to fight in front of the city" (2.801), the tabulation of Greek forces by ships and the imperfect tense of the verbs throughout are more appropriate for a listing of a Greek fleet as it prepares to depart for war, perhaps even from Aulis.

For the view that the Greek catalogue represents a Mycenaean catalogue of an Achaean fleet at Aulis, see V. Burr, *Neon Katalogos: Untersuchungen zum homerischen Schiffskatalog. Klio* Suppl. 49 (1944), 119–28; cf. Webster, *From Mycenae to Homer*, 122. Page, *History and the Homeric "Iliad,"* 137 and 144–45, sees the catalogue as an original Mycenaean document but not one recording a fleet's congregation at Aulis. Simpson and Lazenby, *Catalogue of Ships*, 153–76, argue that the catalogue is of the twelfth century. A. Giovannini, *Etude historique sur les origines du catalogue des vaisseaux* (Berne, 1969), argues that the catalogue reflects conditions in the eighth, if not seventh, century. In his *Commentary*, Kirk reasonably suggests "different dates of origin for various pieces of information over the long span of the heroic oral tradition, from the time of the historical siege of Troy or even earlier down to the latest stages of monumental composition" (p. 238; cf. 168–247). There are some unmistakable anachronisms and certain details that can be datable only to the eighth century, or even later. Especially pertinent for me is Athena's freestanding nēos (cf. 2.546–49), which for linguistic and archaeological reasons must be Ionian and eighth century; cf. J. M. Cook, "Two Notes on the Mycenaean Catalogue," *SMEA* 2 (1967), 103–9.

50. There is another city from southwestern Peloponnese called Aipeia in the *Iliad* (9.152, 294), and the Linear B tablets from Pylos register a city *A-pu?-*, but William Wyatt in "Homeric *Aipu*," *CP* 59 (1964), 184–85, thinks the city here cited is *Aipu* and that it records a misunderstanding of *Od.* 15.193: *Pylou aipu ptoliethron* ("the steep city of Pylos"). The name in the catalogue is therefore, he feels, wholly imaginary. Although there is this one coincidence between the nine towns identified as the Pylian contingent in the Iliadic catalogue and a district of nine towns identified on the Linear B tablets, these two groupings have little else in common; cf. S. Hiller, *Studien zur Geographie des Reiches um Pylos nach den mykenischen und homerischen Texten* (Wien, 1972), who says that the Mycenaean Pylos and the Pylos in the Homeric poems must be considered distinct. In defense of Homer, see J. Chadwick, "*Esti Pylos pro Pyloio*," *Minos* 14 (1973), 39–59, and R. H. Simpson, *Mycenaean Greece* (Atlantic Highlands, N.J., 1981), 144–52. The similarity in names between the priest Khryses, daughter Khryseis, and their home in Khryse (1.11ff., as between Briseis and her father Briseus, 1.392) may look particularly artificial, but the naming of people by place is not uncommon and the name Khryse appears again in the fifth century: cf. Sophocles (*Phil.* 1326ff.) with an altar to a daimon Khryse in an inlet by the same name, near Lemnos. Elsewhere in the *Iliad* within the Troad, children seem commonly to be named after a river (sacred, as rivers generically are): i.e., the Trojan Simoeisios is so named after the river Simoeis where he was born while his mother and grandparents were tending flocks (4.473–77); similarly Satnios is named after the river Satnioeis where his father was tending a herd (14.443–45). Hektor and Andromache name their child after the river Skamandros (sacred and protecting river of Troy), although the townspeople call him Astyanax for reasons of their own (6.402–3).

51. C. M. Bowra, *Tradition and Design in the "Iliad"* (Oxford, 1930), 32.

52. For the preoccupation of the Mycenaeans with the theme of siege warfare in their art, see note 6, above.

53. The Cypriote, Thessalian, and "Mycenaean" spelling of *pt* for *p* is interesting in this regard because this dialectical spelling is attested only in words for city and warfare: i.e., *ptolis* and *ptolietheron* ("citadel") and *ptolemos* ("war"). It is also found in epithets for ptolis-storming men—*ptoliporthos* or *ptoliporthios* ("sacker of cities")—and in proper names of heroes such as Troy-sacking Neoptolemos, Achilles' son. While many agree that the formulaic tradition dates back to the Mycenaean age, there is less agreement about the evolution of the multi-dialectical epic *Kuntsprache* found in Homer and Hesiod. M. L. West argues that epic language, passing through a Lesbian phase (i.e., Aeolic) "early enough to overlap with the last few decades of Troy VIIb2" (164), acquired its definitive and normative form in Euboea (i.e., far from the Ionian east); see his "Rise of the Greek Epic," *JHS* 108 (1988), 151–72. For more on an Aeolian phase, see P. Wathelet, *Les traits éoliens dans la langue de l'épopée grecque* (Rome, 1970) and R. Janko, *Homer, Hesiod, and the Hymns: Diachronic Development in Epic Diction* (Cambridge, 1982), 89–93 and 176–79. D. G. Miller, on the other hand, sees a steady layering from Mycenaean to Ionic forms, without at any time an exclusively "Achaean" or

"Aeolic" phase; see his *Homer and the Ionian Epic Tradition* (Innsbruck, 1982), 139, 147–48, and passim. Cf. W. Wyatt, "Homer's Linguistic Ancestors," *Epistēmonikē Epetēris Thessalonikēs* 14 (1975), 133–47.

54. J. Redfield, *Nature and Culture in the "Iliad"* (Chicago, 1975), 146.

55. C. Whitman, *Homer and the Heroic Tradition* (Cambridge, Mass., 1958), 14 (also quoted by Redfield in ibid.).

56. J. Schafer, from response in *Greek Renaissance*, 208.

57. S. Hiller, "Possible Historical Reasons for the Rediscovery of the Mycenaean Past in the Age of Homer," in *Greek Renaissance*, 14.

58. W. Burkert, "Oriental Myth and Literature in the *Iliad*," in *Greek Renaissance*, 55, and his *Die orientalisierende Epoche in der griechischen Religion und Literatur* (Heidelberg, 1984), esp. 85–99 and 106–10. Cf. T. J. Dunbabin, *The Greeks and Their Eastern Neighbors* (Chicago, 1979; reprinted from *JHS* suppl. 8 [1957]), 35–43, and R. M. Cook, "Origins of Greek Sculpture," *JHS* 87 (1967), 28–31. For a passionately one-sided point of view concerning Phoenician contact with the Greeks beginning in the eighth century, see J. Muhly, "Homer and the Phoenicians: The Relations between Greece and the Near East in the Bronze and Iron Age," *Berytus* 19 (1970), 19–64. For Mycenaean contact with the Hittites, see F. Schachermeyr, *Mykene und das Hethiterreich* (Wien, 1986), and H. G. Güterbock, "The Ahhiyawa problem reconsidered," *AJA* 83 (1983), 133–38. Cf. West, "Rise of the Greek Epic," 169–72, and Miller, *Homer and the Ionian Epic Tradition*, 16–21.

59. H. L. Lorimer, *Homer and the Monuments* (London, 1950), 522, compares the Trojan Horse in this way; the ax comparison may be found in K. Devries, "Greek and Phrygians in the Early Bronze Age," in *From Athens to Gordion*, ed. K. Devries (Philadelphia, 1980), 36 n. 18, with related references. For illustrations of Assyrian siege warfare, see Paul Lampl, *Cities and Planning in the Ancient Near East* (New York, 1968), plates 8 and 9.

60. George Steiner, *Antigones* (Oxford, 1984), 121.

61. Jaeger, *Paedeia*, 55–56. For the significance of the polis in Homer, see also Cook, "Greek Settlement in the Eastern Aegean and Asia Minor," 804, and note 42, above.

7. Oikos and Polis in the Homeric Poems

1. Moses I. Finley, *The World of Odysseus* (London, 1954), 27 and 79, respectively; cf. 33, 111, 124–25. Cf. his *Early Greece: The Bronze and Archaic Ages*, Ancient Culture and Society Series (London, 1970), 84–85.

2. A. W. H. Adkins, *Moral Values and Political Behaviour in Ancient Greece* (New York, 1972), 17; also see his *Merit and Responsibility* (Oxford, 1960), 40.

3. J. M. Redfield, "Household and Community," in *Nature and Culture in the "Iliad"* (Chicago, 1975), 111, and see 123–27.

4. J. Halverson, "Social Order in the *Odyssey*," *Hermes* 113 (1985), 129; cf. his "Succession Issue in the *Odyssey*," *Greece and Rome* 33 (1986), 119–28. See also W. G. Runciman, "Origins of States: The Case of Archaic Greece," *Comparative Stud-*

ies in Society and History 24 (1982), 351–77, and R. Posner, "The Homeric Version of the Minimal State," *Ethics* 90 (1979), 27–46.

5. Many scholars, but by no means all, now believe that *basileus* in Homer does not mean "king," but "high-born leader." The *locus classicus* for the difficulty in interpretation occurs, appropriately enough, in Book 1 of the *Odyssey*. Berating Telemachos, Antinoos says, "May the son of Kronos never make you basileus in Ithaca, *a thing [ho]* which is your inheritance by birth." Telemachos responds: "I would wish to obtain this, Zeus willing. . . . It is not a bad thing *[kakon]* to be king. Straightway one's house is rich and he has more honor *[timeesteros]*. But in truth there are many other basilēes of the Achaeans in Ithaca, young and old, one of whom may hold this (title? office?) *[tode]*, since Odysseus has died" (1.386–96). Many problems are evident in this passage. *Basileus* can stand for "a thing" as well as a person; there is a kind of patrimony that gives Telemachos a preeminent, but contested, right to become basileus, and there is no sign here of royal blood; and the relation between the many basilēes and the one basileus is not self-evident. Among the Phaiakians, there are thirteen famous, scepter-holding basilēes (8.40–41), whom the illustrious Phaiakians call to Assembly *(Boulē)* (6.54–55). Of these, Alkinoos ranks the first among peers (8.390–91). Was this true of Odysseus, as well? But what powers, or offices, did the basilēes collectively, or the basileus individually, exercise in the Boulē? Agreement among scholars is anything but uniform: For J. Halverson, there is no throne, no office of king, and to be sure no real Ithacan state. The title *basileus* is "of prestige only," not of an office; cf. Halverson, "Social Order in the *Odyssey*," 134–36, and "Succession Issue in the *Odyssey*," 119–21. For W. G. Runciman, political organization in Homer is stuck midway between statelessness and statehood. With autonomous oikoi, the basilēes "are nobles, not kings, in the proper sense, and their *poleis* are communities with a residental centre, not states" (Runciman, "Origin of States," 358; cf. 354–67). For R. Posner, a basileus is like a medieval baron—the most powerful man in a district with the largest oikos; cf. his "Homeric Version of the Minimal State," 33–46. On the other hand, for J. V. Luce, thinking of powerful monarchs like Agamemnon, who holds a divinely made scepter handed down through his family, and Priam, who is in a line of kings from Dardanos, sired by Zeus, kings are of a royal line and the polis "is strongly monarchical in flavour. The king under Zeus is the ultimate source of authority. His word is law" (Luce, "The Polis in Homer and Hesiod," *PRIA* 78 [1978], 10 [see Chapter 4, note 14, above]). But for others, and here is where my sentiments lie, the evidence suggests a culture in transition, moving from a Dark Age, oikos-oriented society to that of the emerging polis. E. Lévy sees the role of basileus within that larger picture of social transition; for him, the position of basileus, unlike that of the Mycenaean, monarchical wanax, carries with it public honor *(timē;* cf. *Od.* 1.393) and institutional functions (cf. *Boulē* of *Od.* 6.54–55); on these points, see his "Lien Personnel et titre royal: *ANAX* et *BASILEUS* dans l'*Iliade*," in *Le système palatial en Orient, en Grèce et à Rome,* ed. E. Lévy (Strasbourg, 1987), 291–314. Similarly, B. Quiller sees evidence in the poems of a collective rule of the nobility and of the aristocracy closing ranks as they share political power in a polis; see his "Dynamics of the Homeric Society," *SO* 56 (1981), 109–55, esp. 136–43. Cf. R. Drews, *Basileus: The Evidence for Kingship in*

Geometric Greece (New Haven, 1983); O. Murray, *Early Greece* (Sussex, 1980), 40–41; G. Calhoun, "Polity and Society," in *A Companion to Homer*, ed. A. J. B. Wace and F. H. Stubbings (London, 1962), 434–38.

6. J. Halverson argues passionately for a two-tiered society in Homer: a servile class on the one hand and the dēmos and laoi on the other. For the latter, no class tension, let alone class consciousness, existed between dēmos and basileus; cf. "Social Order in the *Odyssey*," 132–34 (see relevant bibliography there). But can this position hold? At Pylos, there were nine "seats" (*hedrai* and *aguris*—said to be Aeolic for "agora") or congregations of five hundred Pylians each, making a total of forty-five hundred people (cf. *Od.* 3.7 and 31). Such organization suggests *some* division of the dēmos into groups where tensions between a basileus and the populace were inevitable. We hear of one on Ithaca, for example, when Odysseus protected Antinoos' father, Eupeithes, from a furious dēmos (*Od.* 16.424–30). In the *Iliad*, the sons of Priam are said to have plundered their own people (*epidēmioi harpaktēres*, 24.262); cf. Hesiod, *Works and Days* 202ff. Even if the basilēs do not come from a separate noble class, these passages suggest tension, or struggle, between rulers and ruled, a tension that is unmistakable between the Ithacans and Odysseus after he has killed the suitors: like his son Antinoos ("Anti-Mind"), the father Eupeithes ("Good Persuader") leads the throng of Ithacans against the king and his family, although the dēmos had been warned by Halitherses to refrain from war. Punning on Eupeithes' name, Homer says *Eupeithei/peithont'* ("they [the Ithacans] were persuaded by the good persuader," 24.465–66), and he comments further that Eupeithes was their leader in folly (24.469). Pointedly, Antinoos' father will be the only one killed in the ensuing battle (24.523). Criticism of the power of language to move the dēmos, against all sound advice and in spite of past debts (16.424ff.), is clearly intended in this scene. As a separate point, B. Quiller makes the important observation that a king could, and did frequently, it seems, take land away from the dēmos to distribute at his discretion; see *SO* (1981), 132–34. For hostility between the people of Troy and the family of Priam, see Chapter 4, note 14, above; cf. K. Rauflaub, "Homer and the Beginning of Political Thought in Greece," in *Proceedings of the Boston Area Colloquium Series in Ancient Philosophy* 4 (1988), 1–25, and Posner, "Homeric Version of the Minimal State," 37. P. W. Rose, in "Class Ambivalence in the *Odyssey*," *Historia* 24 (1975), 129–49, argues that the poems show an eighth-century clash between older monarchies and rising oligarchies; but see Halverson, "Succession Issue in the *Odyssey*," 126–28.

7. See my "Bard as Custodian of Homeric Society: *Odyssey* 3.263–272," *QUCC* n.s. 8 (1981), 70–73.

8. See P. Stanley, "Ancient Greek Market Regulations and Controls" (Ph.D. diss., University of California at Berkeley, 1976). The agora at Sidonia in the *Odyssey* is also near the harbor, while the one at Pylos is in front of the royal palace. The Phaiakians also put on sporting contests in their agora. For the similarity between agora and boulē, see *Od.* 3.127; for that between agora and *hedrai* (seats), see *Od.* 8.16.

9. It is not clear from the poem whether Telemachos claims his father's seat by inheritance and/or by right of Odysseus' title (and office?) as basileus.

10. Halverson, "Social Order in the *Odyssey*," 138; cf. Runciman, "Origins of States," 357–58.

11. Halverson, "Succession Issue in the *Odyssey*," 121–22. He writes much the same thing in "Social Order in the *Odyssey*," 138: "Ithaka has had no civic assembly, no ruler, and therefore no 'government' for twenty years. And one may well imagine that it had little enough before and will have little enough in the future." Although not compelled by such momentous events, the Phaiakians *call* Alkinoos, and not the other way around, to the boulē (6.54–55). If Ithacans, in their peace and farming quietude, seldom have need of public gatherings, the Phaiakian behavior must seem even more extreme, in Halverson's view of Homeric society, since before Odysseus' arrival they were a people far removed from the dangers of war and humankind.

12. Cf. M. I. Finley, *World of Odysseus*, 78–79: "An assembly is no simple institution. As a precondition it requires a relatively settled, stable community made up of many households and kinship groups; in other words, the imposition upon kinship of some territorial superstructure. That means that the several households and larger family groups had substituted for physical coexistence at arm's length a measure of common existence, a community, and hence a partial surrender of their own autonomy."

13. *Pulon, Neleos euktimenon ptoliethron* (3.4); *Pulou aipu ptoliethron* (3.485 and 15.193).

14. Cf. 3.347–49 and 3.355, 368, 387, 388, respectively.

15. The epithet *piōn* ("rich, fertile") normally describes lands, or countries, sometimes cities, only here oikos.

16. M. Nagler, "Towards a Semantics of Ancient Conflict: Eris in the *Iliad*," *CW* 82 (1988), 81. Cf. Halverson, who says rightly of the beginning of Book 9 and of the poem in general: "Here love and loyalties are focused not on the polis but on the country and, above all, on the family household" ("Succession Issue in the *Odyssey*," 140; cf. 140–44). H. Foley comments in "'Reverse Similes' and Sex Roles in the *Odyssey*," *Arethusa* 11 (1978), 7–26, how the focus on marriage (here reunion) can express a larger range of hierarchical relationships between "strangers" in a society.

17. Nagler, "Towards a Semantics," 81; cf. M. B. Arthur, "The Divided World of *Iliad* VI," in *Reflections of Women in Antiquity*, ed. H. Foley (New York, 1981), 19–43, also cited by Nagler concerning her distinction between the value of *kleos* in the *Iliad*, whereas in the *Odyssey*, *eleos* ("pity") is reclaimed as a dominant value.

18. The narrator describes an angry gang of townspeople standing "before the town [*astu*] with its spacious dancing floors"; cf. Chapter 3, pp. 41–42.

19. Offering what is perhaps the simplest definition of the Homeric polis, G. M. Calhoun writes: "As the individual belongs to a household and to a polis, so the polis is an aggregation of households . . . everywhere in the poems the two salient facts are the polis and the household" (*A Companion to Homer*, 432). Finley captures some of that same spirit when describing "a ceaseless interplay of household, kin and community" in Homeric society (*World of Odysseus*, 110). The lines that distinguish politically defined relationships within the city from blood ties of the

house, as both critics imply, are much less sharply defined in Homer than in classical Athens. Austin and Vidal-Naquet describe this interplay as "une certain tension entre la cité homérique et l'*oikos* aristocratique" (M. Austin and P. Vidal-Naquet, *Les économies et sociétés en Grèce ancienne* [Paris, 1972], 53); cf. Calhoun, *A Companion to Homer*, 434. Their word *cité*, unlike Finley's "community," restores Homeric terminology as well as the "tension" between polis and oikos that is more in line with the classical Greek city-state conflict between these competing modes of identity. Such interplay of city and extended family is perhaps natural in any premodern city. Consider what Leon Battista Alberti living in fifteenth-century Florence says of their interrelatedness: "It seems to me that the city, just as it is made up of many families, is itself almost like a very large family. And, on the other hand, the family might also be a small city" (Alberti, "Deiciarchia," in *Opere volgari*, ed. A. Bonucci [Florence, 1845], 5 vols., 3:122–23). Also see C. Tunnard, *The City of Man* (New York, 1953), 6–11, who quotes Alberti. Compare V. Ehrenberg on the city-state: "The citizens were assembled like one large family round the hearth of the Polis" (*The Greek State* [New York, 1960], 90); and one cannot help but think of Plato's *Republic* where the polis literally replaces, or displaces, the oikos. My point is that, though the interplay of household and polis is ceaseless in Homer, this tension does not cease in the classical polis.

20. E. Mireaux, *Vie quotidienne au temps d'Homère* (Paris, 1967), 50–51.

21. Luce, "The *Polis* in Homer and Hesiod," 8. Cf. Chapter 6, text and notes; M. L. West, "Greek Poetry: 2000–700 B.C.," *CQ* 23 (1973), 182.

22. W. Hoffmann, "Die *Polis* bei Homer," in *Festschrift Bruno Snell*, ed. H. Erbse (Munich, 1956), 156. Cf. Luce, "*Polis* in Homer and Hesiod," 9–10. For a discussion of the difference between the concept of *aretē* in Homer and Tyrtaeus, see C. M. Bowra, *Early Greek Elegists* (London, 1938), 65–67; for a study of narcissism in the Homeric hero, see P. Slater, *Glory of Hera* (Boston, 1968), passim, esp. 26 and 35–36; see also C. Beye, "Male and Female in the Homeric Poems," *Ramus* 3 (1974), 90–93. For a study of heroes who shoulder the responsibility of civic defense, see P. A. L. Greenhalgh, "Patriotism in the Homeric World," *Historia* 21 (1972), 528–37. Cf. M. Arthur, "Origins of the Western Attitude toward Women," *Arestusa* 6 (1973), 9–12.

23. Greenhalgh, "Patriotism," 528.

24. Ibid., 528–29. Cf. *Il.* 12.243 and 3.50.

25. See Chapter 4, pp. 60–61.

26. J. T. Kakridis, in *Homeric Researches* (Lund, 1949), 19–27 and 152–64, has shown how the order of figures in each instance is suited to the dramatic purpose of the scene. For the city in the Meleager story, see Hoffmann, "Die *Polis* bei Homer," 157–58.

27. Cf. M. Lynn-George, *Epos: Word, Narrative, and the "Iliad"* (Atlantic Highlands, N.J., 1988), 211, where much the same is noted: "In this tale a city is saved in the telling of a city destroyed" (cf. 218). For the importance of *philotēs* in Kleopatra's plea and in Phoinix' plea to Achilles, see S. Schein, *The Mortal Hero: An Introduction to Homer's "Iliad"* (Berkeley, Calif., 1984), 112–13.

28. Redfield, *Nature and Culture in the "Iliad,"* 118, where in an excellent study he compares *aidos* and *nemesis* when comparing Hektor and Alexander (113–19;

and see further bibliography on 244 n. 15). In the same year D. Claus studied the word *aidos* in the context of Achilles (*"Adios* in the Language of Achilles," *TAPA* 115 [1975], 13–28).

29. *Il.* 15.561–62; cf. 15.733. In his third and final exhortation, Ajax continues to inspire the struggling Greeks by similar pleas: "Achaean heroes, fighting comrades of Ares, / Be men of battle [*aneres*] and remember your impetuous courage," 15.733–34.

30. In this third address, he exhorts Trojan and ally to set fire to the enemy ships, 15.718–25.

31. Redfield, *Nature and Culture in the "Iliad,"* 119.

32. Ibid., 115.

33. Luce, *"Polis* in Homer and Hesiod," 11.

34. For his important comments about the socially destructive emphasis on individual fame and honor in the Athenian fifth century, see A. W. Gouldner, *Enter Plato: Classical Greece and the Origins of Social Theory* (New York, 1965), 41–77. For the prominence of individual's seeking personal fame and reputation throughout Greek culture, see K. Dover, *Greek Popular Morality in the Time of Plato and Aristotle* (Oxford, 1974), 226–42. For a balanced view of the relation between individualism and cooperative virtues in Greece from Homer to the fifth century, see S. Goldhill, *Reading Greek Tragedy* (Cambridge, 1986), 144–46.

35. For an equation of agora and boulē, see *Od.* 3.127; for the people calling the basileus to the boulē, see *Od.* 6.54–55. For a belief that this anti-Kyklopes world represents a "civil society," see E. Havelock, *The Greek Concept of Justice* (Cambridge, Mass., 1978), 80. Against Havelock, Halverson argues, in "Social Order in the *Odyssey,*" 139, that, in contrast to the wildness and primitiveness of the Kyklopes, the Greek counterexample is only expressive of a "populated, cultivated, built-up farming country." There are no civic institutions or public buildings to suggest a polis ideology, he argues. Seemingly between these two positions, Runciman, "Origins of States," 352 n. 3, says that the contrast is one between civilization and its absence, but not one between statehood and statelessness. Within the context of the poems, the contrast should be understood, it seems to me, as one between oikos and polis.

36. Plato (*Laws* 680b–e) notes this passage as an example of primitive patriarchal government (oikos dominant): "And did not such a state spring out of single inhabitants [*oikoi*] and families [*genos*] who were scattered owing to the distress following the catastrophes; and among them the eldest ruled, because government originated with them in authority of a father and mother whom, like a flock of birds, they followed, forming one troop under the patriarchal rule of sovereignty of their parents, which of all sovereignties is the most just?" Cf. Aristotle, *Pol.* 1252b.16–31. Of the family and nonpolis orientation among the Kyklopes, V. Ehrenberg says: "Diese Erkenntnis zeigt, wie überaus stark das religiöse Moment bei der Entstehung der staatlichen Gemeinschaft der Griechen mitgewirkt hat; zugleich aber enthüllt *themis* die Bedeutung der Gentilizischen Gebilde, die legendige Kraft, die aus den enzelnen Geschlechtern hinüberleitet zum Staat" (*Die Rechtsidee im Frühen Griechentum* [Darmstadt, 1966; originally Leipzig, 1921], 15).

37. Note the emphasis on technology in the parallelism between "builders of

ships who could have made them / strong-benched [*eusselmous*] vessels" and "made this a strong settlement [*euktimenon*]." The prefix *eu-*, as elsewhere, signifies technological skill. For other instances in which human habitation transforms the natural landscape, see the intransitive use of *naiō, naietaō,* and *oikeō;* compare M. Leumann, *Homerische Wörter* (Basil, 1950), 182–94, esp. 191–94 (modified, correctly in my view, by G. P. Shipp, *Essays in Mycenaean and Homeric Greek* [Melbourne, 1961], 42–47). For a different view, see P. Vivante, *The Homeric Imagination* (Bloomington, Ind., 1971), 103.

38. H. Arendt, *The Human Condition* (Chicago, 1959), 37.

39. This last attribute of the polis, its striving for immortality, is a modern classification, not articulated in Aristotle, although perhaps implied in his notion of "perfect self-sufficiency." Most notably see Arendt, "Eternity and Immortality," in *Human Condition,* 17–21. Cf. Redfield, *Nature and Culture in the "Iliad,"* 126, and L. Mumford, *The City in History* (New York, 1961), 48–49. See also N. O. Brown, *Life against Death* (Middletown, Conn., 1970), 282–87.

8. Achilles, Troy, and Hektor: A Configuration

1. J. V. Luce, "The *Polis* in Homer and Hesiod," *PRIA* 78 (1978), 11.

2. W. Schadewaldt, *Von Homers Welt und Werk: Autsätze und Auslegungen zur homerischen Frage,* 3d ed. (Stuttgart, 1959).

3. C. Whitman, *Homer and the Heroic Tradition* (Cambridge, Mass., 1958). So Richmond Lattimore writes in the introduction to his translation of the poem: "The *Iliad* is not the story of Troy. Neither the beginning nor the end of the war is narrated in the *Iliad*. We begin in the tenth year of the siege and we end, some weeks later, still in the tenth year, with the city still untaken" (*The "Iliad" of Homer* [Chicago, 1961], 17). But clearly the fall of Troy resonates, sometimes quietly, sometimes in loud lament, throughout the poem and especially in Books 22 and 24. For M. Lynn-George, in particular (*Epos: Word, Narrative, and the "Iliad"* [Atlantic Highlands, N.J., 1988]), who believes every presence reveals an absence and every absence has about it a presence, Troy is and is not the subject: in his words, the *Iliad* manifests a narrative mode of "indefiniteness which also shapes this determination of limits" (210). Accordingly, he characterizes Troy as "a city suspended between the possibilities of preservation and destruction" (221; cf. 220–27) and asserts its thematic importance to the poem as a whole. Recent scholarship, in general, has increasingly acknowledged the significance of Troy in the *Iliad;* see M. Mueller, *The "Iliad"* (London, 1984), 2–6 for excellent introductory remarks. More attention to Troy is found in S. Schein, *The Mortal Hero* (Berkeley, Calif., 1984); he concludes his book with the chapter "Hektor and Troy," 168–95. I am pleased to observe that this account seems to be in basic agreement with a thesis I advanced in "The *Polis* in Homer: A Definition and Interpretation," *Ramus* 10 (1981), 1–34, esp. 14–26, much of which I have incorporated into this chapter. For another important treatment of the subject, see J. M. Redfield, *Nature and Culture in the "Iliad"* (Chicago, 1975), chap. 3 ("The Hero") and chap. 4 ("Error").

4. This is S. Benardete's translation of Porphyry ("The *Aristeia* of Diomedes and the Plot of the *Iliad,*" *Agon* 2 [1968], 10). I agree with him that criticism of the *Iliad* must look beyond Achilles and his wrath, but surely the broader themes of the *Iliad* go beyond questions of glory (kleos) to those of Troy and its fall.

5. W. Jaeger, "Tyrtaeus on True Arete," *Five Essays* (Montreal, 1966), 121.

6. I wish to thank my student Mary Hannah Jones for this observation. See 18.79–126, esp. 90–96 and 114–16; cf. 16.851–54. The domino effect begins with the death of Sarpedon which precipitates the rest: Patroklos, Hektor, Achilles (cf. Zeus at 15.64–77; cf. 15.612–14).

7. *Il.* 17.737–39, 18.207–14, 18.219–21, 21.522–25. Cf. *Od.* 8.523–30. For the one simile of a city of peace, see *Il.* 15.679–86. Cf. the comparison of a boy who makes sand castles and then ruins them to the figure of Apollo wrecking the bastions of the Achaeans (15.360–66) and Priam's response to the approaching Achilles (21.526–38 and 22.25–30). Cf. Lynn-George, *Epos,* 220–22 and 264–65.

8. Cf. S. Bassett, "The Introduction of the *Iliad,* the *Odyssey,* and the *Aeneid,*" *CW* 27 (1934–35), 105–10 and 113–18. On Achilles' *menis,* see J. Redfield, "The Proem of the *Iliad:* Homer's Art," *CP* 74 (1979), 90–105; see also C. Watkins, "A propos de *MENIS,*" *Bulletin de la Société de linguistique de Paris* 72 (1977), 187–209. In "The Wrath of Thetis," *TAPA* 116 (1986), 1–24, Laura Slatkin says that Thetis possessed a cosmic, theogonic power capable of overthrowing the universe. This power in the *Iliad* is both displaced (onto her son) and renounced (when she, obeying Olympian wishes, convinces Achilles in Book 24 to return Hektor's corpse): "cosmic equilibrium is achieved at the cost of human mortality" (22). She concludes that the *Iliad* "is concerned with the individual's experience of his mortal limitations and the existential choices they demand . . . [as well as] their metaphysical consequences in relation to the entire cosmic structure" (24). This attention on the individual, interesting as it is, in the end limits the *Iliad's* broader "concern" with communal order and the precipitous social consequences of Achilles' *menis.*

9. Cf. *Il.* 3.373–82, 3.445–54, 4.14–19, where Zeus in assembly with the other gods asks whether they should stir up battle again or allow that the city of Priam "still be a place men dwell in." Cf. A. Parry, "Language and Characterization in Homer," *HSCP* 76 (1972), 15. Bride-stealing may originally have motivated epic accounts of siege warfare (see T. B. L. Webster, *From Mycenae to Homer* [New York, 1964], 85–87). but in the *Iliad* that motif is relegated to a back position and incorporated into the central story of Achilles and Hektor. See K. Reckford, "Helen in the *Iliad,*" *GRBS* 5 (1964), 5–20; cf. L. L. Clader, *Helen: The Evolution from Divine to Heroic in the Greek Epic Tradition* (Leiden, 1976). See Chapter 3, pp. 42–44.

10. Benardete, "The *Aristeia* of Diomedes," 20–24.

11. Even this battle has its false start in the short confrontation between Achilles and Hektor aborted by Apollo (20.421–44). The encounter occurs before the great struggle of Achilles with the river in Book 21 and thus is a premature confrontation, without the full associations of the later duel between the two heroes in Book 22.

12. Diomedes is also compared to a star (the same autumnal star) at the beginning, rather than near the end, of his aristeia in Book 5, but that simile stops short

of associating the brillance of the light with its threatening consequences; cf. Whit-man, *Homer and the Heroic Tradition,* 142–44.

13. Cf. 6.459–61. From our perspective, it matters less whether Hektor imag-ines that he will not survive (Schadewaldt, *Von Homers Welt und Werk,* 222, and C. Broccia, "Homerica: La chiusa di Z secundo la critica e secondo l'esegesi," *RFIC* 92 [1964], 392) or whether Astyanax at this point gives him new hope (K. Rein-hardt, *Die "Ilias" und ihr Dichter,* ed. U. Hölscher [Göttingen, 1961], 303), than that Hektor thinks that the *city* will continue. One can take exception, nevertheless, to Reinhardt's terminology when he says that Hektor's departure from Astyanax reawakens his sense "for life and the present." M. B. Arthur describes Hektor's prayer as "a utopian vision of the nuclear family" which provides "the ideal recon-ciliation between opposing interests" of the male and female, of war and peace ("The Divided World of *Iliad* VI," in *Reflections of Women in Antiquity,* ed. H. Foley [New York, 1981], 34). That utopian image of the nuclear family, however, is also a utopian image of a polis that lives without end: the domestic is cast within a public frame. For the fluctuation between this image of urban continuity and the certainty of imminent doom, see Lynn-George, *Epos,* 218–20.

14. *Il.* 6.486–89 (condensed). P. Vivante, *The Homeric Imagination* (Bloom-ington, Ind., 1970), 208, is fundamentally wrong, I think, even from the most distant perspective, in what is for the most part a refreshing book on Homer, when he sees in Hektor a transcendence of the actual human drama, intense as it is, and thinks that he is lifted into a frame of mind where he is "free of heart."

15. For the "self-deluding" aspects of Hektor, see Whitman, *Homer and the Heroic Tradition,* 208–12, and M. Mueller, "Knowledge and Delusion in the *Iliad,*" *Mosaic* 3.2 (1970), 86–103, reprinted in J. Wright, ed., *Essays on the "Iliad"* (Bloom-ington, Ind., 1978).

16. *Il.* 18.115ff.; cf. 19.420–23, 21.99–113, and so on.

17. A. N. Whitehead, *The Aims of Education and Other Essays* (New York, 1949), 26. For the consciousness that entertains a past and future, see L. Mumford, *The City in History* (New York, 1961), 9, and N. O. Brown, *Life against Death* (Mid-dleton, Conn., 1970), 283–85.

18. W. Marg, "Die Schild des Achilleus," *Homer über die Dichter* (Munster, 1971), 38. It seems odd to argue, as Marg does, that the scenes on the Shield are meaningless to Achilles when he alone of the Myrmidons has the courage to look at the intricate armor (19.14–20). As much as most of the individual pictures depict life-continuing activities, in their entirety they present the world from the distance of the Olympians.

19. *Il.* 18.483–85. Compare also the broad temporal frame in which Achilles perceives his own fate. In its magnitude, it equals the spatial frame in which Zeus casts the fate of Troy at 4.41–49. Achilles says to Lykaon: "Yet even I have also my death and my strong destiny, / and there shall be a dawn or evening time [*deilē*] or midday / when some man in the fighting will take the life from me also" (21.110–12). The astronomical component of Achilles' Shield continued to be of particular importance in sixth- and fifth-century Greek literature; see P. R. Hardie, "Imago Mundi: Cosmological and Ideological Aspects of the Shield of Achilles," *JHS* 105 (1985), 11–15.

20. *Il.* 22.179–80; Athena inquires of Zeus: "Do you propose to reprieve a mortal man [i.e. Hektor], whose doom has been long settled, from the pains of death?"

21. F. Scott Fitzgerald, "My Lost City," in *The Crack-up* (New York, 1945), 32, first published by *Esquire* (1934).

22. For the symmetrical correspondences between the first and last books, see Whitman, *Homer and the Heroic Tradition,* and D. Lohmann, *Die Komposition der Rehen in der "Ilias"* (Berlin, 1970), 169ff. But see Lynn-George, *Epos,* 230–50. When referring to the judgment of Paris in Book 24, Malcolm Davies comments that, unlike Achilles and Priam who relent and forgive through suffering, the gods, malicious and unforgiving to the end, demand the destruction of Troy: "The Judgment of Paris and *Iliad* XXIV," *JHS* 101 (1981), 56–62. Such a view sentimentalizes the stern and sweeping vision of the *Iliad,* a poem in which the action of fate far transcends mere personal malice, human or divine. See Chapter 2, 39–40 and notes 69 and 70 to that chapter.

23. See 24.728–29; this reference to the fall of Troy is the last reminder of what is foreshadowed throughout the *Iliad.* All passages are collected in W. Kullmann, *Die Quellen der "Ilias."* Hermes Einzelschriften 14 (Wiesbaden, 1960), 343–49.

Appendix 1. Nature and Technology in Place Epithets

1. The Odyssean numbers increase when predicate adjectives describing place are included (see, for example, the detailed descriptions of Ithaca by speakers at 4.405–6, 9.21–27, 13.242–47).

2. After Homer, it is found with natural elements such as *phaos* (Bacchy. 16.42) and *hudōr* (Simon. 45). It is seldom used of people.

3. It also applies to ambrosia, and in Pindar to *hudōr* (*Olympian* 6.85).

4. C. M. Bowra, "Homeric Epithets for Troy," *JHS* 80 (1960), 17.

5. P. Vivante, *The Epithets in Homer: A Study in Poetic Values* (New Haven, Conn., 1982), 121.

6. Euphony often seems evident as well: Araithureēn t' erateinēn (2.571); Arēnēn erateinēn (2.591); Augeias erateinas (2.532 = 583); but less assonance is felt perhaps in a word beginning with a consonant, such as Mantineēn erateinēn (2.607).

7. The epithet is found seven times with Troy, always with a preposition, usually *proti,* in both speeches and narrative, and once with Enispe in Arkadia, in the Greek Catalogue of Book 2, without preposition.

8. Iolkos, Thebes, Athens, and Mycenae, we know, were dominant in the Mycenaean period and, with the possible exception of Thebes, well-walled. The other three are more difficult to correlate with archaeological evidence.

Appendix 3. Sacred Cities of the East

1. King Sennacherib (705–681 B.C.), *The Annals of Sennacherib,* 2 vols., ed. D. Luckenbill (Chicago, 1924), 2: para. 363.

2. For the fullest and most wide-ranging consideration of the sacredness of capital kingdoms, see P. Wheatley, *City as Symbol,* Inaugural Lecture, University College London (London, 1969), 9–22, but see also the seminal work by A. J. Wensinck, "The Ideas of the Western Semitics concerning the Navel of the Earth," *Verhandelingen der Koninklijke Akademie van Wetenschappen te Amsterdam* n.s. 17 (1916), chaps. 11 and 23–30 (hereafter "Ideas"). Cf. M. Eliade, *The Myth of the Eternal Return,* 2d ed., trans. W. R. Trask (New York, 1965), 6–17, and his *Images et symboles* (Paris, 1952), chap. 1.

3. See *Ancient Near Eastern Texts,* trans. E. A. Speiser 3d ed., ed. J. B. Pritchard (Princeton, 1969), 67 (hereafter cited as *ANET*). For the creation of Babylon after Marduk defeats the forces of chaos, see T. Jacobsen, "The Battle between Marduk and Tiamat," *Journal of the American Oriental Society* 88 (1968), 104–8.

4. Cf. "They (the assembled gods = Anunnaki) raised high the head of Esagila equaling Apsu. / Having built a stage-tower *as high as* Apsu, / They set up *in it* an abode for Marduk, Enlil, (and) Ea. / In their presence he *adorned* (it) in grandeur" (*ANET, Enuma Elish,* emphasis is the translator's). The phrase "the head of Esagila" in this Akkadian text plays on the Sumerian meaning for *Esagila* ("house," "lofty head") and refers to the Esharra itself. For more on the "mountain" as the place where the mysterious potency of the earth is concentrated, see H. Frankfort, *The Birth of Civilization in the Near East* (London, 1951), 49–77 and his *The Art and Architecture of the Ancient Orient,* 4th ed. (London, 1970), 4–9 and 54–56. For a recognition of Babylon and Nippur as cosmic centers, if not cosmic mountains, see R. J. Clifford, *The Cosmic Mountain in Canaan and the Old Testament* (Cambridge, Mass., 1972), 14–25; for general observations of temple and mountain, see O. Keel, *The Symbolism of the Biblical World: Ancient Near Eastern Iconograghy and the Book of Psalms,* trans. T. J. Hallett (New York, 1978), 113–20.

5. M. Green, "Eridu in Sumerian Literature" (Ph.D. diss., University of Chicago, 1975), 180.

6. M. Eliade, *Patterns in Comparative Religion,* trans. R. Sheed (New York, 1974), 376. See the useful summaries in T. Gaster, "Myth and Story," *Numen* 1 (1954), 184–212, esp. 191, as well as in Wheatley, *City as Symbol,* 9; Clifford, *The Cosmic Mountain in Canaan and the Old Testament,* 14–25; Keel, *Symbolism of the Biblical World,* 113–20, 151–63, and 171–6.

7. Keel, *Symbolism of the Biblical World,* 120.

8. Cf. Ps. 87:1 and Isa. 28:16. For further analysis, see J. Dougherty, *The Five Square City: The City in the Religious Imagination* (Notre Dame, 1980), chap. 1; Keel, *Symbolism of the Bibilical World,* 174–75; cf. 118–20 and 179–83; H. Schmidt, *Der heilige Fels in Jerusalem* (Tübingen, 1933). Cf. M. Eliade, *Patterns in Comparative Religion,* 376–77, and Wensinck, "Ideas," 16–23, 30–35, and 54–57. It is from underneath that Holy Rock, according to some, that all the fresh waters of the world derive; compare Wensinck, "Ideas," 35, and Keel, "The Symbolism of the Biblical World," 118 fig. 153a.

9. See S. Safrai, "The Heavenly Jerusalem," *Ariel* 23 (1969), 11–16.

10. See Clifford, *Cosmic Mountain in Canaan and the Old Testament,* 182–89.

11. Ezek. 5:5. Compare Josephus (*Jewish Wars* III.3.5): "The town [of Jerusalem] has sometimes, not inaptly, been called 'the navel of the country,'" and Sibylline

Oracles (V.248–50) which speak of "the godlike heavenly race of the blessed Jews, who dwell around the City of God at the center of the earth."

12. For a study of the Greek term *omphalos* and its relevance to Hebrew religion, see S. Terrain, "The Omphalos Myth and Hebrew Religion," *Vetus Testamentum* 20 (1970), 315–38; with extensive bibliography cited there.

13. Quoted in W. D. Davies, *The Gospel and the Land: Early Christianity and Jewish Territorial Doctrine* (Berkeley, Calif., 1974), 57–60, cf. 8. Cf. his *Territorial Dimension of Judaism* (Berkeley, Calif., 1982), 38–39. See also R. Gordon, "Terra Sancta and the Territorial Doctrine of the Targum to the Prophets," in *Interpreting the Hebrew Bible: Essays in Honor of E. I. J. Rosenthal*, ed. J. A. Emerton and S. C. Reif (Cambridge, 1982), 119–31.

14. G. E. von Grunebaum, "The Sacred Character of Islamic Cities," in *Islam and Medieval Hellenism: Sacred and Cultural Perspectives*, ed. D. Wilson (London, 1976), 32.

15. Ibid., 32; also quoted in Wensinck, "Ideas," 18. For references to the ancient sources, see Wensinck, "Ideas," 36.

16. Von Grunebaum, "Sacred Character of Islamic Cities," 33.

17. Cf. ibid., 27–28 and 31; Wheatley, *City as Symbol*, 26; Dougherty, *Five Square City*, 2.

18. Cf. A. L. Oppenheim, "Mesopotamia—Land of Many Cities," in *Middle Eastern Cities*, ed. I. Lapidus (Berkeley, Calif., 1969), 6, and L. L. Orlin, "Ancient Near Eastern Cities: Form, Function, and Idea," in L. L. Orlin, ed., *Janus: Essays in Ancient and Modern Studies* (Ann Arbor, Mich., 1975), 31. For the late and tenuous unification of the country, see T. Jacobsen, "Early Development in Mesopotamia," *Zeitschrift für Assyriologie und vorderasiatische Archäologie* 52 (1957), 99. The rise and fall of successive cities was explained by a joint and complex decision of all the gods, an account of which is partially recorded in the various city lamentation hymns: see J. Cooper, ed., *The Curse of Agade* (Baltimore, 1983); S. Kramer, *Lamentation over the Destruction of Ur* (Chicago, 1940); M. Green, "Eridu in Sumerian Literature," passim; P. Michalowski, ed., *Lamentation over the Destruction of Sumer and Ur* (Winona Lake, Ind., 1988).

19. S. Kramer, *The Sacred Marriage Rite: Aspects of Faith, Myth, and Ritual in Ancient Sumer* (Bloomington, Ind., 1969), 12; cf. H. Frankfort, *The Birth of Civilization*, 54–56. Each temple and city god was distinctive and expressive of the specific aura of its inhabitant; cf. S. Dalton, "Canal, Wall, and Temple Names of the Old Babylonian Period" (Ph.D. diss., Brandeis University, 1983), 216.

20. The translation is that of A. Heidel, *The Babylonian Genesis*, 2d ed. (Chicago, 1951), 62–63. The transliteration from the Sumerian and Babylonian texts is that of L. W. King, *The Seven Tablets of Creation*, 2 vols. (1902; reprint New York, 1976), 1:130–33, with the one following exception: I altered the spelling *azag* (or *azag-ga*) to *kù* to follow contemporary convention.

21. Cf. A. Falkenstein, *The Sumerian Temple City* (Los Angeles, 1974), 10–13.

22. G. Gragg, *The Kes Temple Hymn*, printed along with and catalogued under A. Sjoberg and E. Bergmann, *The Collection of the Sumerian Temple Hymns* (Locust Valley, N.Y., 1969), Temple I, line 29.

23. Ibid., Temple II, lines 35–36.

24. Ibid., listed under the rubric "unduplicated strophe," 176, lines 12′–13′.

25. The translation comes from Kramer, *Sacred Marriage Rite,* 32.

26. See ibid., passim; see also H. Frankfort, *Kingship and the Gods: A Study of Ancient Near Eastern Religion as the Integration of Society and Nature* (Chicago, 1948), 313–33. Cf. T. Jacobsen, *The Treasures of Darkness: A History of Mesopotamian Religion* (New Haven, Conn., 1976), 39 and 209. See page 154 and note 53, below.

27. Cf. Orlin, "Ancient Near Eastern Cities," 51.

28. "Hymn to Enlil, the All-Beneficent," 573–76, lines 65–73 in *ANET,* describing the Duranki or Eduranki, central temple at Nippur, city of the chief Sumerian god Enlil.

29. T. Jacobsen, *Toward the Image of Tammuz and Other Essays on Mesopotamian History and Culture,* ed. W. Moran (Cambridge, Mass., 1970), 379 n. 49. See notes 31 and 33, below. See also Chapter 2, note 32.

30. Translation and text from G. Gragg, *The Kes Temple Hymn,* from Temple III hymn, 170–71, lines 58–59.

31. Cf. A. L. Oppenheim, *Ancient Mesopotamia: Portrait of a Dead Civilization,* 2d ed. (Chicago, 1977), 362 n. 59. For Oppenheim's excellent observations about sacred cities, see 125–42, esp. 129–33.

32. Sjoberg and Bergmann, *The Kes Temple Hymn,* Hymn 1, 17, lines 1–13. Compare a Kes hymn again: "Temple, great crown, reaching the sky" (Hymn 1, 169, line 33). The metaphor of the temple as a head is equally common. See the *Enuma Elish:* "They raised high the head of Esagila equaling Apsu" (line 100), where the Akkadian text plays on the meaning of the Sumerian *Esagila,* or see another Kes hymn: "The four corners of heaven became green for Enlil like an orchard. / Kes lifted its head for him. / When Kes lifted its head among all the lands. / Enlil spoke the praises of Kes" (Hymn 1, 167, lines 6–9).

33. The inner citadel was called a *kirhu,* neither Akkadian nor Sumerian, implying foreign origin. As a historian, Leo Oppenheim in *Ancient Mesopotamia,* 129–33, draws a sharp distinction between the old cities of the alluvial plains in Lower Mesopotamia, where there is a significant separation between the temple and the palace, and the cities in Upper Mesopotamia, where the separation between temple and palace disappears. Important as this distinction is in terms of political organization of the state, the cities of Lower and Upper Mesopotamia suggest strong similarities from the perspective of comparative religion. Both types clearly demarcate the division between sacred center (whether temple complex or temple/palace complex) and human city. Even when the city of Babylon in the Neo-Babylonian period enclosed both a walled palace complex and a walled temple complex, religious texts, such as the Neo-Babylonian cosmogonic text cited above, described the city in terms of distinct city and temple complex division.

34. Quoted in Luckenbill, *Annals of Sennacherib,* 2:111, lines 50–52. Cf. Frankfort, *Art and Architecture of the Ancient Orient,* 65–79.

35. Translation from T. Jacobsen, *Toward an Image of Tammuz,* 379 n. 49. It is from this text that Jacobsen thinks *uru-kù* is a general term for the temple settlement within a city, but see Chapter 2, note 32.

36. Quoted from D. Luckenbill, *Ancient Records of Assyria and Babylonia,* vol. 1:

Historical Records of Assyria from the earliest times to Sargon (1926; reprint New York, 1968), 244, para. 675–77.

37. Cf. R. Ellis, *Foundation Deposits in Ancient Mesopotamia* (New Haven, Conn., 1968), 32.

38. Quoted from Luckenbill, *The Annals of Sennacherib*, 2:134, para. 94. See C. Faraone, "Hephaestus the Magician and Near Eastern Parallels for Alcinous' Watchdogs," *GRBS* 28 (1987), 266–75.

39. Both quoted from G. Barton, *Miscellaneous Babylonia Inscriptions: Sumerian Religious Texts* (New Haven, Conn., 1938), 29, col. ii.9–10.

40. Cf. Ellis, *Foundation Deposits in Ancient Mesopotamia*, passim, esp. 20–26, 46–57, and 77–93.

41. Ibid., 134; cf. 32 and 133. For magical and religious measures used to secure gates in the Near East, Israel, and Egypt, see Keel, *Symbolism of the Biblical World*, 120–27.

42. For an overview of this unique synthesis, see H. Güterbock, "A View of Hittite Literature," *Journal of the American Oriental Society* 84 (1964), 107–14.

43. O. R. Gurney, *Some Aspects of Hittite Religion* (Oxford, 1977), 39. For the likely connection of this festival (thought to mean "of the earth") with the New Year Festival (associated with the AN-TAH-SUM plant), see Gurney, *The Hittites*, 3d ed. (New York., 1981), 154–57, 183–85, 190–91. For an account of the festival with that plant, see Güterbock, "An Outline of the Hittite AN-TAH-SUM Festival," *Journal of Near Eastern Studies* 19 (1960), 80–89.

44. Quoted from A. Goetze in *ANET*, 2d ed., 356.

45. In addition to the royal palace, a library, storehouses, and administrative buildings have been identified in the citadel. See also K. von Bittel, *Hattuscha, Haupstadt der Hethiter: Geschichte und Kultur einer altorientalischen Grossmancht* (Koln, 1983), 87–132 (hereafter *Hattuscha*), as well as his *Hattusha: The Capital of the Hittites* (New York, 1970), 63–90 (hereafter *Hattusha*), and *Les Hittites* (Paris, 1976), 117–22; E. Akurgal, *The Art of the Hittites*, trans. C. McNab (New York, 1962), 89–96; Gurney, *Hittites*, 153–62.

46. When finally built, the circuit around Hattusas' acres must have been impressive. The double line of outer wall where the city was most vulnerable and the massive main wall, sometimes twenty-five feet thick, reached as high as nineteen feet, topped with mud-brick and fitted with crenellated towers. Unlike the small-stone work of the wall at Troy VI and VIIa, Hattusas' huge polygonal masonry is strikingly similar to the Kyklopean construction typical of Mycenaean citadels, as is its corbel-vaulted tunnel. But similarities between Hittite and Mycenaean craftsmanship break down with regard to other construction details, such as with projecting towers and mud-brick work. Cf. Akurgal, *Art of the Hittites*, 96–99 and 107–8; Bittel, *Hattuscha*, 32–41, as well as his *Hattuscha*, 50–53, and *Les Hittites*, 105–16; Gurney, *Hittites*, 112–15; J. Lehmann, *The Hittites: A People of a Thousand Gods*, trans. J. M. Brownjohn (New York, 1977), 253–58 (hereafter *Hittites: People*).

47. Cf. Bittel, *Hattuscha*, 72–80, as well as his *Hattusha*, 49–50 and 54–60, and *Les Hittites* (Paris, 1976), 122–33; Akurgal, *Art of the Hittites*, 99–103; Lehmann, *Hittites: People*.

48. Cf. Bittel, *Hattusha*, 54–57; Akurgal, *Art of the Hittites*, 107; Gurney, *Hittites*, 146–52.

49. For the king as god's regent, see a tablet quoted by Akurgal, *Art of the Hittites*, 87: "The Country belongs to the Weather-God, heaven and earth and the people belong to the Weather-God. He made Labarna the king (Labarnas I, 1680–1650 B.C.), his regent, and gave him the entire land of Hatti." The king's priestly role is evident from a tablet quoted by Gurney, *Hittites*, 154: King Mursilis II (1339–1306 B.C.) on military command in the south felt it necessary to return to Hattusas to perform the *purulli* festival at Yazilikaya, even though that same spring he had already twice performed it elsewhere.

50. Quoted in Gurney, *Hittites*, 158–59.

51. The Hittite example at Hattusas of city enclosure joined by sacred way to a major "chthonic" fertility sanctuary outside the city is paralleled by similar linkages at many Greek cities on the Asia Minor coast. For example, at Ephesus, the city is joined by sacred road to the important sanctuary of Artemis seven stades outside the city walls. In Pausanias' words, the sanctuary was "far more ancient than the coming of the Greek Ionians" (7.2.6), undoubtedly sacred to the Anatolian mother goddess Kybele and appropriated by the Greeks when they took over Ephesus. When the people of that city were besieged by Croesus, Herodotus says that a rope was stretched from the city to the sanctuary—to no avail (1.26.2). Similarly, Pergamon is linked by sacred road to the Asklepieion a few kilometers outside its city, as Colophon is closely connected by myth with Klaros, slightly farther away, an important nocturnal oracular center of Apollo where Artemis, Leto, and Dionysus were also worshiped. Coins from Colophon also featured cult images from Klaros. Similarly, Miletus was umbilically linked by a sacred road of fifteen kilometers to Didyma, another oracular site sacred long before the Greek arrival (Paus. 7.2.6). In each case, a very prominent religious center of pre-Greek origins and with clear chthonic ties outside the city was intimately bound with the city's religious identity.

52. See Bittel, *Hattuscha*, 133–61, as well as his *Hattusha*, 91–112, and *Les Hittites*, 134–35 and 202–22. See also Güterbock, "An Outline of the Hittite AN-TAH-SUM Festival," 80–89, and his "Yazilikaya," *Mitteilungen der Deutschen Orient-Gesellschaft* 86 (1953), 15–76; J. Garstang, *The Hittite Empire* (New York, 1930), 95–119. E. Laroche, "Le panthéon de Yazilikaya," *Journal of Cuneiform Studies* 6 (1952), 115–23, dates construction of the temple-sanctuary to shortly after 1250 B.C. in the time of Tuthaliya IV, but Hittite scholars generally agree that the site was a holy place long before the last decades of the Hittite Empire. See further, Gurney, *Some Aspects of Hittite Religion*, 19–23 and 40–43, and his *Hittites*, 154–57, 183–85, 190–91, 200–202; Akurgal, *Art of the Hittites*, 76–81 and 118–19.

53. See Jacobsen, *Toward the Image of Tammuz*, 36. See the important remarks by Oppenheim, *Ancient Mesopotamia*, on the sacred road at Babylon, Assur, and Hattusas (115 and 139) and on the Babylonian/Assyrian New Year Festival (122 and 132). For the Assyrian Sennacherib's rebuilding of the temple for the New Year Festival outside Babylon, see his inscription in Luckenbill, *Annals*, 135–43. Before that rebuilding, the text says, the festival was "held in the city." See note 26, above.

54. See Bittel, *Les Hittites*, 187–88 and 223–33; Akurgal, *Art of the Hittites*, 96, 109–10, and 113–16.

55. B. Rutkowski, *The Cult Places of the Aegean*, rev. ed. (New Haven, Conn., 1986), 185; cf. 197.

56. Quoted from Goetze, *ANET* 2d ed., 356.

57. Ibid., 356; cf. Ellis, *Foundation Deposits in Ancient Mesopotamia*, 32–33, 79, 92, 139.

58. Cf. Bittel, *Les Hittites*, 136–40.

59. C. Blegen, J. Claskey, M. Rawson, *Troy: The Sixth Settlement*, vol. 3, part 1 (text), 97, and more generally 96–100 and 252–53. For a judicious comparison of these pillars with the freestanding columns represented in Minoan/Mycenaean art, see M. P. Nilsson, *The Minoan-Mycenaean Religion and Its Survival in Greek Religion*, 2d ed. (Lund, 1950), 236–61. For general discussion of divine images at gateways in the Near East and Greece, see C. Picard, *Les murailles*, vol. 1: *Les portes sculptées à images divines. Etudes Thasiennes VIII* (Paris, 1962).

60. Servius, at *Aen.* 2.13 and 241; cf. W. F. J. Knight, *Vergil: Epic and Anthropology* (New York, 1967), 121–22.

61. Cf. Plautus, *Bacch.* 953–56; source found in Knight, *Vergil*, 132 n. 159.

62. Akurgal, *Art of the Hittites*, 124.

63. For a discussion of the many city shapes in the Near East (ovaloid, rectangular, triangular, diamond-shaped, square, as well as circular), see Oppenheim, *Ancient Mesopotamia*, 133–35. For a study of the circular form of royal residences in a slighter later period of the Near East, see H. P. L'Orange, "Expressions of Cosmic Kingship in the Ancient World," in *Sacred Kingship* (also *La Regalita Sacra*), Studies in the History of Religions IV (Supplements to *Numen*) (Leiden, 1959), 481–92. L'Orange compares the portrait of a king rising out of a ring in Persian, Achaemenian, and later Near Eastern art ("the symbolic, almost hieroglyphic expression of the cosmocratic power of the Eastern king") to the striking iconographic parallel of "the king in the centre of his round city, the king in his revolving throne" (both quotes on 489). For a revival of theriomorphic guardians at gateways to cities and palaces among the Neo-Assyrians and Neo-Hittites, see D. Kolbe, *Die religiös-mythologischen Charakters in neu-assyrischen Palästen* (Frankfurt, 1981); T. A. Madhloum, *The Chronology of Neo-Assyrian Art* (London, 1970), 94–117; E. Akurgal, *The Art of Greece: Its Origin in the Mediterranean and the Near East* (New York, 1966), 60–63, 105–8; L. Delaporte, *Malatya: la porte des lions* (Paris, 1940). See also note 38, above.

Selected Bibliography

Arendt, H. *The Human Condition*. Chicago, 1959.

Arthur, M. B. "The Divided World of *Iliad* VI." In *Reflections of Women in Antiquity*, ed. H. Foley. New York, 1981. 19–44.

Austin, M., and P. Vidal-Naquet. *Les economies et sociétés en Grèce ancienne*. Paris, 1972. *Economic and Social History of Ancient Greece: An Introduction*. Trans. and rev. M. Austin. Berkeley, Calif., 1977.

Austin, N. *Archery at the Dark of the Moon: Poetic Problems in Homer's "Odyssey."* Berkeley, Calif., 1975.

Benveniste, E. "Deux modèles linguistiques de la cité." In *Echanges et communications: Mélanges offerts à Claude Lévi-Strauss*. The Hague, 1970. 589–96. Also in his *Problèmes de linguistique générale*, vol. 2. Paris, 1974. 272–80.

——. *Le vocabulaire des institutions indo-européennes*. Vol. 2: *Pouvoir, droit, religion*. Paris, 1973. = *Indo-European Language and Society*. Trans. E. Palmer. Coral Gables, Fla., 1973.

Blegen, C. W., et al. *Troy: Settlements VIIa, VIIb, and VIII*, vol. 4. Princeton, 1958.

——. *Troy IV: Plates*. Princeton, 1958.

Burkert, W. *Greek Religion*. Trans. J. Raffan. Cambridge, Mass., 1985.

Calhoun, G. M. "The Divine Entourage in Homer." *AJP* 61 (1941), 257–77.

——. "Homer's Gods: Myth and Marchen." *AJP* 60 (1939), 1–28.

——. "Polity and Society: The Homeric Picture." In *A Companion to Homer*, ed. A. J. B. Wace and F. H. Stubbings. London, 1962. 431–51.

Casabona, J. *Recherches sur le vocabulaire des sacrifices en Grèc*. Aix-en-Provence, 1966.

Chantraine, P. *Dictionnaire étymologique de la langue grecque, histoire des mots*. 4 vols. Paris, 1968–80.

Chantraine, P., and O. Masson. "Sur quelques termes du vocabulaire religieux des Grecs: La valeur du mot *agos* et de ses derívés." In *Sprachgeschichte und Wortbedeutung; Festschrift A. Debrunner*. Bern, 1954. 85–107.

Coldstream, J. N. *Geometric Greece*. New York, 1977.

Cook, J. M. *The Greeks in Ionia and the East*. London, 1962; New York, 1963.

———. "Old Smyrna, 1948–51." *BSA* 53–54 (1958–59), 1–34.

Donlan, W. "Homeric *Temenos* and the Land Economy of the Dark Ages," *MH* 46 (1989), 129–45.

———. "The Social Groups of Dark Age Greece," *CP* 80 (1985), 293–308.

Drerup, H. *Griechische Baukunst in geometrischer Zeit*. Archaeologica Homerica. Kap. O. Göttingen, 1969.

Edwards, M. W. *Homer: The Poet of the "Iliad."* Baltimore, 1987.

Ehrenberg, V. *The Greek State*. 2d ed., 1960. Reprint. edition New York, 1964.

———. "When Did the *Polis* Arise?" *JHS* 57 (1937), 147–59.

Eliade, M. *Images et symboles*. Paris, 1952.

———. *Patterns in Comparative Religion*. Trans. R. Sheed. New York, 1974.

Farnell, L. R. *The Cults of the Greek States*. 5 vols. (Oxford, 1896–1909)

Foley, H. "'Reverse Similes' and Sex Roles in the *Odyssey*." *Arethusa* 11 (1978), 7–26.

Gouldner, A. W. *Enter Plato: Classical Greece and the Origins of Social Theory*. New York, 1965.

Griffeth, R., and C. G. Thomas, eds. *The City-State in Five Cultures*. Santa Barbara, Calif., 1981.

Gschnitzer, F. "Stadt und Stamm bei Homer." *Chiron* 1 (1971), 1–17.

Hägg, R., ed. *The Greek Renaissance of the Eighth Century B.C.* Stockholm, 1983.

Hägg, R., and N. Marinatos, eds. *Sanctuaries and Cults in the Aegean Bronze Age*. Stockholm, 1981.

Hammond, M. *The City in the Ancient World*. Cambridge, Mass., 1972.

Hoekstra, A. *Epic Verse before Homer: Three Studies*. New York, 1981.

Hoffmann, W. "Die *Polis* bei Homer." In *Festschrift Bruno Snell*, ed. H. Erbse. Munich, 1956. 151–65.

Hooker, J. T. *Hieros in Early Greek*. Innsbrucker Beiträge zur Sprachwissenschaft 22. Innsbruck, 1980.

———. "Ilios and the *Iliad*." *WS* 13 (1979), 5–21

Hurwit, J., *The Art and Culture of Early Greece, 1100–480 B.C.* Ithaca, N.Y., 1985.

Iakovidis, S. *Vormykenische und Mykenische Wehrbauten*. Archaeologia Homerica. Kap. E. Göttingen, 1977. 166–221.

Kakridis, J. T. *Homeric Researches*. Lund, 1949.

———. "The Role of the Women in the *Iliad*." *Eranos* 54 (1956), 21–27.

Kilian, K. "The Emergence of Wanax Ideology in the Mycenaean Palaces." *OJA* 7 (1988), 291–302.

———. "Zur Funktion der mykenischen Residenzen." In *The Function of the Minoan Palaces*, ed. R. Hägg and N. Marinatos. Stockholm, 1987. 21–38.

Knight, W. F. J. *Vergil: Epic and Anthropology*. New York, 1967.

Korfmann, M. "Beşik Tepe: New Evidence for the Period of the Trojan Sixth and Seventh Settlements." In M. Mellink, ed., *Troy and the Trojan War*, q.v. 17–38.

———. "Troy: Topography and Navigation." In *Troy and the Trojan War*, ed. M. Mellink, q.v. 1–16.

Lesky, A. *Homeros. Sonderausgaben der Paulyschen Realencyclopädie der classischen Altertumswissenschaft.* Stuttgart, 1967.

Lévy, E. "*Astu* et *polis* dans l'*Iliade*." *Ktema* 8 (1983), 55–73.

———, ed. *Le système palatial en Orient, en Grèce et à Rome.* Strasbourg, 1987.

Lloyd, C. "Greek Urbanity and the *Polis*." In *Aspects of Graeco-Roman Urbanism: Essays on the Classical City*, ed. R. T. Marchese, British Archaeological Reports, International Series 188. Oxford, 1983. 11–41.

Loraux, N. *The Invention of Athens: The Funeral Oration in the Classical City.* Trans. A. Sheridan. Cambridge, Mass., 1986.

Luce, J. V. "The *Polis* in Homer and Hesiod." *PRIA* 78 (1978), 1–15.

Lynn-George, M. *Epos: Word, Narrative, and the "Iliad."* Atlantic Highlands, N.J., 1988.

McDonald, W. A., and G. R. Rapp, eds. *The Minnesota Messenia Expedition. Reconstructing a Bronze Age Regional Environment.* Minneapolis, Minn., 1972.

Mellink, M., ed. *Troy and the Trojan War.* Proceedings of a symposium at Bryn Mawr College (October 1984). Bryn Mawr, Penna., 1986.

Momigliano, A., and S. C. Humphreys. "The Social Structure of the Ancient City." *Annali della Scuola Normale* 4 (1974), 331–67.

Morris, I. M. *Burial and Ancient Society: The Rise of the Greek City-State.* Cambridge, 1987.

———. "The Early *Polis* as City and State." In *City and Country in the Ancient World*, ed. J. Rich and A. Wallace-Hadrill London, 1990.

———. "The Use and Abuse of Homer." *CA* 5 (1986), 81–138.

Mueller, M. *The "Iliad."* London, 1984.

Mumford, L. *The City in History.* New York, 1961.

Murray, O. *Early Greece.* Sussex, 1980.

Nagler, M. "Towards a Semantics of Ancient Conflict: Eris in the *Iliad*." *CW* 82 (1988), 81–90.

Nagy, G. *The Best of the Achaeans: Concepts of the Hero in Archaic Greek Society.* Baltimore, 1979.

———. *Greek Mythology and Poetics.* Ithaca, N.Y., 1990.

———. *Pindar's Homer: The Lyric Possession of the Epic Past.* Baltimore, 1990.

Nicholls, R. V. "Old Smyrna: The Iron Age Fortifications and Associated Remains of the City Perimeter." *BSA* 53–54 (1958–59), 35–137.

Nilsson, M. P. *Geschichte der griechischen Religion,* vol. 1, 3d ed. Munich, 1967. Vol. 2, 2d ed. Munich, 1961.

———. *A History of Greek Religion.* New York, 1964.

Parker, R. *Miasma: Pollution and Purification in Early Greek Religion.* Oxford, 1983.

de Polignac, F. *La naissance de la cité grecque.* Paris, 1984.

Quiller, B. "The Dynamics of Homeric Society," *SO* 56 (1981), 109–55.

Redfield, J. M. "The Making of the *Odyssey*." In *Parnassus Revisited,* ed. A. C. Yu. Chicago, 1973. 141–54.

———. *Nature and Culture in the "Iliad": The Tragedy of Hector.* Chicago, 1975.

Reinhardt, K. *Die "Ilias" und ihr Dichter,* ed. U. Hölscher. Göttingen, 1961.

———. "Das Parisurteil." In *Tradition und Geist.* Göttingen, 1960. 16–36.

Renfrew, C. *The Archaeology of Cult: The Sanctuary at Phylakopi.* British School of Arhaeology at Athens Suppl. 18. London, 1985.

Rudhardt, J. *Notions fondamentales de la pensée religieuse et actes constitutifs du culte dans la Grèce classique.* Geneva, 1958.

Sale, W. M. "The Formularity of the Place-Phrases in the *Iliad.*" *TAPA* 117 (1987), 21–50.

Sarkady, J. "Outlines of the Development of Greek Society in the Period between the 12th and 8th Centuries B.C." *AAntHung* 23 (1975), 107–25.

Schein, S. *The Mortal Hero: An Introduction to Homer's "Iliad."* Berkeley, Calif., 1984.

Schmidt, A. "La polarité des contraires dans la rencontre d'Hector et Andromaque." *LEC* 31 (1963), 129–58.

Schmidt, M. "H(I)EROS," in *Thesaurus Linguae Graecae: Lexicon des frühgriechischen Epos,* ed. B. Snell. Göttingen, 1989. No. 13, 1138–45.

Scully, V. J. *The Earth, the Temple, and the Gods: Greek Sacred Architecture.* New Haven, Conn., 1962.

Segal, C. "Andromache's Anagnorisis, Formulaic Artistry in *Iliad* 22.437–76." *HSCP* 75 (1971), 33–57.

———. "Nature and the World of Man in Greek Literature." *Arion* 2 (1963), 19–53.

———. "The Phaeacians and the Symbolism of Odysseus' Return." *Arion* 1 (1962), 17–63.

———. *The Theme of Mutilation of the Corpse in the "Iliad."* Mnemosyne Suppl. 17. Leiden, 1971.

Simpson, R. H. *Mycenaean Greece.* Atlantic Highlands, N.J., 1981.

Simpson, R. H., and J. F. Lazenby. *The Catalogue of Ships in Homer's "Iliad."* Oxford, 1970.

Smith, P. "Aineiadai as Patrons of *Iliad* XX." *HSCP* 85 (1981), 17–58.

Snodgrass, A. A. *Archaeology and the Rise of the Greek State.* Cambridge, 1977.

———. *Archaic Greece: The Age of Experiment.* London, 1980.

———. *The Dark Age of Greece: An Archaeological Survey, c.1200–c.1000 B.C.* Oxford, 1964.

Vidal-Naquet, P. "Land and Sacrifice in the *Odyssey:* A Study of Religious and Mythical Meanings." In *The Black Hunter,* trans. A. Szegedy-Maszak. Baltimore, 1986. 15–38. (Originally *Le chasseur noir.* Paris, 1981.)

Vivante, P. *The Epithets in Homer: A Study in Poetic Values.* New Haven, Conn., 1982.

Webster, T. B. L. *From Mycenae to Homer.* London, 1958; New York, 1964.

Wheatley, P. *City as Symbol.* Inaugural Lecture, University College London, 20 November, 1967. London, 1969.

Whitman, C. *Homer and the Homeric Tradition.* Cambridge, Mass., 1958.

Wright, J., ed. *Essays on the "Iliad."* Bloomington, Ind., 1978.

Wülfing–von Martitz, P. "*Hieros* bei Homer und in derältern griechischen Literatur." *Glotta* 38 (1960), 272–307.

Wust, E. "Hektor und Polydamas. Von Klerus und Staat in Griechenland." *RhM* 98 (1955), 335–49.

General Index

Roman numerals followed by arabic figures refers to chapters and footnotes. Ap. refer to an appendix.

Abzu (subterranean waters), 29
Achaeans, 13, 26, 44, 56, 57, 74, 75, 77, 95
    camp, location of, i.23
    compared to a wall, 58–59
Achaean wall, 26–27, 51, 88–89, 98, ii.67, iii.16, iii.28
Achilles, 4, 11–12, 26, 40, 45, 49, 52–53, 57, 76–77, 93, 97, 107, 110, iii.1, iv.14, iv.33, iv.43, v.1, v.6, v.11
    and Agamemnon, 21, 22
    and Agenor, 55, 109
    and Briseis, 48, 123–24
    epithets of, 53, 114
    and fall of Troy, 36, 37–38
    fate of, 118
    and Hektor, 13–14, 33, 66–67, 98, 104–5, 118
    and magic, 37, 38
    and mortality, 121–23, 124, viii.19
    and Patroklos, 116
    and Priam, 127
    Shield of, 99, 101, 102, 126, viii.18
    shout of, 37
    similes concerning, 117
    visit of assembly to, 95
    wrath of, theme expanded, 114–15, viii.8
Acropolis, 31
Adkins, A., 100, 111
Aduton ("shrine"), 35
Aeneas, 8, 11, 13, 35, 43, 45, 76

and Troy, account of origins, 61–64
Aeolus, iii.16
Agamemnon, 12, 13, 31, 40, 60, 62, 74, 75, 78, 95, 114, 115, iv.14, iv.23
    and the Achaeans, 107–8
    and Achilles, 21, 22
    on breaking of truce by Trojans, 39
    brutality of, 65–66
    and Greek wall, iii.16
Agenor, 6, 12, 13, 77, v.3
    and Achilles, 55, 109
Agora, 18, 23, 46–47, 101–2, 111, vi.5, vii.8
Aiakos and walls of Troy, 37, 50
Aidōs ("respect"), 90, 107–110
Aiskhos ("shame"), 38
Aisepos (river), 94
Aisyetes, tomb of, 12
Ajax, 120, vii.29
    on *aidōs*, 107–8
    shield of, 59, 95, iv.21, iv.45
Akurgal, E., 156
Alberti, L. B., vii.19
Alcaeus, 58
Alcibiades, 15, 110
Alexander, 7, 8, 36, 76, 115, 120, 125, 134, iv.14
    and claim over Helen, iii.7
    and code of hospitality, 38–39
    and Menelaus, duel with, 39
    see also Paris
Alkinoos, 103

Alsos ("grove"), 14
Amata, 45
Amburbium, Roman, founding ritual of, 18–19
Amphion, 48
Amphios, Trojan ally from Paisos, 57
Anat, Ugaritic city goddess, 34
Anatolia, walled cities of, 152–57
Anax ("king"), 103
Anchises, 36
    line of, 62, iv.32
Andromache, 57, 64–68, 93, 98, 109–10, 122, iii.10, iv.487
    and Astyanax, 44, 127
    and Hektor, 42–43, 60–61, 67–68, 106–7, 123
    and *krēdemnon,* 33
    military strategy of, 44, 50, 66
    and Troy, 65–66
Antenor, 39, 43, ii.68, iv.14
    wife of, 23
Antilochus, iv.33
Antimakhos, i.3, iv.14
Antinoos, vii.5
Antiope, daughter of Asopos, 48
Antiphos, son of Priam, 11
Apatē ("deceit"), 39
Aphrodite, 43, 95, 134
    affiliations with Ishtar/Astarte, ii.55
    as protectress of Troy, 35–36
Apolis ("extra-polis space"), 10
Apollo, 7–8, 12, 35, 57, 76–77, iii.28, iv.33, v.3
    and city foundation rituals, 52
    cults of, 35, ii.54
    epithets of, 35, iii.23
    and Hittite Guardian god, 35
    and Semitic god Resys, 35
    temple (*nēos*) of, 23, i.5
    as Troy's defender, 35
    and walls of Troy, 27, 37, 51–53, viii.7
    worship of, at Zeleia, ii.12
Apotropaic figures, 36, 154–55
Arendt, H., 63, 112
Ares, 12, 32, 53, 57, 58
Aretē ("excellence"), 37
Argos, 40, 85, 115, 125
Ariadne, 22
Arinna, Hittite city, 152
Arisbe, 93, 94
Aristeia ("prowess"), 95, 96, 120
Aristotle
    on man, 25, iv.38
    on polis, 112, i.26, ii.33
Arrēktos ("unbreakable"), 26, 32, 125, 127, iii.16, iii.28

Artemis, 35
Arthur, M., 42, iv.42
Assyria, 98, 149–50
Astu ("the lower residential town"), 8–9, i.12, i.15
Astyanax, 42, 98, 122–23
    death of, 44, 127
    and Hektor, 60, 61–64, 122–23
    name of, 61, iv.24, vi.50
Atē ("bewilderment" or "reckless sin"), 39, ii.69
Athena, 12, 37, 101, 125, iii.25
    epithets of, 32, 33, 35, 64–65
    and Troy, 39–40
    temple (*nēos*) of, 23, 35, 38, i.5, vi.49
    worship as polis protectress, 32–34
Athens, 21, 35, 41, 85, 94, ii.36
Austin, N., 79
Ayios Andreas on Siphnos, 86
Azraqī, on Mecca, 144

Babylon, 141–43, 147, 154
Basileus ("chief" or "prince"), 52, vii.5
Batieia (or Thorn Hill), 11–12
Beekes, R. S. P., ii.13
Benardete, S., 120
Benveniste, É., 19, 20, iv.1
Bios politikos ("life befitting a citizen"), 63
Blegen, C., 7, 155, ii.16
Bōmos ("altar"), 14
Bowra, C. M., 95, 133
Bride-stealing, viii.9
Briseis, 48, 93
Burkert, W., 17, 20, 36–37, 97–98, ii.1, ii.19, ii.42

Calhoun, G. M., 14, 105, vii.19
Callimachus, 52
Cape Mimas, 92
Capital cities of ancient Near East, sacredness of, 144
Capitolium, origin of name, 31
Cassandra, 8, 44, iii.8
Catalogues in *Iliad,* 21–22, 91–95, vi.48–50
Cattle raiding, in epic poetry, 96
Cayster (river), 92
Chios, 92
City, 4–5, 8, 18, 40, 84–87, 95, 125
    agrarian economy of, 10–11, iii.12
    Aristotelian view of, 112–13
    definition of, 14–15
    "heads" of, 30–31, 149
    sanctity of: in Near East, 28, 30–33; Rome, 18–19, 30–31; Troy, 23–40
    see also Oikos; Polis; Sacred cities

City wall(s), 3, 5, 10, 20, 89
  ambatos ("scalable"), 50
  anthropomorphized, 58–60
  areion ("martial"), iii.15
  arrēktos ("unbreakable"), 26, 58
  and defense, 7, 26–28, 42–48
  divine construction of, 32, 50–53
  and effeminacy, 58
  epidromos ("scalable"), 50
  female metaphors for, 33, 64–65
  hieros ("sacred"), 20, 32–33, 50–53,
    iii.16
  and the Homeric polis, 41, 47–48
  as ideogram for the city, 9, 32, 48
  importance of, in establishing a city,
    24–25, 32, 45–47, 86
  kalos ("beautiful"), 50
  khthamalōtaton ("nearest to the
    ground"), iii.15
  male and female identities of, 32–34,
    52
  at old Smyrna, 85–87
  at Scheria, 45–47
  skilled construction of, 49–50, 86
  thematic importance of in *Iliad*, 5, 41–
    49
  theodmētoi purgoi ("divinely built tow-
    ers"), 20
  and *toikhos* ("house wall"), 5, 136
  at Troy, importance of, 24–28, 42–45,
    49–50, 105
  see also Achaean wall; Epithets, city;
    Iliad; *Purgos*
City-state, Ionian, 2–3
Coldstream, J., 86
Colophon, Ap.iii.51
Composition, theory of, 95–99
Cook, J., 88, 89, 90–91
Corinth, 85
Cosmic "mountains," Ap.iii.4
Crete, Early Iron Age sites in, vi.14
Crown, Homeric metaphor for, 31
Cyclopes. *See* Kyklopes

Dardania, 61, 93
Dardanos, son of Zeus, 24, 61
Defense, transference of from physical
  rampart to individual, 59
Deikoon, iv.17
Deiphobus, house of, i.4
Delos, 52
Dēmos ("land" or "people"), 55, i.9
Detienne, M., ii.42, iii.25
Diomedes, 12, 33, 38–39, 95, 120, iv.33,
  v.1, viii.12
Dion, in northern Euboia, 94

Dionysus, 22
Dios ("divine"), 20, 140
Domos ("house"), 17, 34
Duel scenes in Homer, 120, 121, iii.6
Dur Sharrukin, 98, 151

É (inner house of the city god), 28, 29,
  146, 147
Eanna, the hallowed sanctuary of Anu and
  Ishtar, 28, 145–46
Ecbatana, capital city of the Medes, 156
Echepolos, 59
Economy, agrarian, 10, 11
Eden, Hebrew story of, 29, 148
Edwards, M., iv.41
Ēgatheos ("very sacred"):
  defined, 19–20
  places used with, 139–40
Ehrenberg, V., 14, vii.36
Eleusis, topography of, ii.45
Eliade, M., 50, 143
Elis, 21
Ellu (Akkadian for "pure"), 147
Emathia, 92
Emporio, on Chios, 85, 87
En, Sumerian priest king, 151
Enuma elish, 31
Epalxeis (breastworks of planks or battle-
  ments), 50
Epeians, 96
Ephesus, Ap.iii.51
Epithets, 4–5, 72–74, 89, 94–95
  in speech and narrative, 4, 50
  verbal force of, 72–73, 76, 79
  see also City wall(s); Epithets, city; Polis
Epithets, city, 5, 21, 54, 129
  aipeinos. See aipus
  aipus and variants ("steep"), 16, 21, 72,
    75, 76, 78, 80
  akrē ("high"), 8
  antheia, anthemoeis ("blooming"), 21
  arrēktos ("unbreakable"), 15, 26, 32, 50,
    53, 125
  dios ("divine"), 19, 20, 22
  eu araruiai ("well-fitted"), applied to
    gates, 49
  eudmētos and variants ("well-built"), 5,
    49, 77, 78, 136
  euktimenos (well-founded), 5, 21, 70, 71,
    75, 78, 104, 136
  euktiton aipu ("well-built Steep" or
    "steep Well-Built"), 22
  eu poiētai ("well-made"), applied to
    gates, 49
  eupurgos and variants ("well-towered"),
    49, 77, 78, 80

Epithets, city (*cont.*)
  euruguia ("of wide ways"), v.10
  eustephanos and variants ("well-crowned"), 31, 49
  euteikheos and variants ("well-walled"), 4, 48–50, 70, 71, 74, 75, 76, 78, 80
  hiera krēdemna ("a sacred veil"), 31
  hieros and variants ("sacred"), 15, 17, 19, 20, 21, 22, 48, 72, v.20, v.21
  hupsēlos ("lofty"), 78
  husipulos and variants ("lofty-gated"), 49, 77, 78
  poiētai ("made"), applied to city gates, 49
  puka ("solid"), applied to city gates, 49
  stibaros ("compact"), applied to city gates, 49
  tetugmenon ("constructed"), applied to city walls, 49
  theios ("divine"), 20, 53, 78
  for Troy, 54, 69–80
Erechtheus, 34, 35
Eretria, 85, 87
Erichthonius, agricultural aspects of, 61, 63–64, iv.37
  and mares of, 15, 63–65, ii.65
Esagila ("House with Lofty Head"), 31, 146, 149
Esharra, temple of Marduk, 141, 142
Eskharē ("hearth"), ii.1
Etēs ("kinsman"), 55
Eukhomai ("to pray" or "boast"), iv.26
Eumaios, 13
Eunir, ziggurat of Eridu, 30–31, 149
Eurypylos. *See* Poseidon
Eustathius
  on sanctity of the polis, 21, 126
Evocatio, 37, ii.63

Farnell, L. R., 51, 52, ii.50
Figurines, copper, as cosmo-magical defense, 151–52
Finkelberg, M., 77, v.17
Finley, M. I., 1, 83–84, 100, 105, 107, 110, 111, vii.12
Fitzgerald, R., 24

Ganymede, son of Tros, 62, 64
Garaistus, southern promontory of Euboea, 92
Gargaros, highest peak of Mount Ida, 92
Garland, significance of, ii.35
Gatekeepers, as sacred, iii.16
Genos ("race" or "family"), 91, 105
Glaukos, 9
Gortyna, in Crete, 41, 87, 94
Gouldner, A. W., iv.33, iv.44

Greece
  depopulation of, vi.10
  Iron Age in, vi.12
  population density of, vi.17, vi.20
Greenhalgh, P., 106
Gudea Cylinder, inscription on, 147
Gyge, Lake, 92

Halverson, J., 100, 102, 105, vii.6, vii.11
Hammond, N. G. L., 85, 93, vi.24
Harbors, and Sheria, 46–47
Hattusas, capital of Hittite Empire, 153–54, Ap.iii.45, Ap.iii.46, Ap.iii.52
Havelock, E., vii.35
Hearth, 17, ii.1
Hekabe, 7, 9, 42, 45, 56, 60
  and Hektor, 66, 67
Hektor, 6–7, 9, 40, 45, 55, 56, 58–64, 66–68, 77, 106–10, iii.8, iii.19, iv.16, iv.44, v.14
  and *aidōs*, 108–9
  and Alexander, 76, iii.9
  and Andromache, 42–43, 66–68, 106
  body of, protected by Apollo and Aphrodite, 36
  choice of, 66–67, 120–26
  as city-defender, 59–60, 110, 123
  death of, 97, 122–23, 126–27, viii.20
  debate with Poulydamas, 117–18
  and exhorts Trojans, 108, vii.30; his captains, 55
  as father, 62–64, 122–25, iv.33, viii.13
  and Greeks, difference between, 63
  motivation for fighting, 59–61, 107
  name of, 59, iv.24
  and Patroklos, 119–20
  as physical rampart, 59, iv.23
  soliloquy of, 45, 117
  as son, 62–64
  as tutelary figure of Troy, 60
  weakness of, 120–25, viii.15
Helen, 22, 36, 38–39, 42, 43, 44, 95, 103, 110, 115, 120, 134, iv.17, iv.47
  and Hektor, 67
  and Priam, iii.6
Helenos, 67
Hellespont, 92
Hephaistos, 38, 53, iii.22
Hera, 26, 39, 75, 92, 115
  contrasts Hektor with Achilles, 60
  regional affiliation with the Argolid, ii.56
  sacrifices her three most beloved cities, 40, 125
  and vengeance upon Priam's family, 57
  and view of human cities, ii.70
  Zeus acquiesces to will of, 78

Herakles, iv.33
Herkos ("bulwark"), 59
Hermes, 24
Hermos (river), 92
Hero-cult, rise of at Troy, i.23
Herodotus, 151, 156
Heroism, and the Iliad, 2, 63, 106–10, 114
    and civic defense, 67, 118, 124
Hesiod, 17, 52, 105
    oriental influence on, 97
Hestia ("hearth"), 17, ii.1
Hiera teikhea ("sacred walls"). See City
    wall(s)
Hieros ("sacred"), 16–23, 53, 78–79
    defined, 19, ii.7, ii.13
    places used with, 137–38
    and theios ("divine"), 20, 32
    see also City; City wall(s); Sacred cities
Hiketaon, son of Laomedon, 62
Hiller, S., 97
Hittite civilization, 152
    and festival, 154
    and foundation offerings, 155
    and king, priestly role of, Ap.iii.49
    magic and Mesopotamian connections,
        154–55, 157
    and Sun-Goddess, 34
    see also Neo-Hittites
Hoditai ("those on the road"), 14
Hoekstra, A., v.13
Hoffmann, W., 105
Homer
    city vision in, 45–48, 112–13
    and geography, 91–95
    and history, 1–4, 81–82, 87–91, 94–99,
        110–12
    and latent references to cosmo-magical
        practices, 36–37
    and monumental composition, 95–99
    see also City; Iliad; Odyssey
Hooker, J. T., 17–18, 23
House. See Domos; Oikos
Hurwit, J., 84
Hyllos (river), 92

Iakovides, S., 88, vi.9
Iasos, 85, 87
Ida, Mount, 62, 64, 92, 94
Iliad
    dramatic setting of, 89–91
    importance of city wall in, 41–45
    oikos and polis in, 55–64
    and siege warfare, 44–45
    single combat in, 120–21
    vision of rooted in city culture, 95, 97–
        98, 114–16
    see also City wall(s); Epithets; Homer;
        Odyssey; Oikos; Polis; Troy

Ilion, Ilios, Ilium. See Troy
Ilos, son of Tros, 12, 62, i.23
Imbros, 91
Inanna/Ishtar, Sumerian/Babylonian city
    goddess, 34, 146
Iolkos in Thessaly, 94
Ionia, urban revolution in, 2
Ionian cities of eighth century, 83, ii.51
Ionian poetry, and reemergence of walled
    cities, 96–97
Ionian League, twelve poleis of, 93
Iris, 43, 44, 56
Ismaros, of the Kikones, 21
Isos, son of Priam, 11
Ishtar. See Inanna/Ishtar
Ithaca, 1, 10, 21, i.27
    and the Odyssey, 42
    as polis, 5, 100–105, 130
    spring at, 13–14

Jacobsen, T., 29, 148, ii.32, Ap.iii.3,
    Ap.iii.35
Jaeger, W., 90, 98–99, 116
Jerusalem, special sanctity of, 141, 143–44
Josephus, Ap.iii.11

Kakridis, J. T., iv.4
Kallikolone ("Beautiful Hill"), landmark,
    12
Kalydon in Aitolia, walled city in Iliad,
    41, 89, iii.1
Kalypso, 24
Kamerbeek, J., ii.18
Kapys, son of Assarakos, 62
Keel, O., 143
Kes, Ap.iii.32
Kes temple, incantation from, 29, 147,
    149, 150
Kholos ("anger"), of Hera, 115. See also
    Koteōn; Lōbē; Mēnis
Khryses, 8, 114, vi.50
Killa, city in Troad, 93
Kirhu, inner citadel, Ap.iii.33
Kirk, G. S., vi.49
Kirke, bēssae ("glens") of, ii.2
Kisseus, king of Thrace, 22–23
Klazomenai, 93
Kleonai, 94
Kleopatra, wife of Meleager, 60, 66, 106
Kleos ("glory"), 119, 120, iv.42
    of Achilles, 121–22
    for Greek and Trojan, compared,
        63
Klytios, son of Laomedon, 62
Knight, W. F. J., 36, 52
Kolbe, D., Ap.iii.63
Kōmē ("village"), i.9

Koteōn ("anger"), of Zeus, 39
Kramer, S., 145
Krēdemna ("veils"), 20, 31, 33
Krisa, in Phocis, 21
Ktistēs ("founder"), 52
Ktizō ("to found"), 48
Kù, Sumerian for pure, 29, 147
Kybele, 34, Ap.iii.51
Kyklopes, 1, 25, 45–46, 91, 110–11, iii.22

Laertes, 101
Laestrygonians, 13
Lakedaimon, 103
Lampos, son of Laomedon, 62
Laoi ("people" or "host"), 55, iv.10
Laomedon, son of Ilos, 39, 62, 125
Latinus, 45
Lattimore, R., viii.3
Lavinia, 45
Lefkandi, vi.18
Lektos (or Lekton), 92
Lemnos, 21, 92
Lesbos, 21
Leto, 35
Lévy, E., 9
Lōbē ("outrage"), 38
L'Orange, H. P., Ap.iii.6
Loraux, N., 32, 54, iv.16, 39
Luce, J. V., 105, 110, 114
Luvian text, 7
Lycia, 35
Lycurgus, 58
Lydians, 59
Lykaon, 11
Lynn-George, M., iii.6, iii.28, viii.3
Lyrnessos, walled city in Troad, 41, 48, 89, 93, v.1
Lysander, 15

Magic
  apotropaic, 151–52
  in Homer, 37–38
  in Near East, Israel, and Egypt, Ap.iii.41
  and song, 37, 52, iii.27
  of Sumerian Ningirsuk, 150
  of Troy, 155

Maier, F. G., vi.26
Marduk, chief Babylonian deity, 141, 154
Martini, S., 95
Mecca, special sanctity of, 141, 144
Medeon, 94
Megaron ("large room"), 25
Melanthos, 14
Meleager, 60

Kleopatra's plea before, 66
  story of, 107, 108
Melie, in Caria, walls of, 85
Menelaos, 5, 13, 43, 62, 65, 75, 103, 115, 120
  duel with Alexander, 39, 43
  boast over slain body of Peisander, 38
Menestheus, compared to a tower, 59
Mēnis ("wrath")
  of Achilles, 116, vi.8
  of Zeus, 38
  see also *Kholos; Koteōn; Lōbē*
Mentor, 101
Mesopotamia, 28–30, Ap.iii.33
Miletos, 93, vi.48, Ap.iii.51
Miller, D. G., 79, ii.13
Mireau, E., 105
Morris, I. M., 84, i.26, vi.9
Mortality, 63, 121
Mourning, iv.13
Muellner, L., 31
Muhly, J., vi.58
Mumford, L., 25–26, 32
Murray, O., 84, 91
Mursilis II, Hittite king, Ap.iii.49
Music, and building of city walls, 37, ii.62
Mycenae (Mykenai), 21, 41, 94, 115, 125, vi.3
  city dear to Hera's heart, 40
  eponymous defender of, 34
  Lion's Gate at, 36
Mycenaean
  citadel, symbolic significance of, 83
  civilization, decay of, 83–84
  cosmo-magical practices, 36
  pictorial tradition, 10
  religion, 155
  settlements, vi.4
Mycenaeans, 2, 82–84
Mylonos, G., 34
Myrine, tomb of, as landmark, 11–12

Nagler, M., 103–4, vii.17
Nagy, G., 31, ii.1
Nature, anthropomorphizing of, 53
Nausikaa, 9, 46, i.18
Nausithoos, 5, 45
Near East
  and cosmo-magical practices, 36, 150–52
  importance of, in understanding Greek religion, ii.24
  sacred cities of, 28–31
Neo-Hittites, 156
Neoptolemos, son of Achilles, 124
Nēos ("temple"), 23, 46
  of Apollo, 7, 35

of Athena, 32–33, 35
Ionic form, ii.15
on Troy's acropolis, 23
see also Temples
Nestor, 5, 31, 48, iii.1, iv.14, v.1
on *aidōs*, 108
in cattle-raiding contests, 96
oikos and *dōmata* of, 103
and story of cattle raids, 105
Nicholls, R. V., vi.25, 38
Nicias, iv.18
Nilsson, M., 17, 34, ii.48
Nineveh, 141, 150
Niobe, figure of, 92
Nippur, city of, Ap.iii.28
Nirek, Hittite city, 152
Nomos, 14–15

Odysseus, 5, 9, 46, 62, 95, 114, iv.33,
    iv.35
as *basileus* ("king") of Ithaca, 101
epithets of, 79
and oikos, 103
and impression of Scheria, 46
and Laestrygonians, 13
and survey of Kyklopes' island, 90
Odyssey
epithets, compared to Iliadic usage, 5,
    v.20–21
oikos and polis in, 105–10
walled cities in, 41
see also Epithets; *Iliad*; Oikos; Polis
Ogygia, 24
Oikonomos on island of Paros, 87
Oikos, 1, 3, 5, 15, 25, 30, 45, 64, 91, 103,
    119, iv.17
arguments for preeminence of, in *Odys-
    sey,* 100–101
as defining a man's life, 84, 100
and guest-friendship bonds, 103
individualistic tendencies of, 90
never called sacred in Homer, 17
with *piōn,* vii.15
and polis, 57, 59–61, 105, 109
role in ethical decisions, 111
see also City; Polis
Old Smyrna, 1, 2–3, 22, 92, 94, vi.25,
    vi.26
added to original Ionian League, 93
first public temple at, 87
and walls of, 85, 86, 87
Omphalos ("navel") and city religion, 29,
    142–44, 147, Ap.iii.12
Oulos ("murderous"), 53

Page, D., iv.15
Palladion, 36

Greek cities claiming possession of,
    ii.58
and Troy, 34, 37, 39, ii.41
Paris, 9, 22, 62, 95, 110
judgment of, ii.69
see also Alexander
Parry, A. A., 73–74
Parry, M., 72–73
Patroklos, 40, 44, 77, 116
addressed by Hektor, 61
Briseis speaks to body of, 123–24
death of, 118
effect of death of, on Achilles, 119, 121
funeral games of, 127
Pausanias, 151
Pedaios, city in Troad, 93
Pedasos, city in Troad, 93
Peisander, boast over slain body of, 38
Peleus, father of Achilles, 124
Penelope, 5, 101
Pergamon, Ap.iii.51
origin of name, 7–8
see also Troy
Pericles, 54, iv.18
Perkote, in the Troad, 94
Phaia (in Elis), 89
Phaiakians, iv.35, vii.11
Phaistos on Crete, walls of, 86
Phēgos ("oak tree"), 12
Pheia, walls of, iii.1
Phera in Messenia, 21
Phoinix, 106, iii.1
Picard, C., iv.3, Ap.iii.59
Pieria, 92
Pindar, 20, ii.11
explains overrunning of god-built walls
    of Troy, 37
explains Greek success at Troy, 50
Pityeia, in Troad, 94
Place
naming of people by, vi.50
predicate adjectives describing, Ap.i
Plato, 112
on primitive patriarchal government,
    vii.36
on weakening nature of fortification
    wall, 58
Plautus, on fate of Troy, 156
Pleuron, walled city, 89
Polias
epithet for guardian deity of city, 59
post-Homeric epithet of Athena, 32
Polieus
epithet for guardian deity of city, 59
title of, ii.39
Polioukhos ("protecting the city" or "hold-
    er of the city"), 59

Polioukhos (*cont.*)
applications of epithet, iv.25
post-Homeric epithet of tutelary deities,
32, 52, iv.25
Polis, 1–4, 86
arrēktos ("unbreakable"), 26, 32, 125,
127
and *astu*, 8–9, 82
and countryside, 9, 10–11, i.16, iii.12
definition of, 14–15, i.27
difficulties of translating, i.25
eutheikheos ("well-walled"), 59–60, 70–
74
and family geneaology, 55–57, 61–64
female associations with, 33–34, 64–66,
iv.4
in Homer, 8–9, 81–82, 87–91, 105–6
Homeric polis vs. city-state, 1–4, 54–
55, 112–13
of Ithaca, relative insignificance of, 102–
3
meropōn anthrōpōn ("of mortal men"),
40, 54, 126
Mycenaean vs. Ionian characteristics, 1–
4, 12–13, 82–83
Odysseus' vision of, 46–47
paradox of, 15, 63–64
polissamen ("citied"), 32
political characteristics of, in Homer,
54–55, 82, 89–90, 100–106, 109–12
and *ptolis*, vi.53
set apart from nature, 24–26, 45–48,
63–64, 112
teikhioessa ("walled"), iii.1
tripartite nature of, 5, 45–46, 54
see also City; City wall(s); *Hieros*; Homer; *Iliad*; Oikos; *Politai*; Troy
Politai (in Homer: "city-inhabitant"), 1,
14, 56, 108, iv.12
Politeia ("citizenship; government; polity"), 14, 112
Polites, son of Priam, 12
and *laoi*, 55
as personification of defense of Troy, 56
Polizō ("to found a city"), 48
Polyphemus, iii.22
Population
density of in post-Mycenaean times, 84
expansion of in eighth century, vi.23
Porphyry, on name of the epic, 114
Poseidon, 32, 60, ii.16
domatites ("builder of the house"), iii.23
double nature of, 51–52
father of Eurypylos ("Wide-Gate"), 52
as guardian of Thebes' crown of towers,
34

and jurisdiction over walls of Boiotian
Thebes, 51
patrigeneios ("father"), iii.24
sacred precinct of, 101
tekhnē of, iii.25
themelioukhos ("holder of city foundation
walls"), 52
and Troy, 24, 27, 35, 37, 51, 53, 77,
iii.19
worship of in Trozen, iii.24
Potnia, ii.16, 38
Poulydamas, 124
advice to companions, 49
debate with Hektor, 117–18
military advice of, 44
and reference to wall of Troy, 77
Praktion, 94
Priam, 8, 9, 12, 24, 42, 52, 59, 60, 75, 77,
78, 122, 125, iv.14, iv.35, v.1, v.5
and Achilles, 53, 98, viii.7
brothers of, iv.32
and *dēmogerontes* ("elders of the city"),
43
and family, as epicenter of Achaean vengeance, 57
laments Hektor's death, 56, 59
palace of, 6, 43–44, 101, i.1
and retrieval of Hektor's body, 43
son of Laomedon, 62
sons of, 57
at Trojan assembly, 62
and union of oikos and polis, 57
Proem, 115
Prometheus, 25
Ptoliethron ("city"), 8, i.15, vi.53
Ptoliporthos ("city-destroying"), 114, vi.53
Ptolis. See Polis
Purgos ("tower"), 8, 20, 59
purgoō ("to tower with a wall" or "to
make a city"), 48
see also City wall(s)
Purulli, festival of Hittites, 152
Pylians, 96
Pylos, 10, 103, ii.16

Queen Arete, influence of, 90

Redfield, J., 62, 96, 100, 107, 109, iv.36,
vii.28
Religion, new civic, in Ionia, 35
Religious terms, blend of, in Homer, 20
Renfrew, C., ii.14
Riverbanks, Homeric descriptions of, 11,
i.20
Rivers, named in main body of *Iliad*, vi.47
Rousseau, J. J., 82

Runciman, W. G., vii.5
Rutkowski, B., 155

Sacred. *See Hieros*
Sacred cities, 54, 78–80
    destruction of, and sacrilege, 38
    Homeric, condition of, 21–22
    see also City
Sacred marriage, of Weather God of Hatti
    and Sun Goddess of Arinna, 154
Sacred places, 137–40
Sacred way, joining city and sanctuary,
    Ap.iii.51
Sacrifice, importance of, 24
Sale, W. M., i.19, iv.14
Samos, *Hecatompedon* ("100-footed") tem-
    ple built at, 87
Sanctuaries, in Dark Ages, vi.30
Sanders, N., vi.11
Sargon II, founder of Dur-Sharrukin, 152
Sarkady, J., 91
Sarpedon, 12, iv.41, viii.6
    rebukes Hektor, iv.23
Schachermeyr, F., vi.58
Schadewaldt, W., 114
Schafer, J., 97
Schein, S., 11
Scheria, 1, 10, 47, 100, 101, 103
    blend of Ionian and Mycenaean settle-
        ment, 87–88
    comparison with Troy, 45
    founding of, 5
    between "mythical" and "real" worlds,
        iii.11
    Odyssean descriptions of, 2–3, 41, 45–
        46, 110
    spring near, 13–14
Schmitt, R., iii.27
Segal, C., iv.38
Selleis (river), 94
Seneca, 59
Sennacherib, king of Assyrian Empire, 141
    boast of, 150
    and naming of city gates of Nineveh,
        151
    and rebuilding of temple for New Year
        Festival, Ap.iii.5
Servius, on Skaian Gate, 155–56
Sestos, 94
Shalmaneser III, Assyrian king, 98, 150
Shaw, T. E., 23
Shrines, 14
Sibylline Oracles, on "blessed Jews,"
    Ap.iii.11
Siege warfare, 3
    Homeric depiction of, compared with

Mycenaean art, iii.8
    subject of Mycenaean "epic" poetry,
        95–96
    theme of, in Mycenaean art, vi.6
Similes, agricultural, i.24
Simoeis (river), 11
Simoeisios, 11
Simpson, L., vi.49
Sipylus, Mount, 92
Skaian Gate, 7, 43, 44, 45, 48, 66, 98, 122
    dramatic place in *Iliad*, 42, 44
    magic of, 156
Skamandrios. *See* Astyanax
Skamandros (river), 11, 53, 116
Slatkin, L., viii.8
Snodgrass, A. A., 5, 82, 86, 87, vi.28
Social organization, systems of, 2
Socrates, iv.18
Song. *See* Magic
Sparta, 10, 40, 115, 125
Springs, 13–14, 56, 93
Stanford, W. B., 45–46, ii.18
Starr, C., 96
Steiner, G., 98
Stele, magical purpose of, 150–51
Stephanus, on Apollo as settlement found-
    er, 52
Stesichorus, endows Hektor with divine
    power, 59
Sthenelos, boast of, iv.33
Strabo, on Homer as geographer, 91
Submycenaean culture, 84
Sumerian cities
    gates of, 147–48
    sacred cities, 145–49
    from second millennium, division of,
        28
Sumerian *Esagila*, Ap.iii.4, Ap.iii.32
Sumerian mythology, and Hebrew story
    of Eden, 148
Sumerians, departure of tutelary deity of,
    37
Sun Goddess of Arinna, 152, 153, 154
Suppiluliuma I, Hittite king, 149

Teikhos ("circuit wall"). *See* City wall(s);
    Purgos
Teikhoskopia ("view from the city wall"),
    3, 42–43
Tekmōr ("mark"), of Ilios (Troy), 26, 36
Telemachos, 101, 103, vii.9
Temenos ("king's estate" or "divine pre-
    cinct"), 46
Temples:
    apsidal structures, vi.31

Temples (*cont.*)
  of Babylon and Jerusalem, comparison
    of, 143
  capitals of, modeled on Near Eastern
    prototypes, vi.33
  and city god, in Sumer, Ap.iii.19
  construction, innovation in, 87
  god's oikos and *domos*, ii.2
  Greek, eighth-century examples of, 87–
    88
  and outer city, strong distinction in
    Mesopotamia, 145–46
  precincts of, ii.16, ii.46
  as vital Sumerian centers, 29
  see also Nēos
Tenedos, 92
Tereia, in Troad, 94
Teucer, 75
Theano, 22–23, 33. *See also* Antenor
Thebes in Boiotia, 89, 94
  attacked by Epigonoi, iii.15
  founding of, 48
  sacred walls of, 50
  walled city in *Iliad*, 41
Thebes in Egypt, 89, iii.1
Thebes in Troad, 8, 41, 48, 89, 107
  hieros, 93
  lofty-gated, 93
  sack of, 109
Themis, 102
Themistes ("laws" or "established
  customs"), 26, 111
Themistocles, iv.19
Theocentric, Near Eastern notion of ur-
  ban sanctity, 30
Theognis, on Apollo and Megara, 52
Thersites, 90
Thetis, mother of Achilles, 13, 118, 121,
  viii.8
Thnētos ("suckled at the breast of a wom-
  an"), 60
Thōkos, Odysseus' seat in assembly, 101
Thomas, C., 14, 84
Thoōkos ("sitting"), 101
Thrēnos ("wailing" or "ritualized lamenta-
  tion"), 42, 43–44
Thucydides
  definition of polis, 14
  on early Greece, i.10
Thymbre, in Troad, 93
Tiamat, and creation of universe, 141
Timē ("honor"), 119
Tiryns, 21, ii.14, vi.3
  excavations at, 36
  walled city in *Iliad*, 41
  walls of, 25, 94
Tithonos, son of Laomedon, 62, iv.31
Tmolos, Mount, 92

Toikhos ("house wall"), 5
Troad, 7, 93
Trojan horse, 98
  proleptic anticipation of, 53
Trojans, iv.15
  compared to city fortifications, 58–59
  and responsibility for ruin, 38
Tros, son of Erichthonios and third king
  of Trojans, 7, 62
Troy (Ilios, Pergamon), 23–40, 48, 54,
    69–72, 89, 93, 94, 97, 100, 115, 116–
    17, 125, 126
  and Achaean camp, contrast with, 26
  Athena's temple at, 32
  blend of Ionian and Mycenaean charac-
    teristics, 87–88
  and Boiotian Thebes, parallels between,
    iii.21
  in context of a contemporary Ionian
    city, 88
  descriptions of, and surrounding ter-
    rain, 10–14, 44, 92
  destruction of, 39–40, 77, 125–26
  and efforts to propitiate city gods, 38–
    39
  fall of, 36, 125, viii.23
  fate of, 121, ii.69
  and Greek impiety in taking of, 38
  Homer's preference for names of, 8–9,
    56–57
  isolation of, 93
  and location of scenes from, 42–43
  names of, 7–8
  paradox of, 76
  political order of, iv.14
  sacredness of, 23–24
  as seen by besieger, 49
  springs of, described, 13
  towers of, 33
  as walled city in *Iliad*, 41
  walls of, 23–24, 32, 36, 44–45, 50, 51
  welfare of, 105
Turnus, 45

Uru, 28, 29, 145
  in *Kes* hymns, 148
Uruk, city of, 28, 145–46
Uru-kù, 28, 29, 141–43, 145–50

Van Effenterre, H., iv.16
Vernant, J.-P., ii.1
Vidal-Naquet, P., 10
Village, no word in Homer for, 8
Virgil
  on breaking of Laomedon's promise, 39
  and Homer, 45
Vivante, P., 42, 72–73, 78, 133
von Grunebaum, G., 144

Walls. *See* City wall(s)
Wanax, Mycenaean, 34, 82
War, motives for
  in Homer, 54–55, 60–61, 107
  in Thucydides, 55
Warriors:
  comparison of Trojan and Achaean, 106
  masculine ethos of, 67
  motivations of, 106–7
Weather God of Hatti, 152, 153, 154
Weaving
  and city foundation, iii.27
  and poetry, iii.5, iii.6
West, M. L., ii.13, vi.53
Whallon, W., v.10
Wheatley, P., Ap.iii.2
Whitehead, A. N., 124
Whitman, C., 96, 114, viii.22
Wordsworth, W., 47, 81–82
Wrath. *See Mēnis*
Writing, existence of, 89
Wulfing-von Martitz, P., 21, iii.18
Wyatt, W., vi.50
Wycherley, R., 51

Xanthos ("river"), 11
Xeinios ("belonging to hospitality"), 38
Xenia ("hospitality"), 103

Zagora on island of Andros, 85
Zatheos ("very sacred"), 19, 20
  places used with, 138–39
Zeleia, 21, 93, 94
Zethos, 48
Zeus, 4, 31, 61, 64, 74, 75, 76, 78, 97,
  102, 115, 119, 126
  and Achilles, 116, 124
  in assembly with other gods, viii.9
  and Athena, 33, 40
  and creation of Homeric polis, 25
  and destruction of Achaean wall, 27–28
  and destruction of Troy, 26, 38, 40,
    125, iv.55, viii.19
  and founding of Troy, 24–25, 32
  and Hera, 78–79
  and Ithaca, 109
  oak tree sacred to, 12
  as protector of cities, 26, ii.23
  on sacrifices, 24
  will of, 15, 77
Zeus Herkeios (Zeus of the Enclosure),
  altar of, 17
Ziggurat, 29, 147
Zingirli, 156

Index of Ancient Passages Cited

Aeschylus
  Agamemnon
    119 65
  Persians
    349 58
Aristotle
  Politics
    1252a29ff. 112
    1252b30–31 112
    1253a 25
    1253a27–29 iv.38
    1253b3 112
Bacchylides
  Ode
    9.55–58 25
    9.69–81 25
Enuma elish
  I.71 142
  I.100 Ap.iii.32
  IV.135–46 141–42
  V.119–30 142
  VI.113 142
Epic of Gilgamesh
  I.1–7 28
  I.9–15 145
Euripides
  Hekabe
    1208–10 iv.19
Herodotus
  I.26.2 Ap.iii.51
  I.87 151
  I.101 156
Hesiod
  Theogony
    253 139
    292 21

Homer
  Iliad
    Book 1
    18–19 71
    37 8
    128–29 54, 70, 75
    164 70
    253 iv.14
    284 120
    349–50
    366 21
    416–17 118
    Book 2
    332 71
    367–68 v.i
    373–74 31
    592 22
    691 48
    786–808 62
    801 44
    110–14 74
    112–13 75
    113 70
    115–17 40
    117 31
    119ff. iv.23
    133 70
    160 iv.17
    176 iv.17
    255–56 57
    259–63 92
    467 11
    775–77 11
    788–89 iv.14
    791–94 12
    806 56

    807ff. 94
    811–15 11–12
    865 92
    Book 3
    116–17 62
    130–31 44
    149 43
    160 43
    175 134
    239 134
    264–317 62
    399–401 134
    443 134
    445 22
    Book 4
    25–49 40
    32–33 78
    34–36 115
    41–49 viii.19
    44–47 40, 125
    44–48 79
    44–49 24, 38
    45 iv.55
    45–46 40, 125
    66–220 39
    160–68 39
    164–65 72, 78
    174 13
    175 iv.17
    308 48
    405ff. iv.33
    406–7 iii.15
    416 72
    462 59
    473–77 vi.50
    474–76 11

Book 5
423   35
446   35
448   35
472–92   iv.23
478–80   iv.41
489   70
512   35
529–32   108
535   iv.17
692–93   12
Book 6
3   10
10   10
55–60   65
80–82   67
87–94   39–40
89   17
177   10
177–78   9
191   10
255–60   67
269   68
269–75   39–40
279   68
280   68
286–311   39–40
287   7
289–92   39
291–94   13
305   33
309–10   33
311   40
327–28   107, iii.9
354–58   67
365   68
386   44
390–92   6–7
402–3   vi.50
413–16   107
429–30   109–10
431   67
431–39   44
433–39   iv.42
434   50
441–46   109
444–49   122
448–49   54
450–53   106
476–81   122
486–89   viii.14
490–93   68
505   7
Book 7
40   120
44–45   10
60   12

71–72   77
73   120
90–91   120
112–13   10
135   iii.1
177–83   120
345   43
345–46   101, iv.14
351–52   39
367   iv.14
379   iv.14
401–2   39
452–53   48
453   32, 51
461–63   27
Book 8
57   54–55
240–43   75
271   iv.45
287–88   70
288   75
517–22   iii.19
551   40
551–52   v.2
Book 9
20–21   75
23–25   40
46   v.1
135–36   70
136   54
150–52   21
151   22
328–29   119
394ff.   123
410–16   118
418–20   26, 36, 76
419   75
529ff.   44
555   107
574–86   106
587–96   106
Book 10
47–50   60
103–8   13
Book 11
104–6   11
170–71   12
485   59
Book 12
8–33   27
15   71, v.2
30–33   28
40–46   58
243   60
373   59
Book 13
54   60

136–54   58
460   iv.35
621–27   38
625   75
683–84   iii.15
772–73   76
Book 14
53–54   iii.16
56   26
66–70   iii.16
122–24   12
225–30   92
280–91   92
443–45   vi.50
Book 15
68–71   40
70–71   7
71   75
215   76
360–66   viii.7
405–746   107
413   107
484–514   107
496–99   108
502–3   107
552–65   107
556–58   108
557–58   72, v.14
558   56, 76
561–62   vii.29
605–38   108
617–20   58
657–58   108
661–66   108
679–86   viii.7
688–94   108
716–42   107
718–25   vii.30
733–41   59
Book 16
57   48, v.6, v.11
61–65   122
69–70   iv.16
100   33
103–4   116
124–30   116
387–88   38
697–701   77
698   72
702   44
830   iv.16
830–36   61, 119–20
854–55   121
Book 17
128   59
144   9
205–11   13–14

220–24 55, iv.23
327–28 76
407 v.1
736–39 109
737–38 viii.7
Book 18
1–242 117
206–14 117
107–14 viii.7
217–20 37
219–20 117
219–21 viii.7
243–313 117
250–52 117
254ff. 77
254–83 44
265 118
274–76 49, 118
277–79 118
287 117
307 118
310–13 117
314–617 117
327 v.i
483–85 viii.19
490ff. 32
497 101
503–4 102
512 133
Book 19
295–300 124
319–33 124
340–54 38
386 38
407–24 38
Book 20
184–86 13
188–94 11
192 40
215–18 24–25
216–17 61
217 iii.14
219ff. 61
221 63
226–29 64
385–92 92
421–44 viii.11
Book 21
37–38 11
105 57
110–12 viii.19
211–384 38
212–384 53
214–15 53, 116
229–32 116
308–14 116
309–10 70

433 70
440–45 35
446–47 32, 50, 77
446–49 52
447 53
450–52 39
463–66 124–25
515–17 77
520–25 119
522–25 viii.7
526 53
526–27 77
526–38 viii.7
536 53
537–38 iv.43
540–46 77
547–49 12
583–89 55
584–88 109
586–88 69
602 13
Book 22
1ff. 45, 67
1–3 49
3 77
25–30 viii.7
25–31 122
77–86 66
99–110 117
121 133
124–29 67
145–52 13
146 12
153–56 13
165 59
179–80 viii.20
346–47 116
355–61 121
410–11 59
447–65 42
Book 23
189–91 36
Book 24
27–28 v.2
28 39
29–30 39
35–37 57
56–63 60
85–86 13
245 v.1
258 59–60
262 vii.6
328–29 12
329 9
499–501 59
614–17 92
681 iii.16

700 8, 44
715 55
725–30 60
727–38 42
732–35 44
784 12
Odyssey
Book 1
2 23
3–4 110
272 101
386–96 vii.5
397–98 103
Book 2
6ff. 102
10 101
14 101
26 101
32 102
44–45 103
68–69 102
120 34
154 109
224–27 101
225–27 101
233–34 101
Book 3
127 vii.35
Book 4
405–6 Ap.i.1
Book 5
101–2 24
Book 6
9–10 5, 45
54–55 vii.5, vii.11,
    vii.35
262–67 46
266 101
267 102
Book 7
43–45 46
44 101
81 31, 34
Book 8
5 101
40–41 vii.5
390–91 vii.5
555 103
Book 9
21–27 Ap.i.1
21–28 103
34–36 103
112–15 111
125–30 111
128–29 46
Book 10
2–3 iii.16

Book 10 (*cont.*)
  82–94 92
Book 11
  187–96 101
  260–65 48
  325 22
Book 13
  103 133
  242–47 Ap.i.1
Book 15
  183 103
  405–6 135
Book 16
  424ff. vii.6
Book 18
  266–70 101
Book 19
  524–31 101
Book 22
  335 17
Book 23
  269 103
Book 24
  420 101
  465–66 vii.6
  468 42, 104
  469 vii.6
  523 vii.6
Homeric Hymn to Apollo
  12ff. 52
Josephus
  Jewish Wars
    III.3.5 Ap.iii.11
The Kes Temple Hymns

I.17.1–13 149,
  Ap.iii.32
I.29 147, ii.27
I.167.6–9 Ap.iii.32
I.169.33 Ap.iii.32
II.35–36 147
II.93 147
III.58–59 ii.31,
  Ap.iii.30
III.170–71.58–
  59 iii.206
V.92, 95 151
Mishnah Kelem
  1.6–9 143–44
Pausanias
  7.2.6 Ap.iii.51
Pindar
  Olympian
    8.40 50
    8.40ff. 37
Plato
  Euthyphro
    2c.7–8 iv.45
  Laws
    680b–3 vii.36
    778d 58
Plutarch
  Lycurgus
    19 58
  Roman Questions
    27 18–19
Seneca
  Troades
    126ff 59

Shield of Heracles
  104–5 34, 51
Sibylline Oracles
  V.248–50 Ap.iii.11
Sophocles
  Ajax
    158–59 iv.19
Stesichorus
  Fragment
    224 Page PMG 59
Sumerian Temple Hymns
  I.11–13 ii.34
Theognis
  773–74 52
Thucydides
  1.8 i.10
  1.93.6
  1.143.5 iv.18
  2.36ff. 54
  7.77.4 iv.18
  7.77.7 14
University Museum,
  Babylonian Section
    XIII.41.20–21 148
Virgil
  Aeneid
    6.515–16 ii.59
    12.1–81 45
  Georgics
    1.501–2 39
Xenophon
  Memorabilia
    3.5.27 iv.18

Library of Congress Cataloging-in-Publication Data

Scully, Stephen, 1947–
  Homer and the sacred city / Stephen Scully.
    p.   cm. — (Myth and poetics)
  Includes bibliographical references and index.
  ISBN 0–8014–2464–X
    1. Homer—Political and social views.   2. City and town life in literature.   3. Cities
and towns in literature.   4. Mythology, Greek, in literature.   5. Cities and towns—
Greece.   I. Title.   II. Series.
PA4037.S4215   1990
883'.01—dc20   90–55130